全国本科院校机械类创新型应用人才培养规划教材

机械制造专业英语

主　编　王中任
参　编　邬国秀　吴艳花　吴春凌

北京大学出版社
PEKING UNIVERSITY PRESS

内 容 简 介

本书是为应用型本科人才培养所编写的教材，注重机械工程师所应具备的专业英语的听、说、读、写能力的培养，以适应制造业全球化背景下的机械制造专业英语教学改革的需要。本书共分10章，分别为：第1章绪论，第2章机械制造专业英语文献阅读，第3章机械制造专业英语汉译英，第4章机械制造专业英语英译汉，第5章国际化企业谋职，第6章进口机械设备说明书，第7章现场交流与口译，第8章英文图纸，第9章标题与摘要的写作，第10章参加专业展会与会议。书后有8个附录，分别为：附录1阅读材料的参考译文，附录2大学校园词汇，附录3机械工程词汇，附录4自动控制词汇，附录5液压传动词汇，附录6企业宣传词汇，附录7数学符号与表达，附录8期末测验样卷。本书每章配有习题，供复习和课堂讨论采用。

全书在章节安排上按照应用型本科院校机械类专业学生从入学到求职到工作后的时间先后顺序，遵循"够用、实用、适应未来"的编写原则，避免重蹈单纯的专业文章堆积的覆辙，按照听、说、读、写能力培养进行了全新设计。

本书适合应用型本科院校机械类专业教师和学生使用，也可作为工程技术人员的实用参考书。

图书在版编目(CIP)数据

机械制造专业英语/王中任主编. ——北京：北京大学出版社，2012.10
（全国本科院校机械类创新型应用人才培养规划教材）
ISBN 978-7-301-21319-3

Ⅰ. ①机… Ⅱ. ①王… Ⅲ. ①机械制造—英语—高等学校—教材 Ⅳ. ①H31

中国版本图书馆 CIP 数据核字(2012)第 230472 号

书　　　　名：	机械制造专业英语
著作责任者：	王中任　主编
策 划 编 辑：	童君鑫　宋亚玲
责 任 编 辑：	宋亚玲
标 准 书 号：	ISBN 978-7-301-21319-3/TH·0317
出　版　者：	北京大学出版社
地　　　址：	北京市海淀区成府路205号　100871
网　　　址：	http://www.pup.cn　http://www.pup6.cn
电　　　话：	邮购部 62752015　发行部 62750672　编辑部 62750667　出版部 62754962
电 子 邮 箱：	pup_6@163.com
印　刷　者：	北京鑫海金澳胶印有限公司
发　行　者：	北京大学出版社
经　销　者：	新华书店
	787 毫米×1092 毫米　16 开本　13.25 印张　302 千字
	2012 年 10 月第 1 版　2016 年 8 月第 3 次印刷
定　　　价：	28.00 元

未经许可，不得以任何方式复制或抄袭本书之部分或全部内容。
版权所有，侵权必究　　举报电话：010-62752024
　　　　　　　　　　　　电子邮箱：fd@pup.pku.edu.cn

Choose an author as you choose a friend
——择书如择友

前　　言

"知人者智，自知者明"，应用型本科院校的专业方向课程改革需要在实用性和适应性方面狠下工夫，以教学内容改革和教材建设为先导，促进教学方法和学业评价方式的改革，这样才能激发学生的学生兴趣，提升学生的就业竞争力。

中国加入 WTO 后的 10 年来，制造业高速发展。除了大量引进外资，中国制造业也勇敢走出国门，融入全球一体化的经济浪潮。这就对机械类专业学生的专业英语水平提出了新的更高的要求。目前，国内的机械类专业英语的教学内容几乎都只是围绕着培养学生的阅读理解能力和笔译能力，提供涵盖该专业主要知识点的英语学习材料，忽视了对学生解决未来在国际性工程实践中的实用能力的培养。例如，如何看懂和翻译机械进口设备说明书，如何看懂国外机械工程图纸，如何与外国技术人员进行机械工程现场的专业英语交流等。

本书是我们在自编的机械制造专业英语课程讲义的基础上发展起来的。内容共分 10 章，包括：绪论、机械制造专业英语文献阅读、机械制造专业英语汉译英、机械制造专业英语英译汉、国际化企业谋职、进口机械设备说明书、现场英语交流与口译、英文图纸、标题与摘要的写作、参加专业展会与会议。

本书内容新、知识面广、实用性强，特别注重对学生在工程实际中应用英语能力的培养，能够反映全球化背景下的机械制造业中最新的科研成果和生产实际。

目前，机械制造专业英语在很多工科院校中都为本科专业选修课，一般为 30～36 学时，因此，本书除了 10 个单元的相对独立的内容外，还增加了一些课后阅读内容和练习，供教学选择。本书致力于提升机械类专业本科生应用专业英语的能力，因此，除了教师教授外，还应多组织学生讨论和表演，从多年来的教学经验来看，教学内容的改革有利于增强学生自主学习的积极性，彻底改变了传统专业英语教学中"教师唱戏，学生看戏"的局面。另外，每一章精选了一个英文 proverb，供广大师生参考。

本书既可作为机械类专业高年级本科生的教材，也可作为广大企业科技人员和高校科研人员的参考用书。

本书由湖北文理学院王中任老师担任主编，参加本书编写的有邹国秀、吴艳花、吴春凌等老师，以及彭畅、王述坤、张明、刘洲、陈洪全、洪俊玲等同学。本书借鉴了同类教材的长处，还吸取了有关国内外期刊论文和企业网站的精华，谨在此一并表示真诚的感谢！

由于水平有限，书中难免存在疏漏之处，希望广大读者批评指正。也欢迎各位专家学者在使用过程中不吝赐教，编者联系邮箱：xfu_wangzhongren@126.com

编者于襄阳
2012 年 7 月

Adversity leads to prosperity
——穷则思变

CONTENTS

Chapter 1 Introduction 1
 1.1 About the Course 1
 1.2 About Professional Program 1
 1.3 About Manufacturing 3
  1.3.1 What is Manufacturing? 3
  1.3.2 Dialogue: Visiting an Automatic Factory 6
 1.4 Reading Materials 6
  1.4.1 About Department of Mechanical Engineering at MIT 6
  1.4.2 History of S. M. Wu Manufacturing Research Center 7
  1.4.3 Role of Engineer 8

Chapter 2 Literature Reading of Technical English for Mechanical Engineering 12
 2.1 Importance of Reading Technical Literature 12
 2.2 About Scientific Journals and Technical Papers 12
 2.3 Skills for Reading Papers 15
  2.3.1 Basic Steps 15
  2.3.2 Doing a Literature Survey 15
 2.4 About Patent 16
 2.5 Reading Materials 17
  2.5.1 Investigation of Dry Machining with Embedded Heat Pipe Cooling by Finite Element Analysis and Experiments(Part 1 & Part 2) 17
  2.5.2 Tool Wear and Chip Formation During Hard Turning with Self-propelled Rotary Tools (Part 1~Part 3) 19
  2.5.3 Rules for The Implementation of The Patent Law of The People's Republic of China (Article 18 to 22) 22

Chapter 3 English to Chinese Technical Translation for Mechanical Engineering 32
 3.1 Basic Requirements of Technical Translation 32
  3.1.1 The Characteristics of Professional English Literature 33
  3.1.2 Requirements of Professional Literature Translation 35
 3.2 Basic Process for Technical Translation 37
 3.3 Common Translation Skills 38

  3.3.1 Conversion of Word Class ························· 38
  3.3.2 Addition and Reduction of Words ························· 38
  3.3.3 Affirmative-negative Expression in Translation ························· 40
  3.3.4 Division and Combination ························· 40
  3.3.5 Translation of Passive Voice ························· 41
  3.3.6 Translation of Attributive Clause ························· 44
  3.3.7 Translation of Double Negative ························· 45
 3.4 Translation of Long Sentences ························· 45
 3.5 Fast Mastering English Vocabulary by Comparison ························· 47
 3.6 Reading Material ························· 50
  3.6.1 Machinability ························· 50
  3.6.2 Shaft Design ························· 53
  3.6.3 Application of Adaptive Control(AC) or CNC Machine ························· 58

Chapter 4 Chinese to English Technical Translation for Mechanical Engineering ······ 63
 4.1 Difference of Structure and Collocation in Chinese and English ························· 63
 4.2 Improving the Skill of Chinese-English Translation in Science and Technology ························· 64
 4.3 Reading Materials ························· 67
  4.3.1 About Bosch Products ························· 67
  4.3.2 Sheet-Metal Forming Processes ························· 69
  4.3.3 Estimating The Costs of Custom Components ························· 70
  4.3.4 DC Motor ························· 73

Chapter 5 Applying for a Job in an International Corporation ························· 76
 5.1 Recruiting Process ························· 76
 5.2 Job Advertisement ························· 77
  5.2.1 A Job Advertisement from ABC Corporation ························· 77
  5.2.2 Job Advertisement for a Product Design and Development Engineer ························· 78
  5.2.3 HR Policy From Shenyang Machine Tools Co.,Ltd ························· 79
  5.2.4 Job Advertisement for Experienced Persons of Siemens ························· 80
 5.3 Cover Letter ························· 81
 5.4 Resume ························· 83
  5.4.1 Introduction to Resume ························· 83
  5.4.2 Resume Tips for Engineers ························· 85
 5.5 Job Interview ························· 89
  5.5.1 Introduction ························· 89
  5.5.2 Common Questions and Answers ························· 90
  5.5.3 Interview Example ························· 94

CONTENTS

Chapter 6 Specifications and Manuals of Imported Machinery & Equipments ········ 97

- 6.1 Introduction ·············· 97
- 6.2 Brochure of Moore Nanotech 350FG ·············· 98
- 6.3 Stylistic Characteristic of English Instruction Manuals for Machinery Equipment ········ 101
- 6.4 Airfel Radiator ·············· 103
- 6.5 HCX320A NC Low Speed Wire-cut EDM ·············· 103
- 6.6 Maintenance for a CNC Machine Tool ·············· 105

Chapter 7 On-site Communication and Interpretation ·············· 107

- 7.1 Introduction ·············· 107
- 7.2 Technical Communication ·············· 108
  - 7.2.1 Introduction to Technical Communication ·············· 108
  - 7.2.2 100 Sentences for On-site Communication ·············· 109
  - 7.2.3 Dialogue: Guide to Visit a Factory ·············· 116
- 7.3 Dialogue: Technical Instruction of Using Multimeter ·············· 117
- 7.4 Technical Translation ·············· 117

Chapter 8 About Foreign Drawings ·············· 120

- 8.1 Introduction to Technical Drawing ·············· 121
- 8.2 Methods of Reading Foreign Mechanical Blueprints ·············· 126
  - 8.2.1 Key Terms on Foreign Drawing ·············· 126
  - 8.2.2 Example of Title Block ·············· 129
  - 8.2.3 Example of Transformation From The First-angle to The Third-angle ········ 130
- 8.3 Reading and Discussion ·············· 131
  - 8.3.1 ASME_Y14.5M-1994 ·············· 131
  - 8.3.2 Turning and Lathe ·············· 133

Chapter 9 Title and Abstract Writing ·············· 136

- 9.1 Title Writing ·············· 136
- 9.2 Abstract Writing ·············· 138
- 9.3 Reading Materials ·············· 140
  - 9.3.1 A Robust Design Approach to Determination of Tolerances of Mechanical Products ··· 140
  - 9.3.2 High-speed Machining of Cast Iron and Alloy Steels for Die and Mold Manufacturing ··· 141
  - 9.3.3 An Overview of Power Electronics in Electric Vehicles ·············· 141
  - 9.3.4 A Tool Planning Approach Considering Cycle Time Constraints and Demand Uncertainty ·············· 141

Chapter 10 Attending Professional Exhibition and Conference ·············· 143

- 10.1 Professional Exhibitions ·············· 143

    10.1.1 Introduction to Four Largest Manufacturing Shows ………………… 143
    10.1.2 At CIMT ……………………………………………………………… 145
  10.2 Academic Conference ………………………………………………………… 146
    10.2.1 Introduction ………………………………………………………… 146
    10.2.2 Opening Remarks on Simulated Conference ……………………… 147
    10.2.3 TIPS for Academic Speech ………………………………………… 148
  10.3 Useful Sentences for Professional Speech …………………………………… 150

Appendix Ⅰ Reference Translation of Reading Materials ……………………… 154

Appendix Ⅱ Terms of College Campus ………………………………………… 169

Appendix Ⅲ Terms of Mechanical Engineering ………………………………… 172

Appendix Ⅳ Terms of Automatic Control ……………………………………… 188

Appendix Ⅴ Hydraulic Transmission …………………………………………… 191

Appendix Ⅵ Enterprise Promotion ……………………………………………… 196

Appendix Ⅶ Mathematic Symbols and Expressions …………………………… 198

Appendix Ⅷ Final Examination Sample ………………………………………… 199

参考文献 ……………………………………………………………………………… 200

A good beginning is half done
——良好的开端是成功的一半

Chapter 1 Introduction

1.1 About the Course

科技英语(English for Science and Technology，EST)是一种用英语阐述科学技术中的理论、技术、实验和现象等的英语体系。专业英语(Specialized English)，是结合各自专业的科技英语，因此，专业英语是科技英语的一种。各个专业文章的语法现象基本相同，它们都遵循科技英语的语法体系及翻译技巧。所以，从狭义上讲，机械制造专业英语是关于机械设计制造及自动化专业的科技英语，而从广义上讲，机械制造专业英语是包含了机械工程学科各个专业内容的科技英语。

本课程围绕机制专业应用型本科人才的未来工作需要，内容包括专业培养方案与制造文献阅读翻译、英汉和汉英翻译、国际化企业谋职、进口机械设备说明书、工程现场交流与口译、英文图纸、标题与摘要的写作、专业展会与会议等方面。

1.2 About Professional Program

1. Program Name

Mechanical Design, Manufacturing & Automation.

2. Program Objectives

We cultivate quality innovative engineering professionals who are knowledgeable of natural science and engineering technology.

We train for practical and innovative engineering, mastering modern manufacturing technology and production management skills, competent in mechanical engineering process design & implementing practice, computer-aided design & manufacturing technology, mechanical operation & maintenance, and industrial production management.

3. Employment Prospects

Our graduates are qualified for product design, manufacturing, development and production for business in machinery, vehicles, electronics, instruments, light industry and daily appliances.

4. Program Strengths

We deal with Mechatronic integration which focus on the application of automation and computer in modern design and manufacturing technology.

(1) It emphasize effective hands-on practice so that graduates are prepared with quality, pragmatic competence and innovative power for engineering industry.

(2) The Program Steering Committee includes industrial professionals who participate in guiding internship and graduation projects to integrate teaching with frontline production.

(3) Corporate culture lectures and corporate study tours are parts of the learning program for students' early familiarity of their future career and working places.

(4) Teachers carry on recharging vocational engineering practice in partner enterprises so that the course learning is closely combined to industrial reality.

5. Courses Modules

(1) general education courses.

(2) specialized foundation courses.

(3) specialized direction courses.

(4) practice and Innovation courses.

6. Courses

1) Degree Courses(10 courses, 29credits)

(1) Course Code:07ZB091109   Course Name:Descriptive Geometry & Mechanical Graphing Credit:3.0.

(2) Course Code:07ZB091111   Course Name:Theoretical Mechanics   Credit:3.0.

(3) Course Code:07ZB091112   Course Name:Material Mechanics   Credit:3.5.

(4) Course Code:07ZB091113   Course Name:Mechanical Principles   Credit:3.5.

(5) Course Code:07ZB091114   Course Name:Mechanical Design   Credit:3.5.

(6) Course Code:07ZB091116   Course Name:The Electronic & Electrical Technology   Credit:2.0.

(7) Course Code:07ZB091118   Course Name:Exchangeability & Technological Measurement   Credit:2.0.

(8) Course Code:07ZX091106   Course Name:Mechatronic Transmission & Control   Credit:2.5.

(9) Course Code:07ZX091101   Course Name:Hydraulic & Pneumatic Transmission   Credit:2.5.

(10) Course Code:07ZX091110,Course Name:Mechanical Manufacturing Technology, Credit:3.5.

2) Other Courses

(1) Higher mathematics.
(2) Probability and statistics.
(3) Mechanical CAD/CAM and Application.
(4) Modern Manufacturing Technology.
(5) Introduction to Mechatronic Integration.
(6) Testing Technology.
(7) Digital Control Technology for Machine Tools.
(8) Engineering materials and heating processing.
(9) Basic Mechanic Engineering Control.
(10) Microcomputer Principles & Application.
(11) 3D modeling of Mechanical product and innovation design.
(12) Modern design method.
(13) Trouble-shooting Technology.
(14) Engineering practice.
(15) Marketing.
(16) Production practice.
(17) Technical English for Mechanical Manufacturing.
(18) Advanced Language Programming(C).
(19) Special Internship.
(20) Graduation Thesis/Project.

7. Duration

Essential studying system 4 years, flexible studying system 3~6 years, full time.

8. Graduation Requirements

To qualify for graduation, students of Mechanical Manufacturing & Automation should complete all the courses and the Internship required to earn a minimum of 168 credits, specifically 43 credits of general educational courses, 52 credits of specialized foundation courses, 31 credits of specialized courses, 42 credits of practice and Innovation courses.

9. Bachelor's degree awarded conditions

Graduation conditions; qualified thesis; qualified English level test; qualified computer level test

1.3 About Manufacturing

1.3.1 What is Manufacturing?

Manufacturing is the use of machines, tools and labor to produce goods for use or sale.

The term may refer to a range of human activity, from handicraft to high tech, but is most commonly applied to industrial production, in which raw materials are transformed into finished goods on a large scale. Such finished goods may be used for manufacturing other, more complex products, such as aircraft, household appliances or automobiles, or sold to wholesalers, who in turn sell them to retailers, who then sell them to end users-the "consumers", as shown in Fig. 1.1.

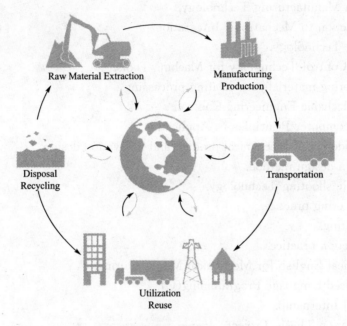

Fig. 1.1　manufacturing cycle

Manufacturing takes turns under all types of economic systems. In a free market economy, manufacturing is usually directed toward the mass production of products for sale to consumers at a profit. In a collectivist economy, manufacturing is more frequently directed by the state to supply a centrally planned economy. In mixed market economies, manufacturing occurs under some degree of government regulation.

Modern manufacturing includes all intermediate processes required for the production and integration of a product's components. Some industries, such as semiconductor and steel manufacturers use the term fabrication instead.

The manufacturing sector is closely connected with engineering and industrial design. Examples of major manufacturers in North America include General Motors Corporation, General Electric, and Pfizer. Examples in Europe include Volkswagen Group, Siemens, and Michelin. Examples in Asia include Toyota, Samsung, and Bridgestone.

General Motors Corporation　通用汽车公司
General Electric　通用电气

Chapter 1 Introduction

> Pfizer 辉瑞(财富500强公司之一,总部所在地美国,主要经营制药)
> Volkswagen Group 德国大众汽车集团
> Siemens 西门子
> Michelin 米其林(财富500强公司之一,总部位于法国,主营轮胎橡胶)
> Toyota 丰田
> Samsung 三星
> Bridgestone 石桥(普利司通)(财富500强公司之一,总部所在地日本,主要经营轮胎橡胶)

Fig. 1.2 shows the process of final assembly of Boeing 787 Section 41. The 787 was designed to become the first production composite airliner, with the fuselage assembled in one-piece composite barrel sections instead of the multiple aluminum sheets and some 50,000 fasteners used on existing aircraft. Boeing selected two new engine types to power the 787, the General Electric GEnx and Rolls-Royce Trent 1000. Boeing claimed the 787 would be near to 20 percent more fuel-efficient than the 767, with approximately 40 percent of the efficiency gain from the engines, plus gains from aerodynamic improvements, the increased use of lighter-weight composite materials, and advanced systems. The 787-8 and-9 were intended to be certified to 330 minute ETOPS capability.

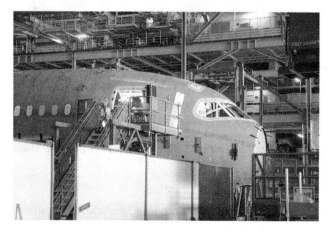

Fig. 1.2 Boeing 787 Section 41 final assembly

After stiff competition, Boeing announced on December 16, 2003, that the 787 would be assembled in its factory in Everett, Washington. Instead of building the complete aircraft from the ground up in the traditional manner, final assembly would employ just 800 to 1200 people to join completed subassemblies and to integrate systems. Boeing assigned its global subcontractors to do more assembly themselves and deliver completed subassemblies to Boeing for final assembly. This approach was intended to result in a leaner and simpler assembly line and lower inventory, with pre-installed systems reducing final assembly time by three-quarters to three days.

1.3.2 Dialogue: Visiting an Automatic Factory

Topical introduction: Tom and Mary are going to visit an automatic factory.

Tom: Hello, Mary. What about paying a visit to a "future" factory?

Mary: It's a good idea. But when shall we go?

Tom: I think we'd better go there this Saturday. Are you free this Saturday?

Mary: I think Saturday would be OK. But I have to have a check with my study plan and see if I can finish my homework for this week.

(Tom and Mary are now in an automatic factory)

Mary: Tom, look here at the assembly line(Fig. 1.3). All the assembly work is done automatically with nobody working inside.

Fig. 1.3 Ball bearing automatic assembly

Tom: Yes. That's true. Everything here is done automatically. Even the quality control is done automatically.

Tom: (To the guide) Excuse me, Ms. Why is there no light in your *workshop*? Do the machines work without light?

Guide: That's true. Most machines here don't need light for their work. They don't need any comfortable temperatures, either.

Mary: But how can all this be made possible?

Guide: Well, you know. It is the computer that has made it possible.

1.4 Reading Materials

1.4.1 About Department of Mechanical Engineering at MIT

Mechanical engineering at MIT is nearly as old as MIT itself, and its impact on the Institute and on society itself is easily demonstrated by noting the alignment of the department's evolution with key events and technological advances in the world.

MechE's origins trace back to the end of the American Civil War, in 1865. Its earliest areas of focus included extensive programs in power engineering and steam engines for both transportation and fixed use. By the mid-1870s, with the Industrial Revolution well underway in North America, the department became known officially. It innovated the use of lab subjects, giving students the opportunity to apply methodology to current engineering problems with hands-on lab work.

The specializations offered at the time reflected the industries of greatest growth, including marine engineering, locomotive engineering, textile engineering, and naval architecture. In 1893, marine engineering spun off from MechE as its own course and remained independent until it merged back (as Ocean Science and Engineering) in 2005. By the turn of the century through the advent of World War I, programs in steam turbine engineering, engine design, refrigeration, and aeronautical engineering set the stage for the technological advances to come.

Between World War I and World War II, automotive engineering was a very popular program in MechE. The Sloan Automotive Laboratory, founded in 1929, became one of the world's leading automotive research centers. Post-World War II, the department's research emphasis gradually shifted from military applications (which continue to be an important component of the overall MechE program in the present day) to "quality-of-life" applications, such as biomedical engineering, energy and environment, and human services.

Mass, motion, forces, energy, design, and manufacturing-these comprise the world of mechanical engineering. Today, MechE attracts and features an extraordinarily rich diversity and quantity of talented individuals, including 400 undergraduates, 500 graduate students, and about 75 faculty, many of whom are members of the National Academies and fellows of prestigious professional societies.

MechE conducts about $35 million worth of sponsored research annually, in a range of areas-such as mechanics, product design, energy, nanoengineering, ocean engineering, control, robotics, and bioengineering-that are diverse and yet also allow for rich collaboration both within the department and with other engineering and science disciplines at MIT and beyond.

These broad areas of focus and our commitment to multidisciplinary research results in an exciting variety of innovative projects, including the use of active control to optimize combustion processes; the design of miniature robots for extraterrestrial exploration; the development of unmanned underwater vehicles; the prevention of material degradation in proton-exchange membrane fuel cells; the development of physiological models for the human liver; and the fabrication of 3-D nanostructures out of 2-D substrates.

1.4.2 History of S. M. Wu Manufacturing Research Center

In 1987, Professor Shien-Ming "Sam" Wu accepted an invitation from Dr. James Duderstadt, then-Dean of Engineering at Michigan to rebuild its manufacturing research programs. Although Professor Wu was already 63 years old, he saw the invitation as an invaluable opportunity to demonstrate, in America's manufacturing heartland, the benefits of his methods of manufacturing science and engineering.

Since the early 1960s, Professor Wu had worked diligently to raise the level of manufacturing science. He was the first to apply advanced statistical techniques and analysis to manufacturing research and practice, and a pioneer in the use of computer technology to do precision machining without precision machinery through the use of error compensation. Additionally, Professor Wu actively sought out industry and insisted upon industrial relevance, as well as academic excellence, in any research undertaken by his group of researchers and students.

Due to Professor Wu's hard work and innovative approaches, the center had become a respected manufacturing engineering research group by the time of Professor Wu's unexpected death in October 1992. His insistence on understanding real-world industrial concerns, using realistic assumptions, and developing generic and industrially relevant theories and methodologies reestablished the University of Michigan's credibility with Michigan's industries and beyond. His emphasis on academic excellence, by learning from the best, encouraging innovative ideas, and setting high levels of standards, earned the group its outstanding reputation as a preeminent center for educating manufacturing engineering researchers. In his honor, the center was named the S. M. Wu Manufacturing Research Center in late 1992.

1.4.3 Role of Engineer

Mechanical engineers research, develop, design, manufacture and test tools, engines, machines, and other mechanical devices. They work on power-producing machines such as electricity-producing generators, internal combustion engines, steam and gas turbines, and jet and rocket engines. They also develop power-using machines such as refrigeration and air-conditioning equipment, robots used in manufacturing, machine tools, materials handling systems, and industrial production equipment. Mechanical engineers are known for working on a wide range of products and machines. Some example are automobiles, aircraft, jet engines, computer hard drives, microelectromechanical acceleration sensors(used in automobile air bags), heating and ventilation systems, heavy construction equipment, cell phones, artificial hip implants, robotic manufacturing systems, replacement heart valves, planetary exploration and communications spacecraft, deep-sea research vessels, and equipment for detecting explosives. Being involved in nearly every stage of a product's life cycle from concept through final production, engineers often work as designers in specifying components, dimensions, materials, and machining processes. A mechanical engineer who specializes in manufacturing is concerned with the production of hardware on a day-to-day basis and with assuring consistent quality. A research and development engineer, on the other hand, works over a longer time frame and is responsible for demonstrating new products and technologies. Engineering managers, for instance, organize complex technical operations and help to identify new customers, markets, and products for their company.

Mechanical engineering is the second-largest field among the traditional engineering disciplines and is perhaps the most general. In 1998, approximately 220,000 people were employed as mechanical engineers in the United States, representing 15% of all engineers. The discipline is closely related to the technical areas of industrial(126,000), aerospace (53,000), petroleum(12,0000), and nuclear(12,000) engineering, each of which evolves historically as a branch or spin-off of mechanical engineering. Together, mechanical, industrial, and aerospace engineering account for about 28% of all engineers. Other specializations that are frequently encountered in mechanical engineering include automotive, design, and manufacturing engineering. Mechanical engineering is often regarded as the broadest and most flexible of the traditional engineering disciplines, but there are many opportunities for specialization within a certain industry or technology that is of particular interest. Within the aviation industry, for example, an engineer will further focus on a single core technology, perhaps jet engine propulsion or flight control systems. An engineer's contribution is ultimately judged based on whether the product function as it should.

Mechanical engineering is driven by the desire to advance society through technology. The American Society of Mechanical Engineers(ASME) surveyed its members at the turn of the millennium in order to identify mechanical engineering's major achivements. This "top-ten" list, summarized here, known as the milestones of modern manufacturing, includes: (1)Automobile, (2)Apollo program, (3)Power generation, (4)Agricultural mechanization, (5)Airplane, (6)Integrated circuit mass production, (7)Air-conditioning and refrigeration, (8)Computer-aided engineering technology, (9)Bioengineering, (10)Codes and standards.

Words

1. recharge 充电
2. vocational 职业的
3. codes 规范
4. preeminent[pri'eminənt]adj. 卓越的;超群的
5. Fabrication 加工
6. fuel-efficient 耗油低的,省油的
7. 比较:innovation 创新,invention 发明,creation 创造,创作
 e.g. innovative power 创新能力
 Necessity is the mother of invention. 需要是发明之母。
 Life is the source of literary creation. 生活是文学创作的源泉。
8. 比较:curriculum n. 课程(正式),(学校等的)全部课程;curricula n. 课程体系;course(有关某学科的系列)课程
 curricular adj. 课程的;curriculum schedule 课程表;syllabus /Course Outline 课程大纲
9. 比较:thesis 本科生或者硕士生论文;dissertation 博士论文;paper/article 一般学术杂志论文

Phrases

engineering practice 工程实训/工程实践	graduation projects 毕业设计
hands-on practice 亲自动手实践	corporate culture 企业文化

steering Committee 筹划指导委员会	corporate study tours 公司考察/游学
production practice 生产实习	frontline production 一线生产
special Internship 专项实习	quality control 质量控制,质量管理
pragmatic competence 语用能力	take turns 轮流
mass production 大量生产	collectivist economy 集体主义经济
at a profit 有利可图	centrally planned economy 中央计划经济
mixed market economies 混合的市场经济	manufacturing sector 制造业,制造部门
government regulation 政府管制	efficiency gain 效率增益
daily appliances 家用电器	stiff competition 激烈的竞争
be certified to 通过了…认证	specialied in 专门从事,专攻
involve in 使参与,陷入,牵扯到	aerodynamic improvements 空气动力学改进
composite materials 轻量级复合材料	Twin-Engine Operations 双引擎操作

Excercises

Task 1 Oral English-Chinese Translation Practice

1. Maybe you've never thought about it before, but it is all around you. It affects every part of your life. Then, What is manufacturing exactly?

2. Actually "manufacturing" is not all around you. But manufactured *products* are.

3. Look around you right now. Name some things you see that were manufactured. Chairs, notebooks, jeans, floor tile, chalkboards, fluorescent lamp, pencils, eyeglasses、mobile phone、computer display、projector, automobile/car—nearly everything around you was manufactured.

4. Manufacturing affects our daily lives—what we wear(jeans), what we eat(breakfast cereal), what we watch(television), how we travel(cars), and many many other things.

Task 2 Oral Chinese-English Translation Practice

1. 请设想一下没有制造业的生活吧：没有自行车骑、没有电视机看、没有鞋穿、没有家具用、也没有飞机坐。缺少人工心脏一类的救护设备更无法想象。制造业就是生产产品，生产出来的产品可大可小，可以简单也可以复杂。

2. 生产零部件并把它们组装起来就是制造。如果你这样做了，那么你就是在制造。但是，现在大多数人一谈起制造，就会想到制造业。

3. 制造业对于我们的社会非常重要，在经济中起着重要作用。经济是一个包括产品生产，销售和服务的运转体系。许多人从事制造业的工作，他们生产产品，同时也用他们赚来的钱购买制造出来的产品。人们买的产品越多，制造的产品也就越多，从事制造业工作的人也就越多。

4. 制造对经济从另一方面讲也非常重要。原材料一旦制造成有用的产品，它将值更多的钱，这就叫附加值。于是，制造过程就为产品增加了附加价值。

Task 3 Match the words or phrases in Column A with their definitions or explanations in Column B

A
1. manufactured product(　)
2. manufacturing(　)
3. economy(　)
4. manufacturing industry(　)
5. value(　)
6. manufacturing processes(　)
7. system(　)

B
a. monetary worth or marketable price
b. output of a manufacturing process
c. the process of converting materials into products
d. a group of related parts working together
e. whole area of manufacturing organizations and factories
f. methods of manufacturing such as milling, grounding, etc.
g. the economic life of a country; the operation of a country's money supply, industry, and trade

If you fail to plan, then you plan to fail
——如果你不去计划,那你就准备着失败

Chapter 2
Literature Reading of Technical English for Mechanical Engineering

2.1 Importance of Reading Technical Literature

  当今的时代是一个信息的时代,无论你本科毕业后是读研究生还是参加工作,都免不了要查阅各种专业文献。文献的种类有:Papers(论文), technical reports(技术报告), instruction manuals(说明书), Abstract(文摘,摘要), Treatise(专题论文), Proposal(申请书), Specification(规范/说明书), Monograph(专题论文/专论); Brochure(小册子); Memoranda(备忘录); Patent(专利); Standard(标准)。

  掌握检索和阅读文献的能力至少有以下三大好处:一是知道前人所做的工作;二是可以产生新的想法;三是可以站在巨人肩膀上继续开展研究。

  本章重点介绍期刊文献、专利以及阅读文献的技巧方法。

2.2 About Scientific Journals and Technical Papers

  In academic publishing, a scientific journal is a periodical publication intended to further the progress of science, usually by reporting new research. There are thousands of scientific journals in publication, and many more have been published at various points in the

Chapter 2 Literature Reading of Technical English for Mechanical Engineering

past. Most journals are highly specialized, although some of the oldest journals such as Nature publish articles and scientific papers across a wide range of scientific fields. Scientific journals contain articles that have been peer reviewed, in an attempt to ensure that articles meet the journal's standards of quality, and scientific validity. Although scientific journals are superficially similar to professional magazines, they are actually quite different. Issues of a scientific journal are rarely read casually, as one would read a magazine. The publication of the results of research is an essential part of the scientific method. If they are describing experiments or calculations, they must supply enough details that an independent researcher could repeat the experiment or calculation to verify the results. Each such journal article becomes part of the permanent scientific record.

1. Types of articles

There are several types of journal articles. The exact terminology and definitions vary by field and specific journal, but often include:

Letters(also called communications, and not to be confused with letters to the editor) are short descriptions of important current research findings that are usually fast-tracked for immediate publication because they are considered urgent.

Research notes are short descriptions of current research findings that are considered less urgent or important than Letters.

Articles are usually between five and twenty pages and are complete descriptions of current original research findings, but there are considerable variations between scientific fields and journals – 80-page articles are not rare in mathematics or theoretical computer science.

Supplemental articles contain a large volume of tabular data that is the result of current research and may be dozens or hundreds of pages with mostly numerical data. Some journals now only publish this data electronically on the internet.

Review articles do not cover original research but rather accumulate the results of many different articles on a particular topic into a coherent narrative about the state of the art in that field. Review articles provide information about the topic and also provide journal references to the original research. Reviews may be entirely narrative, or may provide quantitative summary estimates resulting from the application of meta-analytical methods.

The formats of journal articles vary, but many follow the general scheme recommended. Such articles begin with an abstract, which is a one-to-four-paragraph summary of the paper. The introduction describes the background for the research including a discussion of similar research. The materials and methods or experimental section provides specific details of how the research was conducted. The results and discussion section describes the outcome and implications of the research, and the conclusion section places the research in context and describes avenues for further exploration.

In addition to the above, some scientific journals such as Science will include a news section where scientific developments(often involving political issues) are described. These articles are often written by science journalists and not by scientists. In addition, some journals will include an editorial section and a section for letters to the editor. While these are articles published within a journal, in general they are not regarded as scientific journal articles because they have not been peer-reviewed.

2. Electronic publishing

Electronic publishing is a new area of information dissemination. One definition of electronic publishing is in the context of the scientific journal. It is the presentation of scholarly scientific results in only an electronic (non-paper) form. This is from its first write-up, or creation, to its publication or dissemination. The electronic scientific journal is specifically designed to be presented on the internet. It is defined as not being previously printed material adapted, or re-tooled, and then delivered electronically.

Electronical publishing will exist alongside paper publishing, because printed paper publishing is not expected to disappear in the future. Output to a screen is important for browsing and searching but is not well adapted for extensive reading. Paper copies of selected information will definitely be required. Therefore the article has to be transmitted electronically to the reader's local printer. Formats suitable both for reading on paper, and for manipulation by the reader's computer will need to be integrated.

Electronic counterparts of established print journals already promote and deliver rapid dissemination of peer reviewed and edited, "published" articles. Other journals, whether spin-offs of established print journals, or created as electronic only, have come into existence promoting the rapid dissemination capability, and availability, on the Internet. In tandem with this is the speeding up of peer review, copyediting, page makeup, and other steps in the process to support rapid dissemination.

Other improvements, benefits and unique values of electronically publishing the scientific journal are lower cost, and availability to more people, especially scientists from non-developed countries. Hence, research results from more developed nations are becoming more accessible to scientists from non-developed countries.

Moreover, electronic publishing of scientific journals has been accomplished without compromising the standards of the refereed, peer review process.

One form is the online equivalent of the conventional paper journal. By 2006, almost all scientific journals have, while retaining their peer-review process, established electronic versions; a number have moved entirely to electronic publication. In similar manner, most academic libraries buy the electronic version, and purchase a paper copy only for the most important or most-used titles.

There is usually a delay of several months after an article is written before it is published in a journal, making paper journals not an ideal format for announcing the latest research. Many journals now publish the final papers in their electronic version as soon as they are ready, without waiting for the assembly of a complete issue, as is necessary with paper.

2.3 Skills for Reading Papers

2.3.1 Basic Steps

Reading papers is a skill that takes practice. You can't afford to read in full all the papers that come to you. Generally, reading a paper involves three phases. The first phase is to see if there's anything of interest in it at all. Good places for the first phase are often abstract, conclusion and introduction.

If all else fails, you may have to actually flip through the whole thing. The second phase is to look for the page that has the exciting stuff and read carefully. Finally, you may go back and read the whole paper through if it seems worthwhile. Read with questions in mind:

——How can I use this?
——Does this really do what the author claims?
——What if…?

2.3.2 Doing a Literature Survey

Paper reading skills are put to the test in doing a literature survey. This will require you to read tens of papers, perhaps in an unfamiliar field. What papers should you read? Here is how you can use the three-pass approach to help.

First, use an academic search engine such as Google Scholar or CiteSeer and some well-chosen keywords to find three to five recent papers in the area. Do one pass on each paper to get a sense of the work, then read their related work sections. You will find a thumbnail summary of the recent work, and perhaps, if you are lucky, a pointer to a recent survey paper. If you can find such a survey, you are done. Read the survey, congratulating yourself on your good luck.

Otherwise, in the second step, find shared citations and repeated author names in the bibliography. These are the key papers and researchers in that area. Download the keypapers and set them aside. Then go to the websites of the key researchers and see where they've published recently. That will help you identify the top conferences in that field because the best researchers usually publish in the top conferences.

The third step is to go to the website for these top conferences and look through their recent proceedings. A quick scan will usually identify recent high-quality related work. These papers, along with the ones you set aside earlier, constitute the first version of your survey. Make two passes through these papers. If they all cite a key paper that you did not find earlier, obtain and read it, iterating as necessary.

2.4　About Patent

A patent is a form of intellectual property. It consists of a set of exclusive rights granted by a sovereign state to an inventor or their assignee for a limited period of time in exchange for the public disclosure of an invention.

The procedure for granting patents, the requirements placed on the patentee, and the extent of the exclusive rights vary widely between countries according to national laws and international agreements. Typically, however, a patent application must include one or more claims defining the invention which must meet the relevant patentability requirements such as novelty and non-obviousness. The exclusive right granted to a patentee in most countries is the right to prevent others from making, using, selling, or distributing the patented invention without permission.

Under the World Trade Organization's(WTO)Agreement on Trade-Related Aspects of Intellectual Property Rights, patents should be available in WTO member states for any invention, in all fields of technology, and the term of protection available should be a minimum of twenty years. In many countries, certain subject areas are excluded from patents, such as business methods and computer programs.

A patent is not a right to practice or use the invention. Rather, a patent provides the right to exclude others from making, using, selling, offering for sale, or importing the patented invention for the term of the patent, which is usually 20 years from the filing date subject to the payment of maintenance fees. A patent is, in effect, a limited property right that the government offers to inventors in exchange for their agreement to share the details of their inventions with the public. Like any other property right, it may be sold, licensed, mortgaged, assigned or transferred, given away, or simply abandoned.

The rights conveyed by a patent vary country-by-country. For example, in the United States, a patent covers research, except "purely philosophical" inquiry. A U.S. patent is infringed by any "making" of the invention, even a making that goes toward development of a new invention—which may itself become subject of a patent.

A patent being an exclusionary right does not, however, necessarily give the owner of the patent the right to exploit the patent. For example, many inventions are improvements of prior inventions that may still be covered by someone else's patent. If an inventor takes an existing, patented mouse trap design, adds a new feature to make an improved mouse trap, and obtains a patent on the improvement, he or she can only legally build his or her improved mouse trap with permission from the patent holder of the original mouse trap, assuming the original patent is still in force. On the other hand, the owner of the improved mouse trap patent can exclude the original patent owner from using the improvement.

Some countries have "working provisions" that require the invention be exploited in the jurisdiction it covers. Consequences of not working an invention vary from one country to another, ranging from revocation of the patent rights to the awarding of a compulsory license awarded by the courts to a party wishing to exploit a patented invention. The patentee has the opportunity to challenge the revocation or license, but is usually required to provide evidence that the reasonable requirements of the public have been met by the working of invention.

2.5 Reading Materials

2.5.1 Investigation of Dry Machining with Embedded Heat Pipe Cooling by Finite Element Analysis and Experiments(Part 1 & Part 2)

1. Introduction

Machining is an important manufacturing operation in industry. The purpose of a machining process is to generate a surface having a specified shape and acceptable surface finish, and to prevent tool wear and thermal damage that leads to geometric inaccuracy of the finished part. The thermodynamic approach to the activity at the cutting edge attempts to account for the energy consumed. Research has shown that at least 99% of the input energy is converted into heat by deformation of the chip and by friction of the chip and work piece on the tool. The interface at which the chip slides over the tool is normally the hottest region during cutting. The actual temperature is strongly affected by work piece material, cutting speed, feed, the depth of cut, tool geometry, coolant, and many other variables. Due to the interaction of the chip and tool, which takes place at high pressures and high temperatures, the tool will always wear. The use of fluids in machining is well known. Among the functions of a cutting fluid, cooling and lubrication are generally regarded as the most important, since they directly relate to heat generation and tool wear. However, significant negative consequences for environmental health and safety are associated with the use of cutting fluids.

Numerous methods have also been applied to predict temperatures in machining processes. Tay et al. used a finite element method and Usui et al. used a finite difference method to determine the proportion in which the cutting energy is distributed among the tool, chip, and work piece. Radulescu and Kapoor developed an analytical model for the prediction of tool temperature fields in continuous or interrupted 3-D cutting processes. The analysis predicts time-dependent heat fluxes in the cutting tool, and it only requires the cutting forces as inputs. Stephenson et al. described a method for calculating cutting tool temperatures in contour turning based on Radulescu and Kapoor's model for temperatures in interrupted cutting. Their model is adapted to account for variations in the dimensions of the heat source with time. In addition, insulated conditions are used on the boundaries exposed to the environment, in order to simplify input requirements and reduce computing time.

A heat pipe is a passive heat transfer device with a very high thermal conductance. It is used to transport heat from one location to another by means of evaporation and subsequent condensation of an appropriate fluid, in which circulation of the fluid is maintained by capillary forces. Heat pipes are used for cooling purposes in a wide range of applications, including electronics, die-casting and injection molding, heat recovery, aircraft deicing, the cooling of batteries, and the control of manufacturing temperatures. The objective of this research is to contribute to the fundamental understanding of the new embedded heat pipe technology in metal cutting that can effectively carry away the heat generated at the tool - chip interface in machining, and, thus, reduce tool wear and prolong tool life. In this paper, a finite element model is presented for dry machining. This work departs from previous work in that a more realistic tool design has been adapted for the cutting process with an embedded heat pipe. Because the use of the heat pipe cooling system may reduce or eliminate the need for cutting fluid use, the pollution and contamination of the environment by cutting fluids and the health problems of skin exposure and particulate inhalation in manufacturing can be effectively minimized.

2. Heat generation in machining

In machining operations, mechanical work is converted to heat through the plastic deformation involved in chip formation and through friction between the tool and the work piece. Figure 2.1 shows the subsequent dissipation of that heat in the chip, tool, and the work piece. Most of the analytical methods for steady-state temperature prediction in machining were developed based on Merchant's model for orthogonal cutting, which gives the shear and friction energy in terms of the measured cutting forces, tool-chip contact length, and chip thickness ratio. From Radulescu and Kapoor's model and Stephenson and Ali's approach, the force model predicts the dependence of the forces on the cutting parameters and the work piece's geometry. It can predict the actual force magnitudes or their dependence on material types and cutting conditions.

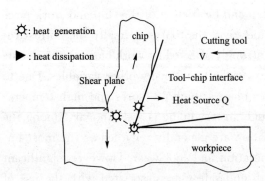

Fig. 2.1 Zones of heat generation and heat dissipation during the metal cutting process

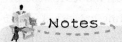

1. It is used to transport heat from one location to another by means of evaporation and subsequent condensation of an appropriate fluid, in which circulation of the fluid is maintained by capillary forces.

分析：in which 引导的非限制定语从句，在这里起补充说明的作用，去掉它，句子仍然完整。

2. heat recovery 热量回收

e. g. We did consider a heat recovery ventilation system, a box and pipes that bring in fresh air.

我们的确曾经考虑过热回收通风系统，用一个机箱和一些管道引入新鲜空气。

3. aircraft deicing 飞机除冰，注意：deicing 是 de＋icing 构成

e. g. These are significant for the study of icing mechanism and the design of anti/deicing equipments.

这些工作对深入认识积冰机理和防/除冰装置的设计具有重要意义。

4. contribute to 是…的部分原因；促成，有助于，起作用

e. g. Your success should contribute to the success of others!

你的成功应能有助于他人的成功！

5. particulate inhalation

微粒吸入

2.5.2 Tool Wear and Chip Formation During Hard Turning with Self-propelled Rotary Tools(Part 1～Part 3)

1. Introduction

Turning instead of grinding hardened steel is an economical method to generate a high quality machined surface. During the past few years, there has been significant industrial interest in using dry machining rather than grinding of hardened steel and other difficult-to-machine materials. As an example, dry hard turning of automotive differential side gears is a successful industrial application of this technology. This technology reduces both the machining time and the specific cutting energy, and eliminates the health and environmental hazards associated with coolant usage in conventional machining operations. Although a large volume of literature exists on hard turning, the control of the tool wear and its effect on the machined surface's physical properties represent a major technical challenge. Understanding the chip formation mechanism is essential to achieve a better insight of the machining process fundamentals. Saw toothed chip formation is observed during hard turning and was the subject of interest by several researchers.

Several models for the chip removal mechanism were presented. Some researchers explained the mechanism of saw toothed chip formation by the adiabatic shear theory. However, other researchers attributed the nature of its morphology to crack propagation. Recent studies using quick stop mechanism confirmed that the saw toothed chip is caused by cyclic crack propagation.

The integrity of the surface produced by hard turning is another important subject. Controlling the machining induced residual stresses is an important aspect for wide spread industrial application of this technology. Hard turning required tool materials that exhibit high wear resistance and an ability to endure the specific cutting forces and high temperature generated. In addition, high indentation hardness of at least three times the workpiece hardness is essential. Since tool wear and plastic deformation of the cutting edge affect the quality and integrity of the machined surface, ceramics and PCBN tools are commonly used for hard turning.

Although in earlier studies rotary tools made of different materials have shown superior wear resistance and prolonged tool life, their performance during hard turning was only investigated using CBN tipped rotary tools. In addition, there were no attempts in the open literature to model the temperature characteristics in machining with rotary tools.

In this paper an attempt to evaluate the cutting performance of rotary tools, made of different materials, during hard turning is presented. In addition a temperature model is presented to describe the heat transfer characteristics and self-cooling feature of this tool.

2. Experimental procedure

A comprehensive testing procedure was carried out to evaluate the rotary tool performance during hard turning. Dry hard turning tests were performed using a 10 hp CNC lathe. Bars of heat-treated AISI 4340 steel (54-56HRC) having a 75 or 100mm diameter, and a 200mm length, were used. The tests were conducted using carbide and TiN coated carbide inserts. Cutting speeds of 100, 130 and 270m/min, with a feed rate of 0.2mm/rev, and depths of cut of 0.1 and 0.2mm were used. Circular inserts having a diameter of 25.4mm were used. The tool wear was measured at four locations, approximately equidistant, along the perimeter of the insert using a tool maker's microscope. These values were then averaged to obtain the value of tool wear. Chips were collected for different cutting conditions. These chips were then mounted in epoxy, ground, polished, and etched using a 1.5% Nital solution. The cross-sections of these chips were examined and photographed using an optical microscope. Optical and scanning electron microscopes (SEM) were used to analyze the collected chips and to analyze the modes of tool failure. The tool spinning speed was measured using an optical tachometer.

3. Essential features of rotary tools

In a pioneer work, Shaw et al. presented a study of a lathe-type cutting tool in the form of a disk that rotates around its center. The continuous spinning of the tool around its center allows for the use of the entire circumference of the insert. As a result of tool spinning, a fresh portion of the cutting edge is provided and therefore a better distribution of tool flank wear over the entire cutting edge is expected. The spinning action of the tool provides a way for carrying the fluid to the tool point at a high cutting speed as in the case of a journal bearing. In addition, this tool offers a self-cooling feature by which the heat is continuously carried away from the cutting zone.

Rotary tools are found in two forms: driven or self-propelled. The tool spinning action in the driven tool is supplied by an independent external source. In the self-propelled tool, the spinning action is achieved by the interaction between the tool and the chip. The driven tool can be either orthogonal or oblique to the cutting speed, while the self-propelled tool requires the cutting edge to be oblique to the cutting speed. The rotational speed of the driven tool is independent of the process parameters. In the self-propelled tool the rotational speed is a function of the cutting velocity and the angle between the workpiece and the rotary cutting edge velocity vectors. Generally, driven rotary tools provide more control over the rotational speed. Fig. 2.2 shows a typical machining process set-up when a rotary tool is used and the main motions encountered in rotary tools.

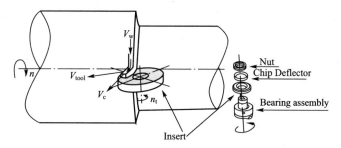

Fig. 2.2 A typical rotary tool during machining.

During machining with rotary tools, three main motions are defined, namely rotational speed of the workpiece(N_{wp}), rotational speed of the tool(N_{toot}), and the feed motion of the tool into the workpiece (f). Due to the rotary motion of the tool the produced chip is dragged along the rake face of the tool. Therefore, the chip velocity is deflected away from its normal direction to the cutting edge in the case of orthogonal machining.

Venuvinod and Rubenstein presented a detailed kinematics analysis of chip formation during machining with the rotary tools. Fundamental experimental and theoretical investigations were also presented by Armarego et al. . Other researchers studied the formation of fluid film at the chip-tool interface when machining with rotary tools. It has been concluded that using a rotary tool is the only way to provide a continuous fluid film at the chip – tool interface. Indeed, this paved the way for a near zero friction at the secondary deformation zone. More recently Kishawy et al. employed a self-propelled rotary tool during face milling operation. The performance of the rotary tool was compared to that of other conventional tools and showed a superior performance and a prolonged tool life.

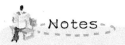

Notes

1. Turning instead of grinding hardened steel is an economical method to generate a high quality machined surface. 分析：instead of 代替，而不是，翻译的时候将"Turning instead of grinding hardened steel"当做一个整体来翻译为"以车代磨淬硬钢"，简洁而通顺。

2. auto chip-removal system 自动排屑系统

e. g. ABC Corporation is a manufacturer and distributor of the highest quality automation components and systems for chip removal operations.

ABC 公司是高质量自动化元件和系统生产商和经销商,其产品用于切屑处理应用。

3. adiabatic[ˌædiəˈbætik] adj. [物]绝热的;隔热的

e. g. This is an adiabatic process. 这是一个绝热过程。

Adiabatic shear theory 绝热剪切理论,是 R. Komanduri 等人最早提出的理论,用来解释高速硬切削时产生锯齿状切屑的原因。

4. morphology [mɔːˈfɔlədʒi] n. 形态学,形态,形貌

e. g. surface morphology 表面形态

Although the different wear mechanism is corresponded to different surface morphology, there exists the formation and propagation of crack in all wear.

各种摩擦磨损虽然有其相关的表面形貌,但其磨损过程都存在裂纹的形成和扩展机制。

5. crack propagation [力]裂纹扩展

近义词有:crack growth,crack extension

e. g. cyclic crack propagation 循环裂纹扩展

The behaviours of fracture,fatigue and fatigue crack propagation in a cast magnesium alloy are systematically studied.

本文系统地研究了铸造镁合金的断裂,疲劳和疲劳裂纹扩展性能。

6. surface integrity 表面完整性

e. g. Surface integrity in abrasive processing 磨粒加工的表面完整性

Analyzing the influence factors and their contributions is useful to obtain the required surface integrity. 分析已加工表面质量的影响因素和变化规律,有助于在零件加工时,获得规定的表面质量要求。

7. indentation n. 凹痕,压痕

indentation hardness 压痕硬度

8. spin vt./vi. (使)旋转

spinning action 旋转动作

9. circumference=perimeter 圆周,周长

10. oblique adj. 斜的 同近义词:sloped;pitched

2.5.3 Rules for The Implementation of The Patent Law of The People's Republic of China (Article 18 to 22)

1. Article 18

The specification of an application for a patent for invention or utility model shall indicate the title of the invention or utility model as it appears in the written request. The specification shall include:

(1) the field of technology: indicating the field of technology to which the technical so-

Chapter 2　Literature Reading of Technical English for Mechanical Engineering

lution under the request for protection belongs;

(2) the background technologies: indicating the background technologies useful to the understanding, retrieval and examination of the invention or utility model; and if possible, citing the documents which reflect these background technologies;

(3) the contents of invention: indicating the technical problems to be solved for the invention or utility model and the technical solution adopted for solving the technical problems, and indicating the beneficial effects of the invention or utility model by comparison with the technology currently available;

(4) the statement of the appended drawings: if the specification is appended with drawings, briefly stating each appended drawing;

(5) the specific method of use: indicating in details the best method considered by the applicant to use the invention or utility model; when necessary, illustrating with examples; and comparing with the appended drawings, if any.

An applicant for a patent for invention or utility model shall present the specification in accordance with the manner and order provided in the preceding paragraph, and shall indicate the heading in front of each portion of the specification, unless a different manner or order would afford a more economical presentation and a more accurate understanding due to the nature of the invention or utility model.

The specification of the invention or utility model shall be written in standard terminologies and clear sentences, and shall not contain such phrases as: "as described in Part... of the claim," or any commercial advertising diction.

Where an application for a patent for invention contains one or more sequences of nucleotide or amino acid, the specification shall include a sequence table in conformity with the provisions of the administrative department for patent under the State Council.

The applicant shall submit the sequence table as an independent portion of the specification, and submit a copy of the sequence table which can be read by the computer in accordance with the provisions of the administrative department for patent under the State Council.

2. Article 19

The same sheet of appended drawings may contain several figures of the invention or utility model, and the figures shall be numbered and arranged in numerical order consecutively as "Figure 1, Figure 2…".

The scale and the distinctness of the appended drawings shall be such that a reproduction with a linear reduction in size to two-thirds would still enable all details to be clearly distinguished.

Appended drawing reference signs not mentioned in the text of the specification of the invention or utility model shall not appear in the appended drawings. Appended drawing reference signs not appearing in the appended drawings shall not be mentioned in the text of the specification.

The appended drawing reference signs for the same composite part used in the application documents shall be consistent throughout.

The appended drawings shall not contain any other explanatory notes, except for words that are indispensable.

3. Article 20

The patent claim shall state the technical features of the invention or utility model, and define clearly and concisely the scope of the requested protection.

Where there are several claims in the patent claim, they shall be numbered consecutively in Arabic numerals.

The technical terminology used in the patent claim shall be consistent with that used in the specification.

The patent claim may contain chemical or mathematical formulas but no drawings, and shall not contain such dictions as: "as described in Part... of the specification" or "as illustrated in Figure..." unless such dictions are absolutely necessary.

The technical features mentioned in the claim may quote the corresponding reference signs in the appended drawings of the specification, and such reference signs shall follow the corresponding technical features and be placed between parentheses, so that the claim can be easily understood.

The appended drawing reference signs shall not be construed as limiting the claim.

4. Article 21

The patent claim shall have an independent claim, and may also contain subordinate claims.

An independent claim shall outline the technical solution of an invention or utility model and record the technical features necessary for solving technical problems.

Subordinate claims shall further define the quoted claim with additional technical features.

5. Article 22

An independent claim of an invention or utility model shall contain a preamble portion and a characterizing portion, and be presented in the following forms:

(1) The preamble portion: indicating the subject title of the technical solution to the invention or utility model which is claimed to be protected and those essential technical features that are common to the subject of the invention or utility model and the closest technology currently available;

(2) The characterizing portion: stating, in such diction as "characterized in that..." or in similar diction, the technical features of the invention or utility model, which distinguish it from the closest technology currently available;

These features, in combination with the features indicated in the preamble portion, serve to define the scope of protection of the invention or utility model.

An independent claim may be presented in any other form if the nature of the invention

Chapter 2 Literature Reading of Technical English for Mechanical Engineering

or utility model is not appropriate to be expressed in the form provided in the preceding paragraph.

Each invention or utility model shall have only one independent claim, which shall precede all the subordinate claims of the same invention or utility model.

Words

dissemination 传播	survey 调查
arbitration 仲裁	invalidation 无效
invention 发明	inventor 发明人
novelty 新颖性	originality 独创性
patent 专利	patent act 专利法
patentee 专利权人	specification 说明书
assignee 受让人	assignment 转让
claim 权项	disclosure 公开
co-applicants 共同申请人	co-inventors 共同发明人
drawing 附图	evidence 证据
examination 审查	treatise 专题论文

Phrases

peer review 同行评审	print publishing 印刷出版
electronic publishing 电子出版	exclusive rights 专利权
working of a patent 实施专利	correction slip 勘误表
patent claim 专利要求书,专利权限	design patent 外观设计专利
utility certificate 实用证书	patent right 专利权
utility model 实用新型	patent documentation 专利文献
patent for an invention 发明专利	patent agent 专利代理人
patent number 专利号	owner of a patent 专利所有人
withdrawal of an application 撤回申请	examination for novelty 新颖性审查
title to patent 发明名称	duration of patent 专利有效期
term of a patent 专利有效期	complete specification 完整的说明书
data of application 申请日期	certificate of addition 增补证书
certificate of correction 更正证明书	certificate of patent 专利证书
date of grant 授予日期	author of the invention 发明人
date of publication 公布日期	applicant for patent 专利申请人
application date 申请日期	application for patent 专利申请
dependent claim 从属权项	technical data 技术资料
technology transfer 技术转移	substantive examination 实质性审查
joint applicants 共同申请人	joint inventors 共同发明人

industrial applicability　工业实用性　　　industrial design　工业品外观设计
infringement of a patent　侵犯专利权　　　intellectual property　知识产权
service invention　职务发明

Excercises

Task 1 Access to the springerlink and CNKI, to search the following papers and download them.

(1) On-line monitoring of tool wear in turning operation in the presence of tool misalignment

(2) An Investigation of a Heat Pipe Cooling System for Use in Turning on a Lathe

(3) 复合刀具及其在阀类零件加工中的应用

Task 2 Login in the website of USPTO and SIPO to search some American and Chinese patents, and translate the description of Pat 4575330.

1. Pat 4575330: Apparatus for production of three-dimensional objects by stereolithography(Acess at: www. uspto. gov or http://www. pat2pdf. org/.)

Description:

BACKGROUND OF THE INVENTION

This invention relates generally to improvements in apparatus for forming three-dimensional objects from a fluid medium and, more particularly, to stereolithography involving the application of lithographic techniques to production of three-dimensional objects, whereby such objects can be formed rapidly, reliably, accurately and economically.

It is common practice in the production of plastic parts and the like to first design such a part and then painstakingly produce a prototype of the part, all involving considerable time, effort and expense. The design is then reviewed and, oftentimes, the laborious process is again and again repeated until the design has been optimized. After design optimization, the next step is production. Most production plastic parts are injection molded. Since the design time and tooling costs are very high, plastic parts are usually only practical in high volume production. While other processes are available for the production of plastic parts, including direct machine work, vacuum-forming and direct forming, such methods are typically only cost effective for short run production, and the parts produced are usually inferior in quality to molded parts.

In recent years, very sophisticated techniques have been developed for generating three-dimensional objects within a fluid medium which is selectively cured by beams of radiation brought to selective focus at prescribed intersection points within the three-dimensional volume of the fluid medium. Typical of such three-dimensional systems are those described in U. S. Pat. Nos. 4,041,476, 4,078,229, 4,238,840 and 4,288,861. All of these systems rely upon the buildup of synergistic energization at selected points deep within the fluid volume, to the exclusion of all other points in the fluid volume, using a variety of elaborate multibeam techniques. In this regard, the various approaches described in the prior art include the use of a pair of electromagnetic radiation beams directed to intersect at specified coordinates, wherein the various beams may be of the same or differing wavelengths, or where beams are used sequentially to intersect the same points rather than simultaneously, but in all cases only the beam intersection points are stimulated to sufficient energy levels to accomplish the necessary curing process for forming a three-dimensional object within the volume of the fluid medium. Unfortunately, however, such three-dimensional forming systems face a number of problems with regard to resolution and exposure control. The loss of radiation intensity and image forming resolution of the focused spots as the intersections move deeper into the fluid medium create rather obvious complex control situations. Absorption, diffusion, dispersion and refraction all contribute to the difficulties of working deep within the fluid medium on any economical and reliable basis.

Yet there continues to be a long existing need in the design and production arts for the capability of rapidly and reliably moving from the design stage to the prototype stage and to ultimate production, particularly moving directly from computer designs for such plastic parts to virtually immediate prototypes and the facility for large scale production on an economical and automatic basis.

Accordingly, those concerned with the development and production of three-dimensional plastic objects and the like have long recognized the desirability for further improvement in more rapid, reliable, economical and automatic means which would facilitate quickly moving from a design stage to the prototype stage and to production, while avoiding the complicated focusing, alignment and exposure problems of the prior art three dimensional production systems. The present invention clearly fulfills all of these needs.

SUMMARY OF THE INVENTION

Briefly, and in general terms, the present invention provides a new and improved system for generating a three-dimensional object by forming successive, adjacent, cross-sectional laminae of that object at the surface of a fluid medium capable of altering its physical state in response to appropriate synergistic stimulation, the successive laminae being automatically integrated as they are formed to define the desired three-dimensional object.

In a presently preferred embodiment, by way of example and not necessarily by way of limitation, the present invention harnesses the principles of computer generated graphics in combination with stereolithography, i. e. , the application of lithographic techniques to the production of three dimensional objects, to simultaneously execute computer aided design(CAD) and computer aided manufacturing(CAM) in producing three-dimensional objects directly from computer instructions. The invention can be applied for the purposes of sculpturing models and prototypes in a design phase of product development, or as a manufacturing system, or even as a pure art form.

"Stereolithography" is a method and apparatus for making solid objects by successively "printing" thin layers of a curable material, e. g. , a UV curable material, one on top of the other. A programmed movable spot beam of UV light shining on a surface or layer of UV curable liquid is used to form a solid cross-section of the object at the surface of the liquid. The object is then moved, in a programmed manner, away from the liquid surface by the thickness of one layer, and the next cross-section is then formed and adhered to the immediately preceding layer defining the object. This process is continued until the entire object is formed.

Essentially all types of object forms can be created with the technique of the present invention. Complex forms are more easily created by using the functions of a computer to help generate the programmed commands and to then send the program signals to the stereolithographic object forming subsystem.

Of course, it will be appreciated that other forms of appropriate synergistic stimulation for a curable fluid medium, such as particle bombardment (electron beams and the like), chemical reactions by spraying materials through a mask or by ink jets, or impinging radiation other than ultraviolet light, may be used in the practice of the invention without departing from the spirit and scope of the invention.

By way of example, in the practice of the present invention, a body of a fluid medium capable of solidification in response to prescribed stimulation is first appropriately contained in any suitable vessel to define a designated working surface of the fluid medium at which successive cross-sectional laminae can be generated. Thereafter, an appropriate form of synergistic stimulation, such as a spot of UV light or the like, is applied as a graphic pattern at the specified working surface of the fluid medium to form thin, solid, individual layers at that surface, each layer representing an adjacent cross-section of the three-dimensional object to be produced. Superposition of successive adjacent layers on each other is automatically accomplished, as they are formed, to integrate the layers and define the desired three-dimensional object. In this regard, as the fluid medium cures and solid material forms as a thin lamina at the working surface, a suitable platform to which the first lamina is secured is moved away from the working surface in a programmed manner by any appropriate actuator, typically all under the control of a micro-computer of the like. In this way, the solid material that was initially formed at the working surface is moved away from that surface and new liquid flows into the working surface position. A portion of this new liquid is, in turn, converted to solid material by the programmed UV light spot to define a new lamina, and this new lamina adhesively connects to the material adjacent to it, i. e. , the immediately preceding lamina. This process continues until the entire three-dimensional object has been formed. The formed object is then removed from the container and the apparatus is ready to produce another object, either identical to the first object or an entirely new object generated by a computer or the like.

The stereolithographic apparatus of the present invention has many advantages over currently used apparatus for producing plastic objects. The apparatus of the present invention avoids the need of producing design layouts and drawings, and of producing tooling drawings and tooling. The designer can work directly with the computer and a stereolithographic device, and when he is satisfied with the design as displayed on the output screen of the computer, he can fabricate a part for direct examination. If the design has to be modified, it can be easily done through the computer, and then another part can be made to verify that the change was correct. If the design calls for several parts with interacting design parameters, the method of the invention becomes even more useful because all of the part designs can be quickly changed and made again so that the total assembly can be made and examined, repeatedly if necessary.

After the design is complete, part production can begin immediately, so that the weeks and months between design and production are avoided. Ultimate production rates and parts costs should be similar to current injection molding costs for short run production, with even lower labor costs than those associated with injection molding. Injection molding is economical only when large numbers of identical parts are required. Stereolithography is useful for short run production because the need for tooling is eliminated and production set-up time is minimal. Likewise, design changes and custom parts are easily provided using the technique. Because of the ease of making parts, stereolithography can allow plastic parts to be used in many places where metal or other material parts are now used. Moreover, it allows plastic models of objects to be quickly and economically provided, prior to the decision to make more expensive metal or other material parts.

Hence, the stereolithographic apparatus of the present invention satisfies a long existing need for a CAD and CAM system capable of rapidly, reliably, accurately and economically designing and fabricating three-dimensional plastic parts and the like.

The above and other objects and advantages of this invention will be apparent from the following more detailed description when taken in conjunction with the accompanying drawings of illustrative embodiments.

BRIEF DESCRIPTION OF THE DRAWINGS

Fig. 1 and Fig. 2 are flow charts illustrating the basic concepts employed in practicing the method of stereolithography of the present invention;

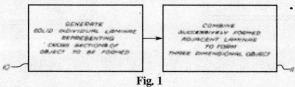

Fig. 1

Fig. 3 is a combined block diagram, schematic and elevational sectional view of a presently preferred embodiment of a system for practicing the invention;

Fig. 4 is an elevational sectional view of a second embodiment of a stereolithography system for the practice of the invention;

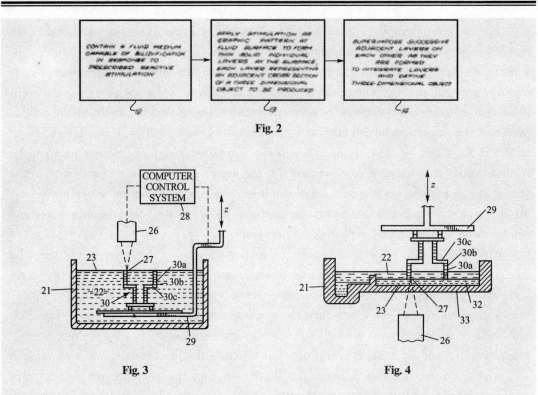

Fig. 2

Fig. 3   Fig. 4

Fig. 5 is an elevational sectional view, illustrating a third embodiment of the present invention;

Fig. 6 is an elevational sectional view illustrating still another embodiment of the present invention; and

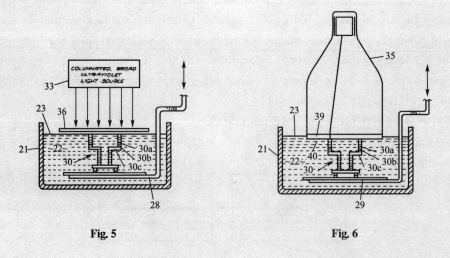

Fig. 5   Fig. 6

Fig. 7 and 8 are partial, elevational sectional views, illustrating a modification of the stereolithographic system of Fig. 3 to incorporate an elevator platform with multiple degrees of freedom.

2. 碳钢芯不锈钢复合管材及其制造工艺(中国知识产权局：www.sipo.gov.cn)

Chapter 2 Literature Reading of Technical English for Mechanical Engineering

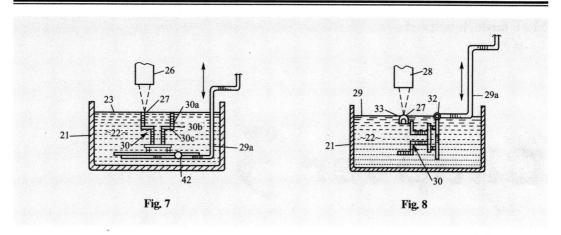

Fig. 7   Fig. 8

More haste, less speed
——欲速则不达

Chapter 3
English to Chinese Technical Translation for Mechanical Engineering

3.1 Basic Requirements of Technical Translation

翻译是把一种语言所表达的信息用另一种语言表示出来的语言活动。早在 18 世纪末，爱丁堡大学历史教授亚历山大·F·泰特勒(Alexander Fraser Tytler，1749—1814)在《论翻译的原则》一书中系统地提出了进行翻译和评判翻译标准的三条基本原则：

1. A translation should give a complete transcript of the ideas of the original work.
译文应完全复写出原作的思想。
2. The style and manner of writing should be of the same character as that of the original.
译文的风格和笔调应与原文的性质相同。
3. A translation should have all the ease of the original composition.
译文应和原作同样流畅。

鲁迅先生认为："凡是翻译，必须兼顾两面，一当然力求其易解，一则保存原作的风姿"。即指出了翻译应该把握的最基本的原则：要能忠实地表达出英文原文的内容和风格；要符合中文的表达习惯。

因此，我们每做完一次翻译，都需要拿出泰特勒先生的翻译三原则，来审视自己的译文，看看自己的译文是否符合泰特勒的翻译三原则，养成良好的翻译习惯，才可以不断地在翻译方面取得进步。

Chapter 3 English to Chinese Technical Translation for Mechanical Engineering

3.1.1 The Characteristics of Professional English Literature

1. 专业词汇多

机械工程专业英语所涉及的大多是机械工程领域的专业知识，这就要求在翻译的时候能准确使用机械工程领域专业术语，不能望文生义。

e.g. The main components of the lathe are the headstock and tailstock at opposite ends of a bed, and a tool post between them which holds the cutting tool.

译文：车床的主要部件是主轴箱、尾座和刀架，主轴箱与尾座位于床身的两端，用于夹持刀具的刀架置于主轴箱与尾座之间。

e.g. All pumps may be classified as either positive-displacement or non-positive-displacement. Most pumps used in hydraulic systems are positive-displacement.

译文：泵可以分为容积式泵和非容积式泵，液压系统采用的大多数泵都是容积式泵。

e.g. Direct-drive technology contributes to higher machine (or system) throughput with quicker acceleration and higher top speeds compared with gear-or belt-driven designs.

译文：直接驱动技术和常规的齿轮、皮带传动相比，由于具有更高的加速度和最高转速，因而可以提高所驱动的机械设备或系统的生产能力。

2. 复杂长句多

科技文献资料、科学实验报告以及仪器设备说明书等科技英语文章，其语言运用的特点之一是句子所含信息量大，长句较多，成为理解和翻译时的难点。为了解开这一难题，首先要弄清长句形成的原因，从中找出分析的思路和脉络。

长句形成的第一种原因：在句子的基本结构前后，常用单词、短语或从句修饰作定语或状语，使句子展开得很长。

e.g. Applied sciences, on the other hand, is directly concerned with the application of the working of pure science to the practical affairs of life, and to increasing man's control over his environment, thus leading to the development of new techniques, processes and machines.

分析：这是一个简单句，主语是 Applied sciences，短语动词 be concerned with 的宾语 the application 带有很长的定语，从 of 到 to increasing man's control over his environment，共包括5个介词短语，并有短语套短语的现象。

译文：另一方面，应用科学直接关系到如何将理论科学研究成果用于生活实践，用于加强人们对外界环境的控制，从而导致新技术、新工艺和新机器的不断产生。

长句形成的第二种原因：并列成分多（如单词、短语和从句）。

e. g. The kinds of materials to be machined, variation in the types of machine tools chosen for a particular operation, the speeds at which the machining is performed, the selection of coarse and fine feeds, the kinds of cut(whether light or heavy), and the kinds of fluids used for cooling and lubricating are factors determining which material, of the several available, is best suited to the purpose in mind.

分析：本句有 6 个并列主语，而且每个主语本身又带有短语或从句作为修饰语。该句的谓语是 are，factors 为表语。实际上，本句的基本结构是"并列主语＋谓语＋表语"并不复杂。

译文：需要加工材料的种类，某种加工所选择的机床种类，操作时的速度，粗细工件进给量的选择，冷却液和润滑液的种类，这些都是确定（刀具）材料的因素，据此确定现有的几种材料中哪一种最合适。

长句形成的第三种原因：存在着从句作为句子成分和短语套短语及从句套从句的复杂语言现象。

e. g. Perhaps the simplest flexible coupling permitting small amounts of axial misalignment and/for torsional flexibility consists of a piece of elastic material bonded to two separated collinear cylindrical members which in turn can be fastened onto the two shafts by means of setscrews or other fasteners.

分析句子成分：分词短语 permitting … torsional flexibility 作主句主语 flexible coupling 的定语；主句的谓语动词为 consists of，宾语是 a piece of elastic material，bonded … members 作定语修饰 material；which … fasteners 为定语从句修饰 members。

主干部分：flexible coupling consists of a piece of elastic material（柔性联轴器由一个弹性材料构成）。

添加修饰成分：flexible coupling(permitting small amounts of axial misalignment and/for torsional flexibility)（允许少量轴向对中偏差和（或）扭转弹性的柔性联轴器）；material(bonded to two separated collinear cylindrical members)（固接在两个分离共线的圆筒形构件上的材料）；which in turn can be fastened onto the two shafts by means of setscrews or other fasteners（通过定位螺钉或其他紧固件将其固定在两个轴上）。

译文：也许，允许少量轴向对中偏差和（或）扭转弹性的最简单的柔性联轴器具有如下结构：将一个弹性材料固接在两个分离共线的圆筒形构件上，再通过定位螺钉或其他紧固件将其固定在两个轴上。

3. 被动语态多

被动语态是一种动词形式，表示动词的主语与该动词所表示的动作之间的主动和被动关系。当主语是动作的执行者，即主语为施事者时动词用主动语态，如果主语是动作的承受者也称受事者时动词使用被动语态。被动语态把所要论证、说明的科技问题放在句子的

Chapter 3　English to Chinese Technical Translation for Mechanical Engineering

主语位置上，就更能引起人们的注意。此外，被动语态比主动语态更少主观色彩，这正是科技作品所需要的。因此在科技英语中，凡是在不需要或不可能指出行为主体的场合，或者在需要突出行为客体的场合都使用被动语态。

机械工程英语使用被动语态的占 1/3 以上，大量使用的原因主要有以下几个方面：
(1) 被动语态，强调主语，突出重要性。

例 1：Springs are used as cushions to absorb shock.
弹簧被用作吸收振动的缓冲器。
例 2：Gears are used to transmit power positively from one shaft to another by means of successively engaging teeth.
齿轮通过连续的啮合齿，被用作从一个轴向另一个轴传递动力。
例 3：Much progress has been made in electrical engineering in less three decades.
在过去的三十年里，电力工程获得了巨大的进步。
例 4：Good safety practices should be followed to ensure safe machining.
必须遵守良好的安全操作规程以保证安全加工。

(2) 采用被动语态，因不需要指出动作的执行者。

例 1：When a force is applied to a material, it produces a stress in the material.
当给材料施加力时，就会产生应力。
例 2：If a machine part is not well protected, it will become rusty after a period of time.
如果机器零件不好好防护，过一段时间后就会生锈。

(3) 采用被动语态，因无法指出动作执行者。

例 1：In most machine members, the deformation must be kept low.
大多数的机械零件其变形量都求很低。
例 2：An engineering drawing must be properly dimensioned in order to convey the designer's intent to the end user.
为了将设计者的意图传达给最终用户，工程图纸都必须合理地标注。

3.1.2　Requirements of Professional Literature Translation

专业英文文献具有客观性(Objectivity)、规范性(Normalization)、科学性(Scientificity)和现实性(Reality)等特点，专业文献的翻译更侧重于翻译的"信"和"达"，对译文"雅"的要求不高。

专业英语的翻译要求符合"ABC"标准：Accuracy(准确)、Brevity(简练)、Clarity(通顺)。

e.g. Heat-treatment is used to normalize, to soften or to harden steels.
热处理用来使钢正常化、软化或者硬化。(×)
热处理可用来对钢正火、退火或者淬火。(√)

e. g. The importance of computer in the use of manufacturing cannot be overestimated.

计算机在制造业应用上的重要性不能被估计过高。（×）

计算机在制造业应用上的重要性怎么估计也不会过高。（√）

如何提高专业英语翻译的水平？建议大家从以下五个方面着手。

（1）准确翻译专业词汇。这需要大家掌握一定的专业英语词汇和表达。附录中给出了机械制造专业的常用专业词汇，但仅供参考，不需要死记硬背，而是需要大家在阅读专业英文文献中，多总结归纳，不断积累。

e. g. Tool magazines are designed in various styles and sizes. CNC machining centers are usually equipped with a tool magazine that can hold a range of twenty to over one hundred tools.

刀库可以设计成不同的形式和大小，CNC 加工中心通常配备有可以容纳 20 至 100 把刀具的刀库。

（2）熟练掌握常用结构。

● S+V(主+谓)

e. g. This machine can work. 这台机器可以工作。

● S+V+P(主+谓+表)

e. g. White cast iron is very hard. 白铸铁是很坚硬的。

● S+V+O(主+谓+宾)

e. g. This steel has excellent ductility. 钢有很好的塑性。

● S+V+O+O(主+谓+间接宾+直接宾语)

e. g. This machine gives me great surprise. 这台机器给我很大惊喜。

● S+V+O+OC(主+谓+宾+宾补)

e. g. The pressure causes a crater to form in the liquid metal pool. 这种压力使液体金属熔池中形成弧坑。

（3）透彻分析深层含义。语言学家吕叔湘先生在《英文汉译述例》中，将只生搬硬套的肤浅的翻译评价为："望文生义，简直是开玩笑。"要透彻分析深层含义，常常需要结合上下文来进行理解。

e. g. A well-developed, competitive world is requiring that manufacturing begins to settle for more, to become itself sophisticated.

译文：一个高度发展的、充满竞争的世界正在要求制造业开始满足更多的需求，并使其自身采用先进高端的技术进行装备。

Chapter 3　English to Chinese Technical Translation for Mechanical Engineering

（4）努力学习专业知识。扎实的专业知识，对于专业英语的翻译有重要的作用，即使最新的专业文献的翻译，也是建立在已有专业知识的基础上的。

> e. g. Computer integration provides widely and instantaneously available, accurate information, improving communication between departments, permitting tighter control, and generally enhancing the overall quality and efficiency of the entire system.
>
> 译文：计算机集成可提供广泛的、及时和精确的信息，可以改进各部门之间的交流与沟通，实施更严格的控制，从而提高整个系统的整体质量和效率。

（5）不断提高汉语水平。要做好翻译，外语重要，母语同样重要。这一方面是理解的需要，另一方面是表达的需要。遇到一些专业英语长句，没相当的汉语水平是很难翻译好的。另外，在国际工程实际英语翻译中，只有良好的汉语水平才能搭起顺畅的沟通桥梁。

> e. g. A workpiece which is relatively short compared to its diameter is stiff enough that we can safely turn it in the three-jaw chuck without supporting the free end of the work.
>
> 差的译文：与其直径相比起来相对短的工件刚性足够好，我们可以安全地车削它，装夹时只用三爪卡盘而不用支撑工件的自由端。
>
> 好的译文：长径比较小的工件有足够的刚性，因此，我们可以安全地进行车削，装夹时只用三爪卡盘，而不用支撑工件的自由端。

3.2　Basic Process for Technical Translation

翻译的基本过程可以简单地分为三步，即：理解（Understanding），表达（Expression），校核（Check）。

1. 理解——语法分析

从语法的角度去剖析原文句子里的语法结构，弄清句子所传递的含义。要求我们学会基本句型，学会从长句中找出基本句型。

2. 表达——语言转换

译者把自己理解的内容用译入语准确而又自然地传递给译入语读者。在表达阶段，着重于如何使用译入语传递原文作者所说的东西。理解是表达的前提，表达是理解的结果。

3. 校核——精益求精

校核是对理解和表达的最终审核阶段，是使译文能符合忠实、通顺的翻译标准所必不可少的环节。校核除了要对原文内容及语言等大的方面检查外，还对很多细节方面进行检查，包括数字等的格式、标点符号的使用、译文中是否有生僻或过时的词汇等。

3.3 Common Translation Skills

3.3.1 Conversion of Word Class

采用词类转换译法的理由是语系不同、难以对号入座，常常需要转换。

1. 英语名词—汉语动词

e. g. A steady increase of load on a part will cause it to deform gradually.
逐渐增加零件上的载荷，可使零件逐渐变形。

2. 英语动词—汉语名词

e. g. The electronic computer is chiefly characterized by its accurate and rapid computation.
电子计算机的主要特点是计算准确而迅速。

3. 英语形容词—汉语动词

e. g. Grinding has better surface roughness than milling.
磨削产生的表面粗糙度优于铣削。

4. 英语形容词—汉语名词

e. g. Glass is much more soluble than quartz.
玻璃的可溶性比石英大得多。

3.3.2 Addition and Reduction of Words

1. 增词的情况

增词的情况有两种：
（1）根据句法需要而增词。

e. g. Brittle materials have high compressive strength but only a moderate tensile strength.
脆性材料抗压强度较高，抗拉强度只有中等水平。

（2）根据意义或修辞需要而增词。

e. g. This soft silver-gray metal could be converted into a superhard substance that could cut glass and many other substances, including itself when soft.
这种银灰色的软金属可以转换成一种超硬的物质，该物质可以切削玻璃和许多其他物质，包括处于软状态的该物质本身。

Chapter 3　English to Chinese Technical Translation for Mechanical Engineering

e. g. The constant temperature workshop consists of large parts machine line, middle and small shell parts machine line, shaft and plate parts machine lines, precision machine line, unit assembly line, powder spraying line, final assembly line, automatic solid storehouse, and precision quality test.

恒温车间建有大件加工线、中小壳体类零件加工线、轴类及盘类零件加工线、精密加工线、部件装配线、涂装作业线、总装作业线、全自动立体仓库、精密检测室。

根据句意，precision quality test可以增译为"精密检测室"。

2. 减词的情况

减词的情况至少有以下七种：

（1）省略代词。

e. g. A shaft can have a nonround cross section and it need not necessarily rotate.
轴可以有非圆形截面，而且不一定需要旋转。

e. g. The advantage of rolling bearing is that they cause less friction.
滚动轴承的优点在于产生的摩擦较小。

（2）省略系动词be。

e. g. White cast iron is too hard to be machined.
白口铸铁太硬，不能进行机加工。

（3）虚词"it"省略。

e. g. It is apparent that shafts can be subjected to various combination.
很明显，轴可以连接多种连接件。

（4）省略冠词。

e. g. The knee provides the vertical movement of the table.
升降台能使机床工作台垂直运动。

（5）省略连词。

e. g. The lathe is one of the most useful and versatile machines in the workshop.
车床是车间里最有用最通用的机床之一。

（6）省略介词。

e. g. Gears provide a positive-ratio drive for transmitting rotary motion from one shaft to another.
齿轮能以恒定的传动比将旋转运动从一根轴传递到另一根轴。

（7）意译省略。

e. g. Workers should avoid using these materials wastefully.
工人们应节约实用这些材料。

3.3.3 Affirmative-negative Expression in Translation

根据需要，把肯定式译成汉语的否定式，或把英语的否定式译成汉语的肯定式。

e. g. 1. The demand for our products exceeds the supply.
我们的产品供不应求。

e. g. 2. Metal do not melt until heated to a definite temperature.
金属要加热到一定的温度才会熔化。

e. g. 3. We cannot be too careful in doing experiments.
我们做实验越仔细越好。

e. g. 4. After the introduction of interexchangeable parts, we take for granted that we can replace a broken bolt of a certain size with an identical one purchased form any local hardware store.
在可互换性零件出现之后，对于一个损坏的螺栓，从当地任何一家五金店后置的完全一样的零件来替代是完全不成问题的。

3.3.4 Division and Combination

1. 分译(Division)

分译是把原句中的某些成分分出来另作处理，可以译成独立的句子。使译文更加简明、明确。

e. g. Matter is composed of molecules that are composed of atoms.
物质由分子组成，而分子则是由原子组成。

e. g. His failure to observe the safety regulations resulted in an accident to the machinery.
因为他没有遵守安全规则，机器出了故障。（名词短语）

e. g. Care shall be taken at all times to protect the instrument from dust and damp.
应经常保护仪器，勿使沾染尘土，勿使受潮。

e. g. The tube consists of a short copper section followed by a longer steel section with a flange at the end.
管子由两段组成：前段短，是铜的；后段长，是钢的，末端带法兰。

e. g. The control unit is an important part of the computer, which can cause the machine to operate according to man's wishes.
控制装置是计算机的重要部件，它能使机器按照人的意志进行操作。

e. g. A statement by many designers, that failure occurs when a body ceases to perform its allotted function and that most machine elements will not properly work after they have received a permanent deformation, approves of the practice of referring the factor of members with steady loads to the stress of the elastic limit(or yield point).

分析：这个长复合句是以 and 连接了两个 statement 的同位语从句 that failure … function 和 that most … deformation。

Chapter 3 English to Chinese Technical Translation for Mechanical Engineering

译文：许多设计人员认为，当一物体不再具有规定的功能时即认为物体失效，大多数机器部件出现塑性变形后就不再工作。因此，根据弹性极限（或屈服极限）确定静载荷构件的安全系数是可行的。

2. 合译（Combination）

合译是当英语中两个以上的简单句关系密切，可不限于原文表层结构，把它们合译成一个汉语单句（或者复句），避免不必要的重复。主从复合句和并列复合句的合译是为了更加清晰和通顺。

1) 单句的合译

e. g. The king of the oilfield is the driller. He is a very skilled man.

油田的主角是技术熟练的钻井工。

e. g. The chemist makes frequent use of catalysts. He adds them in small quantities to reacting materials.

化学工作者经常通过把少量催化剂加入反应物中的方式利用催化剂。

2) 主从复合句的合译

e. g. By then ironworkers had not learned how to heat the iron ore enough that they could melt it.

那时候，炼铁工人还不知道如何把铁矿石加热而使其熔化。

e. g. With all its beams advancing in step with each other, the laser possesses very particular properties which no ordinary light ever has.

由于激光束前进时是同步的，所以激光具有任何普通光线所没有的特性。

3) 并列复合句的合译

e. g. It was in mid-August, and the repair section operated under the blazing sun.

八月中旬，修理组人员在烈日下工作。

总之，分译还是合译，都要在分析句子的语法结构，搞清楚各层意思之间的逻辑关系后，根据目的语的表达习惯，灵活掌握，以避免出现生硬的译文。

3.3.5 Translation of Passive Voice

1. 译成汉语的无主语句

当无法知道或无法说出动作发出者时，往往可以把英语的被动语态译成汉语的无主句。

e. g. To get all the stages off the ground, a first big push is needed.

为了使火箭各级全部离开地面，需要有一个巨大的第一推动力。

e. g. Work is done, when an object is lifted.

当举起一个物体时，就做了功。

e. g. Attention must be paid to safety in handling radio active materials.

处理放射性材料时必须注意安全。

2. 译成汉语的主动句

(1) 用"人们"、"大家"、"有人"、"我们"等含有泛指意义的词作主语,从而使汉语译文呈"兼语式"句式。

e. g. The mechanism of fever production is not completely understood.
人们还不完全清楚发烧的产生机理。

e. g. Sun is known to rise in the east.
我们都知道,太阳从东方升起。

e. g. He was seen to have turned off the current.
有人看见他把电流断开了。

(2) 由 it 引导的主语从句,译成无人称或不定人称句。

e. g. It is said that the production of transistor radios was increased six times from 1970 to 1974.
据说从 1970 年至 1974 年间,晶体管收音机的产量增长了五倍。

e. g. It is demonstrated that the conductivity of silver is higher than that of copper.
已经证明银的导电率比铜的导电率高。

这类句型还有:It is reported/supposed/must be admitted/pointed out that (据报道/据推测/必须承认/必须指出);It is believed/generally considered/well-known that(有人相信/大家认为/众所周知)。

(3) 当被动语态中的主语为无生命的名词或由 under、in、on 等少数几个介词短语构成时,译成主动句。

e. g. That computer is under repair.
那台计算机正在修理。

e. g. A new design method is on trial.
这种新的设计方法正在试用。

e. g. This kind of electronic equipment is in great demand.
这种电子设备需求量很大。

e. g. The plan is being carried out.
计划正在实施。

(4) 当 need、want、require 等动词后接主动形式的动名词,表示被动意义时,译成主动句。

e. g. This device needs repairing.
这套设备需要修理。

e. g. This phenomenon is worth mentioning.
这一现象值得一提。

3. 译成汉语被动句

(1) 译成明显的"被"字句,通常带有"by+动作发出者"或"be+…ed"。

e. g. The number of TTL devices that one TTL output will drive is called an out.
一个 TTL 输出所能驱动的 TTL 装置的数量被称为输出能力。

e. g. Gears are used in place of belt drivers and other forms of friction rivers.
齿轮(传动)被用来代替带传动及其他的一些摩擦传动形势。

e. g. In this case, the molecule is polarized by the field.
在这种情况下,该分子被场极化了。

e. g. Smith's forging is usually used for making very large forges.
自由锻通常被用来锻造大型锻件。

(2) 译成"由、由……组成、用、用于……"等,通常带有"be made up of"、"be composed of"、"be used in/to"。

e. g. The magnetic field is produced by an electric current.
磁场由电流产生。

e. g. Usually alloy is composed of a base metal(the largest part of the alloy)and a smaller amount of other metals.
通常,合金由一种贱金属(合金中最多的那部分)和少量的其他金属组成。

e. g. They are used to support and position a shaft and to reduce the friction created by the rotating part, particularly when under load.
它们用于轴的支承、定位,并降低由转动件带来的摩擦,特别是在载荷作用下。

e. g. Forging operations may be carried out using forging hammers.
锻造操作可由锻锤来完成。

(3) 译成判断句式"是……的"。如果英语句子本身所强调的是与某一静态动作有关的具体情况,如时间、地点、方式、方法等;或着重说一件事情是"怎样做"、"什么时候、什么地点做"的等,这时我们就可以把这些情况放在"是……的"这种判断句式中,使之突出。这种判断句式能够清楚地表达作者的意图和客观事实。

e. g. Everything in the world is built up from atoms.
世间万物都是由原子构成的。

e. g. The first CNC machine tool was developed by MIT in 1950s.
第一台数控机床是由 MIT 在 20 世纪 50 年代研发出来的。

e. g. Iron is extracted form the ore of the blast furnace.
铁是用高炉从铁矿中提炼出来的。

(4) 在谓语动词前面添加"予以"、"加以"、"受到"、"得以"等词。

e. g. The translation technique should be paid enough attention to.
翻译技巧应予以足够的重视。

e. g. Other mistakes of this dictionary will be corrected in the next edition.

这本辞典的其他错误将在下一版中予以修正。

e. g. Coal and oil are the remains of plants and animals. Crude mineralores and crude oil must be purified before they can be used.

煤和石油是动植物的残骸。原矿石和原油必须加以精炼才能使用。

e. g. The temperature must be controlled to produce the desired qualities in the steel.

为了得到(人们)想要的性能，热处理时钢的温度必须加以控制。

e. g. Technology have been rapidly developed because of the discovery of electricity.

由于电的发现，科学技术得以迅速发展。

总之，英语中被动语态的翻译不能一概采用所谓"语言等值"的顺译法，必须根据汉语的语法和习惯，发挥汉语的优势，用规范化的汉语表达方式，忠实而恰当地反映出原作语言的真实涵义，使译文的形式与原文内容辩证地统一起来，才能收到良好的翻译效果。

3.3.6 Translation of Attributive Clause

定语从句(attributive clause)有限制性和非限制性两种。限制性定语从句是先行词不可缺少的部分，去掉它主句意思往往不明确；非限制性定语从句是先行词的附加说明，去掉了也不会影响主句的意思，它与主句之间通常用逗号分开。

1. 限制性定语从句的译法

限制性定语从句对所修饰的先行词起限制作用，关系密切，不用逗号分开，翻译时一般采用前置法、后置法或融合法。

(1) 前置译法——当定语从句比较简单时，可译成带"…的"的短语。

e. g. Object that do not transfer light cause shadows.

不透光的物体会造成阴影。

(2) 后置译法——当定语从句结构比较复杂或前置时不符合汉语习惯，可译成后置的并列分句。

e. g. This condenser consists of a tube surrounded by a water jacket through which cold water circulates.

这个冷凝器有一根围绕着水套的管子，冷水是通过水套循环流动的。

(3) 融合法——将主语与从句融合为一体。

e. g. The species that accepts electrons in an oxidation-reduction reaction is referred to as the oxidizing agent.

在氧化还原反应中接受电子的物质称为氧化剂。

2. 非限制性定语从句的译法

非限制性定语从句对所修饰的先行词不起限制作用，只对它加以进一步的描写、

Chapter 3 English to Chinese Technical Translation for Mechanical Engineering

解释或叙述，而且要用逗号分开，翻译时一般采用独立译法，也可以不译成定语从句。

（1）独立译法——常用方法。

e. g. This was the beginning of the science of radar, which finds aircraft by the reflections of radio waves sent into the sky.

这就是雷达科学的开端。雷达利用射入天空中的电波的反射来发现飞机。

（2）偏正短语译法——适合有些定语从句兼具状语从句的职能，说明原因、结果、目的、让步、假设等关系。

e. g. To make an atom bomb we have to use uranium 235, in which all the atoms available for fission.

制造原子弹需用铀235，因为它的所有原子都可裂变。

3.3.7 Translation of Double Negative

双重否定句(Double Negative)是相对于单纯否定句而言的，是指一句话里同时有两个否定词，或一个否定词和一个具有否定意义的词语。

（1）"not/no+dis" "不能不/不得不 …"。

It could not disobey.

（2）"no … no" "没有 … 没有"。

With no changes there is no new substances.

（3）"scarcely/hardly … not" "几乎没有 … 不"。

There is scarcely any sphere of industry where electricity may not find useful application.

（4）"in the absence of' … not/no/nothing" "没有 … 不"。

In the absence of gravity, we could not do anything.

（5）"never … without" "每当 … 总是"。

Heat can never be converted into a certain energy without something lost.

（6）"but for … no/not/nothing" "要不是 … 就没有"。

But for substances, there could be nothing in the world.

3.4 Translation of Long Sentences

科技英语中有很多长句，主要是因为其具有严谨、准确、详尽、完整、逻辑性强等特点。长句不单纯就句子的长度而言，也指语法结构比较复杂、从句和修饰语较多、包含的内容层次在一个以上的句子。

翻译长句时，首先分析和弄清从句的语法结构，从句与主句等之间的语法关系和逻辑关系；然后，采用相应的手段译成汉语。

语法结构分析的步骤为：首先找出句子的主干或核心句(kernel sentence)——主谓结构或主谓宾结构；然后分析从句的具体语法作用。

e. g. The mixture of oils of which it is composed must be separated out into a number of products such as petrol, aviation spirit, kerosene, diesel oils and lubricants, all of which have special purposes.

本句的核心结构：

The mixture of oils … must be separated out into a number of products; of which it is composed 为定语从句，修饰 oils; all of which have special purposes 为非限定性定语从句，用来说明以上产品。

译文：组成石油的油质混合物必须分离成为一系列的石油产品：汽油、航空汽油、煤油、柴油及润滑油。所以这些产品都有其特殊用处。

根据英、汉语的不同特点，在对长句的语法结构、逻辑层次和时间顺序等有清楚了解的基础上，可采用如下翻译方法：顺译法、逆译法、分译法、重排法。

1. 顺译法

有的英语长句其行文方式与汉语基本相同，即按时间顺序、前因后果，先介绍后总结，先次要后主要等，对这类句子，就可按原文结构顺序翻译。

e. g. 1. This approach is not suitable to these countries which have to establish law and order before their economies can take off.

这个方法不适应这些国家，因为它们必须先建立法制，经济才能腾飞。

e. g. 2. If a hard grade wheel was to be used for grinding a hard material, the dull grains would not be pulled off from the bond quickly enough, thus impeding the self dressing process of the surface of the wheel and finally resulting in clogging of the wheel and burns on the ground surface.

如果使用硬砂轮磨削硬的材料，磨钝的磨粒就不能很快从粘结体上脱落，这样便妨碍砂轮表面的自修整过程，最终导致砂轮的堵塞并在被磨表面留下灼斑。

2. 逆译法

由于英、汉语在表达顺序上的不同，汉语一般是"先发生的事情先说，后发生的后说"，"先原因，后结果"，"先次要，后主要"的习惯；而英语有许多时候跟汉语正好相反：更多地把主句放在句首，分析说明部分置后；有时为了强调，把某些部分放在句首或反常的位置。翻译时要根据汉语的表达方式，对原语顺序进行调整；有时还要重新组合译文，以达到画龙点睛、突出主题的目的。

e. g. This chapter discusses key trends in telecommunications and explores their relationships with language services mainly from the perspective that the new telecommunications technologies are creating new demand for new cross-cultural communication service.

主要基于新的电信技术正对新的跨文化交流服务提出新要求，本章将讨论电信的主要发展趋势，并探讨与语言服务的联系。

3. 分译法

由于英、汉两种语言的表达差异，在英语长句翻译成汉语时，要尽可能"化整为零"。

Chapter 3　English to Chinese Technical Translation for Mechanical Engineering

按在原句的关系代词和关系副词引导的从句处、主谓连接处、并列或转折连接处,切断分成几个意义片段,分别译成汉语分句。

e. g. The very important oil industry,which has done much to rejuvenate the economy of the South since the end of World War II,made considerable headway especially in the five states of Arkansas,Louisiana,Mississippi,Oklahoma and Texas.

第二次世界大战后石油工业对振兴南部经济起了很大的作用。这个十分重要的工业部门特别在阿肯色、路易斯安那、密西西比、俄克拉荷马和得克萨斯五个州取得了很大的进展。

4. 重排法

由于英汉思维习惯和表达方式的差异,对于结构复杂的长句,需要在语法和语义结构理解的基础上,对深层结构进行切分,翻译时通过改变语序、重组结构,按照逻辑或时间顺序译出。重排法是长句翻译的一种常用手段。

e. g. Manufacturing processes may be classified as unit production with small quantities being made and mass production with large numbers identical parts being produced.

制造过程可以分为单件生产和批量生产。单件生产就是生产少量的零件;批量生产就是生产大量相同的零件。

3.5　Fast Mastering English Vocabulary by Comparison

比较是确定客观事物彼此之间差异点与共同点的思维方法。有比较才有鉴别,不经比较,就难以辨别事物的特征,就难以认定事物的本质,就难以弄清事物的相互关系,就难以区别事物的异同之点。所谓比较记忆法,就是对相似而又不同的识记材料进行对比分析,弄清以至把握住它们的差异点与相同点,用以进行记忆的方法。

科技文章中有很多近义词,如果我们加以比较,并结合专业短语来记忆,就能够深刻明白,应用自如。

(1) manufacture,fabricate,make。

Manufacture:一般指工业上批量的、成熟的、有一定规模的制造;

Fabricate:一般指具有技巧性手工方式的制造,而且一般是小批量甚至单件的制作;

Make:泛指做和制造。

(2) transform, transfer, transmit, convert。

Transform:指根本的转换、变换、改造,常跟into,e. g. technological transformation 技术改造;Transfer 和 Transmit:指传递、传送、发射等,e. g.,technology transfer 技术转让,heat transfer 传热,data transmission 数据传输,power transmission 功率传递,TV transmission tower 电视发射塔,hydraulic transmission 液压传动;

Convert:只指物理形式的转换,如模数转换,A/D converter。

e. g. We should try to transform heat into power.

His plans were transformed overnight into reality.

（3）tool，cutter，tooling，device，equipment，installation，facility，utility，implement，utensil，appliance，instrument apparatus。

Tool(工具)，cutter(刀具)，tooling(无复数形式，工装、模具)，device(小装置)，equipment(无复数形式，设备)，installation(成套装置设备)，facility(常用复数形式，设备，机组，设施，＜附属＞装置)，utility(公用事业设备)，implement(工具、器械)，utensil［juːˈtensl，juːˈtensəl］(器皿厨具)，appliance(家用器具)，instrument(仪器仪表，乐器)，apparatus(电器、机电设备)。

e. g. The technicians whom we met yesterday had worked out a new automatic device.
我们昨天碰到的那位技术员设计了一种新的自动化装置。

experimental facility 实验装置；sport facilities 体育设施；recreational facilities 娱乐设施；power utility 发电站。

What implements are needed for gardening?
园艺需要些什么工具？

（4）element(单元，零件)，part(零件)，component(组件，元件)，subassembly(组件)。

（5）machine(机器)，machine tool(机床)，machinery(机械总称)。

（6）accuracy(精度)，precision(精密)。

e. g. machining accuracy 加工精度

location accuracy 定位精度

measuring accuracy 测量精度

precision machining 精密加工

precision instrument 精密仪器

precision mold 精密模具

（7）Location，position。

Location：只做名词，位置、定位，指将某个物体放在或者固定在空间某个具体位置；position：既是名词，又是动词，指确定或找到物体的确切位置。

e. g. six-point location principle 六点定位原理

Location pin 定位销

Locating accuracy 定位精度

GPS(global positional system)全球定位系统

Positional tolerance 位置公差

（8）Transducer，sensor。

Transducer：换能器，变换器，传感器，指将输入能量转换成为另一种形式的能量的装置；sensor：传感器，指将物理、化学等量转换为电信号或者计算机可用的数据。

一般而言，transducer 需要有转化(放大)电路，而 sensor 则不一定。

e. g. Image sensor 图像传感器

inductive displacement transducer 电感式位移传感器

（9）Intensity，strength。

Intensity：指强化的程度、力度；

strength：指材料受力后能承受而不被破坏的能力；优势，实力。

e. g. strength the training intensity 提高训练强度

increase the investment intensity 加大投资力度

fatigue strength 疲劳强度

ultimate strength 极限强度

（10） Figure, picture, diagram, chart, curve, illustration, drawing, image, graph, plot, map。

drawing/map/picture 这 3 个词在日常用语中常见，而 chart/diagram/graph/image 这 4 个是计算机软件中司空见惯的单词，其余的 figure/illustration/plot/curve 这 4 个词则在书面行文中屡见不鲜。如图 3.1 所示。

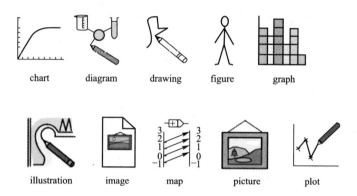

Fig. 3.1　comparision of chart, diagram, etc.

● Chart:变化趋势图，反映某个量在一段时间内变化关系的图线，是以数据信息为基础的，最终呈现出的图线完全依赖于各种详细的数据，如果没有数据作为支撑，则对应的图线或趋势根本无从谈起。

● Diagram：示意图，用简单的图线框对产品或过程所作的图示和解释(结构/功能/逻辑/过程的可视化)，diagram 更强调位置关系，它指的是描述产品的结构或服务的流程的一串图形(通常是示意图，如产品解剖图、组织架构图、作业流程图、程序执行图等)。

● Drawing:图纸。

e. g. This drawing shows what the front elevation of the house will look like when it is built.

这张图显示这幢房子建成后正面的外观。

● Figure:图形,图表,在科技论文中很常用。

e. g. Our textbook has many figures to help explain the lessons.
我们的教科书有许多图表帮助解释课文。

● graph:用手在某个介质(如地面/纸面/屏幕等)上画出来的东西(最终以画面形式呈现出的东西)。只强调把图形画出来，所以不管图形的种类如何，只要能画出来就是 graph，它甚至可以不需要用手去动作(所以 graph 的外延比 drawing 还要大)。

● illustration:插图，配图，为了让文字性的内容更加易懂而配置的图形或图片(借重图形以帮助理解)。

e. g. The text is accompanied by illustration.
正文附有插图。

● image：图像，画像，印象，形象，肖像。

e. g. 1. You can add an Image control to display an image.
您可以添加 Image 控件来显示图像。
e. g. 2. How can we improve our image?
我们该怎样来改善自己的形象呢？

● map：地图，映射图，用于跟实际事物一一对应的概念性的图示（与实物之间的一一对应）。

e. g. He unfolded the map and set it on the floor.
他打开地图，放在了地板上。

● picture：绘画，照片，图画，首先指是别人眼中看到的东西，然后通过他们的绘画、描述或解说在我们的脑海中形成形象。

e. g. I tried to put the picture from my mind.
我试图将这幅画面从脑海中抹去。

● plot：描点绘图，按某个既定方案或限制条件通过描点而形成的线条或形状，强调"思维的脉络性"或"意图"。

e. g. We plot about eight points on the graph.
我们在图表上绘制出大约 8 个点的曲线。

● curve：曲线，弧线。

e. g. Each firm will face a downward-sloping demand curve.
每一家企业都将面临需求曲线的下滑。

3.6　Reading Material

3.6.1　Machinability

The machinability of a material usually defined in terms of four factors:
(1) Surface finish and integrity of the machined part;
(2) Tool life obtained;
(3) Force and power requirements;
(4) Chip control.
Thus, good machinability indicates good surface finish and integrity, long tool life, and

low force and power requirements. As for chip control, long and thin(stringy) cured chips, if not broken up, can severely interfere with the cutting operation by becoming entangled in the cutting zone.

Because of the complex nature of cutting operations, it is difficult to establish relationships that quantitatively define the machinability of a material. In manufacturing plants, tool life and surface roughness are generally considered to be the most important factors in machinability. Although not used much any more, approximate machinability ratings are available in the example below.

1. Machinability of Steels

Because steels are among the most important engineering materials, their machinability has been studied extensively. The machinability of steels has been mainly improved by adding lead and sulfur to obtain so-called free-machining steels.

Resulfurized and Rephosphorized steels. Sulfur in steels forms manganese sulfide inclusions(second-phase particles), which act as stress raisers in the primary shear zone. As a result, the chips produced break up easily and are small; this improves machinability. The size, shape, distribution, and concentration of these inclusions significantly influence machinability. Elements such as tellurium and selenium, which are both chemically similar to sulfur, act as inclusion modifiers in resulfurized steels. Phosphorus in steels has two major effects. It strengthens the ferrite, causing increased hardness.

Harder steels result in better chip formation and surface finish. Note that soft steels can be difficult to machine, with built-up edge formation and poor surface finish. The second effect is that increased hardness causes the formation of short chips instead of continuous stringy ones, thereby improving machinability.

Leaded Steels. A high percentage of lead in steels solidifies at the tip of manganese sulfide inclusions. In non-resulfurized grades of steel, lead takes the form of dispersed fine particles. Lead is insoluble in iron, copper, and aluminum and their alloys. Because of its low shear strength, therefore, lead acts as a solid lubricant and is smeared over the tool-chip interface during cutting. This behavior has been verified by the presence of high concentrations of lead on the tool-side face of chips when machining leaded steels.

When the temperature is sufficiently high - for instance, at high cutting speeds and feeds-the lead melts directly in front of the tool, acting as a liquid lubricant. In addition to this effect, lead lowers the shear stress in the primary shear zone, reducing cutting forces and power consumption. Lead can be used in every grade of steel, such as 10xx, 11xx, 12xx, 41xx, etc. Leaded steels are identified by the letter L between the second and third numerals (for example, 10L45). (Note that in stainless steels, similar use of the letter L means "low carbon," a condition that improves their corrosion resistance.)

However, because lead is a well-known toxin and a pollutant, there are serious environmental concerns about its use in steels(estimated at 4500 tons of lead consumption every year in the production of steels). Consequently, there is a continuing trend toward eliminating the use of lead in steels(lead-free steels). Bismuth and tin are now being investigated as possible substitutes for lead in steels.

Calcium-Deoxidized Steels. An important development is calcium-deoxidized steels, in which oxide flakes of calcium silicates(CaSo) are formed. These flakes, in turn, reduce the strength of the secondary shear zone, decreasing tool-chip interface and wear. Temperature is correspondingly reduced. Consequently, these steels produce less crater wear, especially at high cutting speeds.

Stainless Steels. Austenitic(300 series) steels are generally difficult to machine. Chatter can be a problem, necessitating machine tools with high stiffness. However, ferritic stainless steels(also 300 series) have good machinability. Martensitic(400 series) steels are abrasive, tend to form a built-up edge, and require tool materials with high hot hardness and crater-wear resistance. Precipitation-hardening stainless steels are strong and abrasive, requiring hard and abrasion-resistant tool materials.

The Effects of Other Elements in Steels on Machinability. The presence of aluminum and silicon in steels is always harmful because these elements combine with oxygen to form aluminum oxide and silicates, which are hard and abrasive. These compounds increase tool wear and reduce machinability. It is essential to produce and use clean steels.

Carbon and manganese have various effects on the machinability of steels, depending on their composition. Plain low-carbon steels(less than 0.15% C) can produce poor surface finish by forming a built-up edge. Cast steels are more abrasive, although their machinability is similar to that of wrought steels. Tool and die steels are very difficult to machine and usually require annealing prior to machining. Machinability of most steels is improved by cold working, which hardens the material and reduces the tendency for built-up edge formation.

Other alloying elements, such as nickel, chromium, molybdenum, and vanadium, which improve the properties of steels, generally reduce machinability. The effect of boron is negligible. Gaseous elements such as hydrogen and nitrogen can have particularly detrimental effects on the properties of steel. Oxygen has been shown to have a strong effect on the aspect ratio of the manganese sulfide inclusions; the higher the oxygen content, the lower the aspect ratio and the higher the machinability.

In selecting various elements to improve machinability, we should consider the possible detrimental effects of these elements on the properties and strength of the machined part in service. At elevated temperatures, for example, lead causes embrittlement of steels(liquid-metal embrittlement, hot shortness), although at room temperature it has no effect on mechanical properties.

Sulfur can severely reduce the hot workability of steels, because of the formation of iron sulfide, unless sufficient manganese is present to prevent such formation. At room temperature, the mechanical properties of resulfurized steels depend on the orientation of the deformed manganese sulfide inclusions(anisotropy). Rephosphorized steels are significantly less ductile, and are produced solely to improve machinability.

2. Machinability of Various Other Metals

Aluminum is generally very easy to machine, although the softer grades tend to form a built-up edge, resulting in poor surface finish. High cutting speeds, high rake angles, and high relief angles are recommended. Wrought aluminum alloys with high silicon content and cast aluminum alloys may be abrasive; they require harder tool materials. Dimensional tolerance control may be a problem in machining aluminum, since it has a high thermal coefficient of expansion and a relatively low elastic modulus.

Beryllium is similar to cast irons. Because it is more abrasive and toxic, though, it requires machining in a controlled environment.

Cast gray irons are generally machinable but are abrasive. Free carbides in castings reduce their machinability and cause tool chipping or fracture, necessitating tools with high toughness. Nodular and malleable irons are machinable with hard tool materials.

Cobalt-based alloys are abrasive and highly work-hardening. They require sharp, abrasion-resistant tool materials and low feeds and speeds.

Wrought copper can be difficult to machine because of built-up edge formation, although cast copper alloys are easy to machine. Brasses are easy to machine, especially with the addition pf lead (leaded free-machining brass). Bronzes are more difficult to machine than brass.

Magnesium is very easy to machine, with good surface finish and prolonged tool life. However care should be exercised because of its high rate of oxidation and the danger of fire (the element is pyrophoric).

Molybdenum is ductile and work-hardening, so it can produce poor surface finish. Sharp tools are necessary.

Nickel-based alloys are work-hardening, abrasive, and strong at high temperatures. Their machinability is similar to that of stainless steels.

Tantalum is very work-hardening, ductile, and soft. It produces a poor surface finish; tool wear is high. Titanium and its alloys have poor thermal conductivity (indeed, the lowest of all metals), causing significant temperature rise and built-up edge; they can be difficult to machine.

Tungsten is brittle, strong, and very abrasive, so its machinability is low, although it greatly improves at elevated temperatures.

Zirconium has good machinability. It requires a coolant-type cutting fluid, however, because of the explosion and fire.

3.6.2 Shaft Design

Shafts are usually of circular cross section; either solid or hollow sections can be used. A hollow shaft weighs considerably less than a solid shaft of comparable strength, but is somewhat more expensive. Shafts are subjected to torsion, bending, or a combination of these two; in unusual cases, other stresses might also become involved. Careful location of bearings can do much to control the size of shafts, as the loading is affected by the position of mountings. After a shaft size is computed, its diameter is often modified(upward only) to fit a standard bearing. Calculations merely indicate the minimum size.

1. Common Shaft Sizes

Table 3-1 lists some of the common available sizes for steel(round, solid) shafting. These are nominal sizes only. A designer must accurately compute the exact size so that it will fit properly into bearings. Since any machining is costly, a minimal amount of metal should be removed from stock sizes. Any metal removed in certain locations changes the shaft diameter in various axial positions. Therefore, proper radii must be provided to minimize stress concentrations. Abrupt changes in diameter without sufficient radii produce so-called 'stress raisers'. Thus it is desirable-from the standpoint of stress——to provide large radii. However, large radii also make it difficult to mount such other components as pulleys, cams, gears, and so on because of radius interference. Often, the bore of such other components has to be chamfered to clear radii at the point where a shaft changes diameter. In the final analysis, a compromise has to be made between ideal shaft radii and the undercutting of other components.

Table3-1 Some of common shaft sizes(solid circular, in.)

0.5	1.625	2.75	3.875
0.625	1.75	2.875	4
0.75	1.875	3	4.25
0.875	2	3.125	4.5
1	2.125	3.25	4.75
1.125	2.25	3.375	5
1.25	2.375	3.5	5.25
1.375	2.5	3.625	5.5
1.5	2.625	3.75	6

2. Metric Shaft Sizes

The diameters of shafts made compatible with metric-sized bores of mechanical components(such as antifriction bearings) are specified in millimeters. Although any shaft size can be turned to provide extremely accurate fits, Table 3-2 shows popular nominal sizes.

Table3-2 Typical metric shaft diameters(mm)

4	40	110
5	45	120
6	50(1.969")	130
7	55	140
8	60	150(5.901")

Chapter 3 English to Chinese Technical Translation for Mechanical Engineering

(续)

9	65	160
10	70	170
12(0.472")	75(2.953")	180
15	80	190
17	85	200
20	90	220(7.784")
25(0.984")	95	240
30	100(3.937")	260
35	105	280(11.02")

3. Torsion

Equations for a shaft in pure torsion are listed below; these equations are for round solid and round hollow sections only:

$$T = S_s \frac{J}{c} = \frac{S_s \pi D^3}{16} = \frac{63000(\text{hp})}{N} \text{(for solid shafts)}$$

$$T = S_s \frac{J}{c} = \frac{S_s \pi (D_o^4 - D_i^4)}{16 D_o} = \frac{63000(\text{hp})}{N} \text{(for hollow shafts)}$$

where

$T =$ torque(in-lb);

$S_s =$ design stress in shear(psi);

$D =$ diameter of solid shaft(in.);

$D_o =$ outside diameter of hollow shaft(in.);

$D_i =$ inside diameter of hollow shaft(in.);

hp = horsepower;

$N =$ revolutions per minute(rpm);

$J =$ polar moment of inertia(in.);

$c =$ distance from neutral axis to outermost fiber(in.).

Example 1

Compute the diameter of a solid shaft that rotates 100rpm and transmits 1.2hp. The design stress for shear is to be 6000psi and the shaft is subjected to torsion only.

Solution

$$T = \frac{63000(\text{hp})}{N} = \frac{(63000)(1.2)}{100} = 756 \text{in-lb}$$

$$D = \sqrt[3]{\frac{16T}{\pi S_s}} = \sqrt[3]{\frac{(16)(756)}{(3.14)(6000)}} = 0.863 \text{in. (minimum)}$$

Use $\frac{7}{8}$-in. diameter.

4. Torsional Deflection(Solid Shaft)

The amount of twist in a shaft is important. One rule of thumb is to restrict the torsional deflection to one degree in a length equal to 20diameters. For example, if the active part of a shaft is 40in. and the shaft diameter is 2in. ,1 deg of torsional deflection would be permitted. In some applications, the angle of twist must be smaller than this. The following equation applies to torsional deflection:

$$D=\sqrt[4]{\frac{32TL}{\pi G\theta}}$$

where

L=length of shaft subjected to twist(in.);
G=shear modulus of elasticity(psi);
θ=angle of twist(rad).

Fig. 3.2 shows the angle of twist(greatly exaggerated) that appears when torque is applied to a shaft.

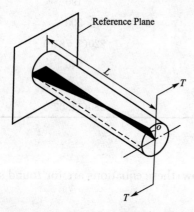

Fig. 3.2 **Torsional deflection of shaft**

Example 2

A 2-in. lineshaft transmits 20hp and rotates at 200rpm. Two pulleys spaced 30in. apart cause a torsional deflection. If the shear modulus of elasticity is 12,000,000psi, find the angle of twist in degree.

Solution

$$T=\frac{63000(\text{hp})}{N}=\frac{(63000)(20)}{200}=6300\text{in}-\text{lb}$$

$$\theta=\frac{32TL}{\pi GD^4}=\frac{(32)(630)(30)}{(3.14)(12,000,000)(2)^4}=0.0100\text{rad};$$

$$0.0100\times57.3=0.573\text{deg}.$$

5. Combined Torsion and Bending(Solid Shaft)

A shaft is often subjected to combined torsion and flexure. There are numerous ways of computing a shaft diameter under these conditions. The simplest is to compute equivalent bending and twisting moments for the shaft and then substitute these values into the regular equations for torsion and bending. Equations for equivalent moments are as follows:

$$T_E=\sqrt{M^2+T^2}$$

$$M_E=\frac{M+T_E}{2}$$

where

T_E=equivalent twisting moment(in-lb),
M_E=equivalent bending moment(in-lb),

The torsion equation then becomes

Chapter 3 English to Chinese Technical Translation for Mechanical Engineering

$$D=\sqrt[3]{\frac{16T_E}{\pi S_S}}$$

and the bending(or flexure)equation becomes

$$D=\sqrt[3]{\frac{32M_E}{\pi S}}$$

Both equations must be solved; the larger of the two diameters is then used for the calculated size. It is important to remember that the allowable shearing stress is used in the torsion formula; the allowable stress in tension is used in the flexure(or bending)formula. The following example shows how the method is applied.

Example 3

In Fig. 3.3, the shaft transmits 10hp at 500rpm. Assume that the design stresses are 6000psi(shear)and 8000 psi(torsion). Compute the diameter(Neglect shaft weight).

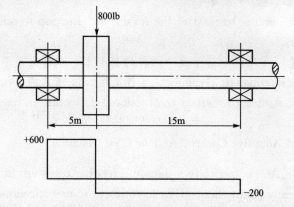

Fig. 3.3 Combined bending and torsion

Solution

First compute the two reactions. Here, these are 600lb on the left bearing and 200lb on the right bearing. The maximum moment is then $600\times5=3000$in-lb. Thus

$$T=\frac{63000hp}{N}=\frac{63000\times10}{500}=1260(\text{in-lb})$$

$$T_E=\sqrt{M^2+T^2}=\sqrt{(3000)^2+(1260)^2}=3260\text{in-lb};$$

$$M_E=\frac{M+T_E}{2}=\frac{3000+3260}{2}=3130\text{in-lb};$$

$$D=\sqrt[3]{\frac{16T_E}{\pi S_E}}=\sqrt[3]{\frac{(16)(3260)}{\pi(6000)}}=1.40\text{in}.$$

$$D=\sqrt[3]{\frac{32M_E}{\pi S}}=\sqrt[3]{\frac{(32)(3130)}{\pi(8000)}}=1.59\text{in}.$$

The safe shaft size for the given conditions is the larger of the two, or 1.59in.

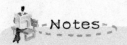
Notes

1. A hollow shaft weighs considerably less than a solid shaft of comparable strength, but is somewhat more expensive.

"but somewhat more expensive"是省略句,相当于"but a hollow shaft is somewhat more expensive than a solid shaft"。

2. The diameters of shafts made compatible with metric-sized bores of mechanical component(such as antifriction bearings)are specified in millimeters.

与机械零件(如滚动轴承)的米制尺寸的孔相配合的轴,其直径用 mm 来规定。

句中,过去分词短语 made compatible with metric-sized bores of mechanical components(such as antifriction bearings)作定语,修饰主语 the diameters of shafts.

3. in-b 英制扭矩单位:英寸磅

psi 英制应力单位:磅/平方英寸

4. One rule of thumb is to restrict the torsional deflection to one degree in a length equal to 20 diameters.

一种经验方法是:在每二十倍于至今的轴的长度上,扭转变形不超过1度。

句中,形容词短语 equal to 21 diameters 作定语,修饰名词 length;介词短语 in a length m 修饰词不定式短语 to restrict the torsional deflection to one degree.

3.6.3 Application of Adaptive Control(AC) or CNC Machine

Adaptive control(AC)is basically a dynamic-feedback system in which the operating parameters automatically adapt themselves to conform to new circumstances; it is a logical extension of computer numerical control systems. Human reactions to occurences in everyday life already contain dynamic-feedback control. For example, driving a car on a smooth road is relatively easy; on a rough road, however, we have to steer to avoid potholes by visually and continuously observing the condition of the road directly ahead of the car. Moreover, our body feels the car's rough movements and vibrations; we then react by changing the direction or the speed of the car to minimize the effects of the rough road.

An adaptive controller continuously checks road conditions, calculates an appropriate desired braking profile(e. g. ,an antilock brake system and traction control), and then uses feedback to implement it. As described before, the part programmer sets the processing parameters on the basis of the existing knowledge of the workpiece material and relevant data on the particular manufacturing operation. In CNC machines, on the other hand, these parameters are held constant during a particular process cycle; in AC, on the other hand, the system is capable of automatic adjustment during the operation, through closed-loop feedback control(Fig. 3.4). Several adaptive-control systems are available commercially for a variety of appliance.

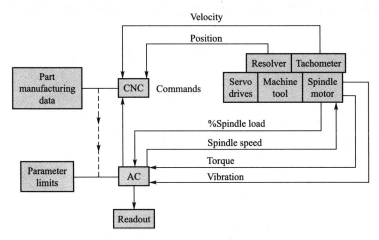

Fig. 3. 4 Schematic illustration of the application of adaptive control(AC) for a turning operation. The system monitors such parameters as cutting force, torque, and vibrations. If these parameters are excessive, it modifies process variables(such as feed and depth of cut) to bring them back to acceptable levels.

The main purpose of adaptive control in manufacturing are to(a)optimize production rate, (b)optimize product quality, and(c)minimize production cost. The application of AC in manufacturing is particularly important in situations where, for example, quality is not uniform, such as in castings from a poorly controlled process or parts that have been improperly heat treated.

Let's consider a machining operation, such as turning on a lathe. The adaptive control system senses parameters in real time, such as cutting forces, spindle torque, a rise in temperature during machining, tool wear rate, tool condition, and surface finish produced on the workpiece. The AC system converts this information into commands that then modify the process parameters on the lathe to hold them within certain limits and thus optimize the machining operation.

Those systems which place a constraint on a process variable(such as force, torque, or temperature)are called adaptive-control constraint(ACC) system. Thus, if the thrust force and the cutting force(and hence the torque)increase excessively(due, say, to the presence of a hard region in a casting), the system modifies the cutting speed or the feed in order to lower the cutting force to an acceptable level(Fig. 3. 5). Without adaptive control or the direct intervention of the operator(as is the case in traditional machining operations), high cutting forces may cause tool failure or may cause the workpiece to deflect or distort excessively. As a result, workpiece dimensional accuracy and surface finish begin to deteriorate. Those systems which optimize an operation are called adaptive-control optimization(ACO) systems. Optimization may invole maximizing the material-removal rate between tool changes or improving the surface of the part.

Response time must be short for AC to be effective, particularly in high-speed machining operations. Assume, for example, that a turning operation is being performed on a lathe at a spindle speed of 1000 rpm, and the tool suddenly breaks, adversely affecting the surface finish and dimensional accuracy of the part. Obviously, in order for the AC system to be effective, the sensing system must respond within a very short time; otherwise the damage to the workpiece will become extensive.

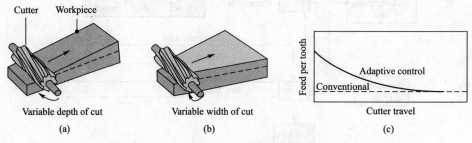

Fig. 3. 5 An examples of adaptive control in milling.
As depth of cut(a) or the width of cut(b) increases, the cutting forces and the torque increase. The system senses this increase and automatically reduces the feed(c) to avoid excessive forces or tool breakage in order to maintain cutting efficiency.

For adaptive control to be be effective in manufacturing operations, quantitative relationships must be established and coded in the computer software as mathematical models. If, for instance, the tool-wear rate in a machining operation is excessive, the computer must be able(a) to calculate how much of a change in speed or in feed is necessary and(b) to decide whether to increase it or decrease the speed, in order to term also should be able to compensate for dimensional changes in the workpiece due to such causes as tool wear and temperature rise(Fig. 3. 6).

If the operation is grinding, the computer software must reflect the desired quantitative relationships among independent process variables(such as wheel and work speeds, feed, and type of wheel) and dependent parameters(such as wheel wear, dulling of abrasive grains, grinding forces, temperature, surface finish, and part deflections). Similarly, in bending sheet metal in a V-die, data on the dependence of springback on relevant material and process variables must be stored in the computer memory. It is apparent that, coupled with CNC, adaptive control is a powerful tool in optimizing manufacturing operations.

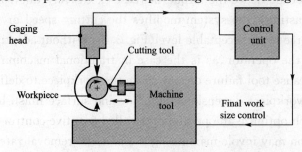

Fig. 3. 6 In-process inspection of workpiece diameter in a turning operation. The system automatically adjusts the radial position of the cutting tool in order to produce the correct diameter.

Chapter 3 English to Chinese Technical Translation for Mechanical Engineering

Words

shaft 轴	section 截面	hollow 空心的
bearing 轴承	modify 修改，更改	stock 原料
radii 半径	mount 安装	pulley 滑轮
cam 凸轮	gear 齿轮	radius 半径
interference 冲突，干涉	bore 孔	chamfer 斜切
compromise 妥协，折中	component 零件，部件	metric 米制的
compatible 一致的，兼容的	antifriction 减少摩擦	
specify 规定	turn 车削	fit 配合
equation 等式，方程式	torsion 扭转	torque 扭矩，转矩
inertia 惯性，惯量	fiber 纤维	restrict 限制
modulus 模数，模量	elasticity 弹性	equivalent 想等的
feedback 反馈	springback n. 回弹，反弹	programmer 编程器
V-die V形弯曲模	compensate 补偿	in-process 在加工(制造)过程中的

Phrases

be subjected to 受到	one rule of thumb （一个）经验方法
antifriction bearing 滚动轴承	stress raisers 应力集中
Adaptive control(AC) 自适应控制	response time 响应时间
adapt to 适应	sensing system 传感系统
conform to 符合，遵照	mathematical model 数学模型
computer numerical control 计算机数控	tool wear 刀具磨损

Excercises

Task 1 Translate the following into Chinese

1. circular cross section
2. equations for a shaft in pure torsion
3. diameter of solid shaft
4. outside diameter of hollow shaft
5. torsional deflection

Task 2 Translate the following sentences into English

1. 实时监控。
2. 自适应控制优化。
3. 车削工件尺寸的在线检测。
4. 产品质量优化。
5. 切屑变形及控制。

6. 从世界上第一台机器人诞生以来，机器人技术得到了迅速的发展。

7. 数控机床通常由输入介质、数控装置、伺服系统和机床本体四个基本部分组成。

8. 伺服系统是把来自数控装置的脉冲信号转换为机床移动部件的运动，使工作台精确定位或按照规定的轨迹作严格的相对运动，以加工出符合图纸要求的零件。

9. ABC是中国最大、全球第六的工程机械制造商。

10. 近年来，ABC连续获评为中国企业500强、工程机械行业综合效益和竞争力最强企业、福布斯"中国顶尖企业"、中国最具成长力自主品牌、中国最具竞争力品牌、中国工程机械行业标志性品牌、亚洲品牌50强。

Practice Makes Perfect
——熟能生巧

Chapter 4

Chinese to English Technical Translation for Mechanical Engineering

随着我国科技现代化的不断提高,越来越多的中国生产制造的机电产品开始步入国际市场,外商在购买我们的产品之前,首先要熟悉该产品的技术特点、功能、用途、使用和维修等方面的情况。如果外商所阅读的是一篇翻译腔十足,汉语味明显的晦涩难懂的文章,就势必产生不良影响。因此,以准确和地道的英文完整无误地表达出中文的等值概念,是专业英语汉英翻译的首要任务。本章首先介绍中英文在结构和用词搭配方面的区别,然后提出英汉翻译的方法技巧,最后通过大量的汉英翻译实例,给大家以示范和启发。

4.1 Difference of Structure and Collocation in Chinese and English

中、英文结构和用词搭配上的差异有以下两个方面。

1. 结构差异

中文的行文基本上是以并列结构为基础,语言比较简练,概括性很强,句间关系由上下文的语义来衔接。英文则以主从结构为主,从句短句相互嵌连,语句很长,但结构严谨,层次分明,逻辑严密。两种语言结构不同,翻译时就不能以汉语形式来书写英文,这就要求翻译者在翻译时应进行自然转换,用不同的句型和句法来表达等值的语义。如果生搬硬套,逐字翻译,往往让人费解。

例:本厂是生产液压阀的专业厂家,拥有职工 312 人,其中技术人员 58 人,高级工程师 16 人。本厂拥有固定资产原值为 1500 万元,固定资产净值为 1200 万元。

译文 1:Our factory is a specialized factory for producing hydraulic valves and has 312 workers, among them there are 58 technicians and 16 senior engineers. We have 1,5000,000RMB of the original value of fixed assets and 1,2000,000RMB of the net value of fixed assets.

译文 2:We, specializing in producing hydraulic valves, have 312 workers among which the technician are 58 and the senior engineers are 16, in possession of 1,5000,000RMB of the original value and 1,2000,000RMB of the net value of the the fixed assets.

译文 1 从语法,用词上都没有明显错误,看上去也还可以明白,但翻译味十分明显,中文结构处处可见,语流平铺直叙,而译文 2 则是充分理解了中文含义之后,按英文结构重新组成的。开始的一个现在分词结构做插入语,指明厂家类别,随后又利用一个介词前置的定语从句来表明职工总数与技术人员之间的比例,最后再加上一个介词短语来表达第二个"拥有"概念,整句流畅、自然、一气呵成。

2. 中、英文用词搭配差异

中、英文在词的搭配能力方面往往有差异,按照中文习惯和词语的搭配来书写英文,就会产生不伦不类的句子。

例:本产品具有 80 年代技术水平。
译文 1:This product owns 1980's technical level.
译文 2:This product is characterized by 1980's technical level.

显然,产品并不是有生命的人活着团体,所以译文 1 用 own 并不合适。而译文 2 则符合英文搭配要求。

4.2 Improving the Skill of Chinese – English Translation in Science and Technology

要提高科技英文汉译英能力,首先要提高学生的中文理解能力,然后要提升专业知识掌握水平和翻译技巧,这样就可以逐步提高汉英翻译水平。

1. 提升汉语理解能力

汉译英翻译过程一般也是分为三个阶段,即理解、表达和校核。其中,理解是关键,表达是目的,校核是保证。所谓理解,就是要正确理解原文的词义、语法关系以及涉及的专业内容。因而,在汉译英过程中,首先对汉语原文中大到大小语篇,小到句子和词语都要有准确的理解。

例 1:大部分数控机床是全防护或半防护的,最大程度上减少了工人暴露在噪声、切屑碎片和工件冷却润滑液中的可能性。

Chapter 4 Chinese to English Technical Translation for Mechanical Engineering

翻译说明：这句结构并不复杂，但是"防护"、"最大程度上减少"的翻译还是需要用一些技巧，如果能够对数控机床的结构多一些了解，在"防护"的选词上就不会用 shelter，protect cover，defend 等词，而会选用 enclose，"最大程度上减少"直接可以用 minimize。

参考译文：Most computer-controlled machines tools are partially or totally enclosed, minimizing the exposure of worker to noise, debris, and the lubricants used to cool workpiece during machining.

例2：自动化工厂是指从原材料到成品出厂极少需要或不需要人的干预。这就需要计算机辅助设计/制造系统对工业机器人和数控机床进行编程，以将原材料变成成品，还需要测量机器人完成自动检测。

翻译说明：自动化工厂是一种工厂，所以第一句的翻译需要增加"a place"才能通顺合理，这是在中文理解的基础上才做得好。

参考译文：An automation factory is a place where raw materials enter and finished products leave with litter or human intervention. This requires CAD/CAM to program the industrial robots and CNC machines to convert the raw materials to finished products, and robotic measuring machines to perform automatic inspection.

2. 更好地掌握的专业知识背景

与科技资料的英译汉一样，在汉译英时，除了具备较好的外语水平外，还应具备一定的科技知识。许多词句中所表达的科技含义必须借助一定的科技知识并在头脑中形成条理清晰的概念才能确保译文的准确。

例1：为了确保各部件运转正常，必须定期对设备进行干或湿润滑。

如果直译为"dry 和 wet lubrication"肯定会贻笑大方，反之，如果具备一定的机械知识便会明白干湿润滑指的是油脂润滑，由此，问题便迎刃而解，译文应为：

The equipment should be lubricated regularly with oil or grease so as to ensure a satisfactory performance of each part.

例2：此开关有两个触点，用于控制电机的通/断。

触点是电气开关的一个接点，是一个不可缺少的部件，这对于一个电工来说是最基础的常识，因此不可以翻译为"touching point"，正确的译文为：

The two contacts in the switch are provided aiming at controlling ON/OFF motor.

3. 词汇平时多积累，用时随手拈来

不少科技工作者在进行专业文献汉译英时，确饱受词穷之累。这就是缺乏积累的后果。英译汉的译者在平时应大量阅读和翻译专业英文资料，同时，有意识地归纳并记住一切你认为是有用的、地道的英语表达法和词汇，为以后的汉译英打下基础。

1）近义词

做、开展、进行、从事：do, make, carry out, perform, conduct(research, study, experiment, survey,investigation,exploration,coorperation…

制造、制作：make,fabricate,build,manufacture,construct…

改变、改换、修改、重建、重组：convert,transform,change,modify,adapt,alter,reform,correct,reconstruct,rebuild,reconfigure,reorganize…

建议、提出：advise,recommend,suggest,propose,introduce,put forward,present,develop…

建立：establish,set up,form,construct,formulate,build…

给、提供：give,offer,provide,supply,furnish

改善、改进：improve,enhance,raise,better

开发、利用：develop,exploit,take advantage of,make use of,employ,tap,open up…

验证、证明：verify,prove,check,test,identify,justify,affirm,confirm

占有、构成：constitute,make up,account for,cover,hold,occupy

2) 选用科技味的词汇

足够的/充分的：adequate(替代 enough)

获得：obtain/achieve(替代 get)

错误：error(替代 mistake)

去除：eliminate(替代 get rid of)

要求：request/require(替代 ask)

热的：thermal(替代 hot)

燃烧：combustion(替代 burning)

4. 直译和意译相结合

(1) 直译(literal translation)：直译是科技文章汉译英中常用的方法，大部分句子均可采用直译方法，可以为译入语输入新的语言元素，在丰富译入语的同时提高译入语的表述能力。

例：该产品是我们为电动车用户设计制造的专用充电器。
This product is a designated battery charger we have designed and manufactured for electric bike users.

(2) 意译(free translation)：有时为了更好地为译入语读者所理解和接受，科技英语中也采用意译的方法。主要表达原文所传达的内容和信息，不注重语言表达形式的对应。

例："雪域神舟"号机车的成功研制填补了我国高原机车的空白，具有国际先进技术水平。
译文：The successful development of the "Divine Ship on the Snow Land" locomotive has established it as the first of its type to be used on the highland in China, which is characterized by the international advanced technical level.

5. 被动语态与主动态相结合

汉语中虽也有被动语态，但使用范围较狭窄，科技汉语文章中大多是主动句式，主语多是人或有生命的东西，有时则为无主句。在科技英语中，第一、二人称使用过多，会造成主观臆断的印象，因此应尽量使用第三人称来进行叙述，采用被动语态。

例：要多应当注意机器的工作温度。
译文：Attention must be paid to the working temperature of the machine.

尽管在科技英译文中大量采用被动语态，但仍有很多句子需用主动句式来进行翻译处理。在汉译英中应灵活使用主动句式与被动句式，不可生搬硬套。

例：安装在床身导轨上的升降台，能使机床工作台垂直运动。
The knee, mounted on the column guideways, provides the vertical movement of the table.

例：由一个以上零件构成的产品都需要装配。对年产量不超过几十万件的产品，其装配几乎都是手工进行的。
Products made of more than one part require assembly. For products made in quantities of less than several hundred thousand units per year, this assembly is almost always performed manually.

4.3　Reading Materials

4.3.1　About Bosch Products

"博世"品牌代表了汽车安全系统的发展和前瞻性技术。博世分别于 1978 年和 1995 年在全球第一个把 ABS(防抱死制动系统)和 ESP(电子稳定系统)投放市场，从而确定了车辆制动技术上的领导地位。

1996 年，博世并购了制动产品的著名品牌——联信公司(Bendix)，业务从而扩大到完整的制动系统上。博世一直努力寻求研究液压技术和电子技术间的协同优势。2001 年，第一台博世的电液制动系统(电子单元将制动力分配到卡钳上)成为了原厂装备。

博世制动系列

博世"舒适型"制动摩擦片

"舒适型"制动摩擦片定位于中高档车型以及原厂配套产品。本条产品线采用了两款半金属和少金属配方，符合欧洲 ECE 要求。所有的两款配方都是主机配套配方，经过了 OE 的各项试验验证，能满足 OE 各项要求。

博世"安全型"制动摩擦片

"安全型"制动摩擦片定位于中低档车型，产品包括制动片与制动蹄，覆盖大多数国内车型。本条产品线采用了博世专门为中国用户提供的大颗粒配方，符合 GB 5763—1998 的要求。

鼓式制动蹄

对于乘用车来说制动蹄主要应用于车辆的后制动，但对于大部分的皮卡和轻型商用车来说制动蹄也应用于前刹。一旦制动起动，车轮制动缸就会驱动制动蹄作用于制动鼓内壁。

博世制动液

制动液是在制动系统中用来传输动力的液态介质。高品质的制动液才能保证制动系统可靠的工作。其基本评价指标包括：平衡沸点、湿式沸点、黏度、可压缩性、腐蚀防护、橡胶膨胀。

参考译文：

The name Bosch stands for development and forward-looking technology in the field of automotive engineering. Bosch started its worldwide pioneering work in brakes with the launching of the first ABS and the first ESP in 1978 and 1995.

In 1996, with the acquisition of Allied Signal(Bendix), a leading name in brakes, Bosch has extended its business to the development of complete braking systems, searching constantly for synergies between hydraulics and electronics. As a result, in 2001, the first electro-hydraulics(braking force transmitted electronically to the caliper)brake was installed in the OE-series.

Bosch brake series

Bosch "comfort" brake friction pad

The "comfort" brake pad is oriented for medium and high grade vehicles and OE products. This product line applies two kinds of formulations of semi-metallic and low metallic, which is in compliance with the requirements of ECE in Europe. All the two kinds of formulations are matched with that of the main body, which have passed all OE authentication test and satisfied all OE requirement.

Bosch "safety" brake friction pad

The "safety" brake pad is oriented for medium and low grade vehicles, consisting of brake pads and brake shoes which cover most of the national vehicle types. This product line applies the Bosch specially chosen large particle formulations tailored to the Chinese clients, which complies with the requirements of GB 5763—1998.

Drum brake shoes

For passenger vehicles, brake shoes mainly rely on the braking of rear wheels whilst, for pickup and light commercial vehicles, on the braking of the front wheels. Once the brake is in operation, wheel cylinders will drive the brake shoes to act on the internal wall of brake drums.

Bosch brake fluid

Brake fluid acts as the transmission medium in the brake system. The high quality brake fluid guarantees the reliable operation of brake system and the basic evaluation indexes include: equilibrium boiling point, wet boiling point, viscosity, compressibility, corrosion protection and rubber expansion.

Notes

1. 车身电子稳定系统(Electronic Stability Program, ESP)，是博世(Bosch)公司的专利。10年前，博世是第一家把电子稳定程序(ESP)投入量产的公司。因为ESP是博世

Chapter 4 Chinese to English Technical Translation for Mechanical Engineering

公司的专利产品,所以只有博世公司的车身电子稳定系统才可称之为 ESP。

2."ABS"(Anti-locked Braking System)中文译为"防抱死刹车系统"。它是一种具有防滑、防锁死等优点的汽车安全控制系统。Bosch(博世)1936 年申请"机动车辆防止刹车抱死装置"的专利。1964 年,Bosch 公司再度开始 ABS 的研发计划,最后有了"通过电子装置控制来防止车轮抱死是可行的"结论,这是 ABS(Antilock Braking System)名词在历史上第一次出现。

4.3.2 Sheet-Metal Forming Processes

由钣金成形工艺制造出来的产品在我们周围比比皆是,包括金属桌子、档案柜、家电、汽车车身、飞机机身以及饮料罐等。薄板成形可以追溯到公元前 5000 年,那时候的家具用品和珠宝首饰都是通过捶打和压制金、银、铜等金属制造出来的。

与铸造、锻造出来的零件相比,薄板成形的零件有着重量轻、形状多变的优点。由于低碳钢价格低,具有足够的强度及良好的成形性能,所以它是最常用的金属薄板料。而在飞机和航空领域的应用中,常选用铝和钛薄板料。表 4-1 描述了各种钣金加工工艺的特点。

表 4-1 各种钣金成形方法的特点

成形方法	特 点
轧制成形	适于生产具有恒定的复杂截面的长件;良好的表面粗糙度;生产率高;工具成本高
拉伸成形	适于生产轮廓较浅的大型零件;适于小量生产;劳动成本高;工具及设备成本取决于零件尺寸
拉深	适于生产形状相对简单的浅或深的零件;生产率高;工具及设备成本高
冲压	包括各种不同的工艺,例如冲压、落料、压花、弯曲、翻边、压印;简单或复杂形状的零件;生产率高;工具和设备成本高,但劳动成本低
橡皮成形	用于拉伸或压印简单或复杂形状;板料表面被橡胶膜保护;操作灵活;工具成本低
旋压	成形轴对称的小或大的零件;良好的表面粗糙度;工具成本;除非自动化加工,否则劳动力成本较高
超塑性成形	可成形形状复杂、细部精致、高精度的零件;成形时间长,因而生产率较低;零件不适于在高温下使用
锤击成形	在大型板料上捶打出浅的轮廓;操作和设备成本可能较高;此工艺也可用于校直零件
爆炸成形	可成形相对复杂的大型板料,尽管通常是轴对称的形状;工具成本低,但劳动成本高;适于少量生产;生产周期长
磁脉冲成形	在相对低强度制定的板料上进行浅成形、涨形、压印操作;大多数适合管状零件;生产率高;需要专门工具

参考译文：

Products made by sheet-metal forming processes are all around us; they include metal desks, file cabinets, appliances, car bodies, aircraft fuselages, and beverage cans. Sheet forming dates back to 5000 B. C. , when household utensils and jewels were made by hammering and stamping gold, silver, and copper.

Compared to those made by casting and by forging, sheet-metal parts offer the advantages of light weight and versatile shape. Because of its low cost and generally good strength and formability characteristics, the common sheet materials are aluminum and titanium. Table 4-1 describes the characteristics of sheet-metal forming processes.

Table 4-1 Characteristics of sheet-metal forming processes

Process	Characteristics
Roll forming	Long parts with constant complex cross-sections; good surface finish; high production rates; high tooling costs.
Stretch forming	Large parts with shallow contours; suitable for low-quantity production; high tooling and equipment costs depends on part size.
Drawing	Shallow or deep parts with relatively simple shapes; high production rates; high tooling and equipment costs.
Stamping	Includes a variety of operations, such as punching, blanking, embossing, bending, flanging, and coining; simple or complex shapes formed at high production rates; tooling and equipment costs can be high, but labor cost is low.
Rubber forming	Drawing and embossing of simple or complex shapes; sheet surface protected by rubber membrances; flexibility of operation; low tooling costs.
Spinning	Small or large axisymmtric parts; good surface finish; low tooling costs, but labor costs can be high unless operations are automated.
Superplastic forming	Complex shapes, fine detail and close tolerances; forming times are ling, hence forming production rates are low; parts ot suitable for high-temperature use.
Peen forming	Shallow contours on large sheets; flexibility of operation; equipment costs can be high; process is also used for straightening parts.
Explosive forming	Very large sheets with relatively complex shapes, although usually axisymmetric; low tooling cost, but high labor cost; suitable for low low-quantity production; long cycle times.
Magnetic-pulse forming	Shallow forming, bulging, and embossing operations on relatively forming low-strength sheets; most suitable for tubular shapes; high production rates; requires special.

在对表格内容进行翻译时，注意英文有很多省略的情况，目的是为了更加简洁。

4.3.3 Estimating The Costs of Custom Components

非标件，即为某产品而设计的零件。它由制造商自己或某个供应商来生产。大多数非标件的生产工艺与标准件相同(例如，注塑、冲压、切削加工等)。然而，非标件是典型的专门用途的零件，它们只能用于某个特定的制造商的产品中。

当非标件是一个单独的零件时，我们把其原材料、加工和工装成本加起来就是它的估计成本。当非标件实际上是多个零件装配而成的部件时，我们就把它当做一个"产品"。要得到这个"产品"的成本，我们分别估算各部分的成本，再加上装配成本和运营成本。为了便于解释，我们暂时假定目前的非标件是一个单独的零件。

要估算原材料成本，先计算零件的重量，先考虑一定的废料(例如，注塑件的废料重量是 5%~50%，钣金件的废料为 25%~100%)，然后乘以原料成本(单位重量价格)。

加工成本包括设备操作者的工资以及使用设备本身的成本。大多数标准的加工设备的成本在每小时 \$25(简单的冲床)到 \$75(中型数控铣床)之间，其中包括折旧、维护、工具和人工成本。估计加工时间通常需要有对所使用设备的经验。然而，理解常用工艺的大致范围成本是很有用的。

工装成本是因为要使用某种机器加工零件，所以需要设计和制造刀具、铸模、冲模或卡具而产生的成本。例如，注塑机需要为它生产的每一种不同的产品定制注塑模。这些模具的成本从 \$10000 到 \$50000。单位工装成本是工装成本除以该工装寿命内所制造的零件总数。高质量的注塑模或冲模通常可以生产几百万个零件。

原来机加工的铸造进气歧管的成本估算见表 4-2。注意，该估算表明，成本主要是铝材成本。我们将会看到，使用复合材料的新设计不仅降低了材料成本，而且消除了切削加工，并允许在注塑件上增加许多特征。

表 4-2 原先的进气歧管的成本估计

项　　目	描　　述	分项单件成本
变动成本		
材料	5.7kg 铝材，\$2.25/kg	\$12.83
工艺(铸造)	150 件/h，\$530/h	\$3.53
工艺(机加工)	200 件/h，\$340/h	\$1.70
固定成本		
铸造工装	寿命为 50 万零件的工装 \$160000/套	\$0.32
切削刀具和卡具	寿命为 1 千万零件的生产线 \$1800000/条	\$0.18
总的直接成本		\$18.56
运营成本		\$12.09
总的单件成本		\$30.65

参考译文:

Estimating the Costs of Custom Components

Custom components, which are parts designed especially for the product, are made by the manufacturer or by a supplier. Most custom components are produced using the same types of production processes as standard components(e. g. , injection molding, stamping, machining); however, custom parts are typically special-purpose parts, useful only in a particular manufacturer's products.

When the custom component is a single part, we estimate its cost by adding up the costs of raw materials, processing, and tooling. In cases where the custom component is actually an assembly of several parts, then we consider it a "product" we estimate the cost of each subcomponent and then add assembly and overhead costs. For the purpose of this explanation, we assume the component is a single part.

The raw materials costs can be estimated by computing the mass of the part, allowing for some scrap(e. g. , 5 percent to 50 percent for an injection molded part, and 25 percent to 100 percent for a sheet metal part), and multiplying by the cost(per unit mass)of the raw material.

Processing costs include costs for the operator(s)of the processing machinery as well as the cost of using the equipment itself. Most standard processing equipment costs between $25 per hour(a simple stamping press)and $75 per hour(a medium-sized, computer-controlled milling machine)to operate, including depreciation, maintenance, utilities, and labor costs. Estimating the processing time generally requires experience with the type of equipment to be used. However, it is useful to understand the range of typical costs for common production processes.

Tooling costs are incurred for the design and fabrication of the cutters, molds, dies, or fixtures required to use certain machinery to fabricate parts. For example, an injection molding machine requires a custom injection mold for every different type of part it produces. These molds generally range in cost from $10,000 to $50,000. The unit tooling cost is simply the cost of the tooling divided by the number of units to be made over the life of the tool. A high-quality injection mold or stamping die can usually be used for a few million parts.

The cost of the original intake manifold's machined casting is estimated as shown in table 4 – 2. Note that the estimate reveals that the cost is dominated by the expense of the aluminum material. We will see that the redesign using a composite material not only reduced the material costs but also eliminated machining and allowed many features to be formed into the molded body.

Table4 – 2 Cost estimate for the original intake manifold

Items	Description	Cost per unit
Variable Cost		
Materials	5. 7kg aluminum at $2. 25/kg	$12. 83
Processing(Casting)	150 units/hr at $530/hr	$3. 53
Processing(Machining)	200 units/hr at $340/h	$1. 70
Fixed Cost		
Tooling for casting	$160000/tool at 500K units/tool(lifetime)	$0. 32
Cutting tools and fixtures	$1800000/line at 10M units(lifetime)	$0. 18
Total Direct Cost		$18. 56
Overhead charge		$12. 09
Total Units Costs		$30. 65

Chapter 4 Chinese to English Technical Translation for Mechanical Engineering

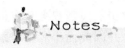

Notes

custom components 非标件
manufacturer 制造商
supplier 供应商
depreciation 折旧，贬值（反义词 appreciation）
intake manifold 进气歧管
stamping die 冲模

4.3.4 DC Motor

定子和转子都是由铁磁材料构成。对于大多数电机，在转子的外圆周和定子的内圆周都刻有许多槽。导体就放置在这些槽里。铁芯用于使放置在转子和定子中的线圈（由导体构成）之间的耦合最大，以增加电机的磁通密度以及减小电机尺寸。如果定子和转子都同时受到时变磁场的影响，就将铁芯许多薄片组成，以减小涡流损耗。

Both stator and rotor are made of ferromagnetic materials. In most motors, slot are cut on the inner periphery of the stator and outer periphery of the rotor structure. Conductors are placed in these slots. The iron core is used to maximize the coupling between the coils (formed by conductors) placed on the stator and rotor, to increase the flux density in the machine and to decrease the size of machine. If the stator or rotor (or both) is subjected to a time-varying magnetic flux, the iron core is laminated to reduce eddy current losses.

放置在定子或者转子的槽中的导体相互连接，形成了绕组。产生感应电压的绕组称为电枢绕组。电流通过其在电机中产生主磁通的绕组称为励磁绕组。在一些电机中采用永磁体以产生主磁通。

The conductors placed in the slots of the stator or rotor are interconnected to form windings. The winding in which voltage is induced is called the armature winding. The winding through which a current is passed to produce the primary source of flux in the machine is called the field winding. Permanent magnets are used in some machines to provide the major source of flux in the machine.

在电枢绕组的各条边所感应的电压是交变的。通过使用换流器电刷的组合作为一个机械整流器以使得电枢的端电压为单方向的同时也使得由电枢电流所产生的磁动势在空间是固定的。电刷是这样安排：当电枢绕组（或者线圈）的边通过励磁磁极区域中部时，流经其的电流就会改变方向。这样就可以保证流经导体的电流在一个磁极下的方向不变。因此，由电枢电流所产生的磁动势沿着相邻的两个磁极，并称为正交轴。

The voltage induced in the terms of the armature winding is alternating. A commutator-brush combination is used as a mechanical rectifier to make the armature terminal voltage unidirectional and also to make the mmf wave due to the armature current fixed in space. The brushed are so placed that when the sides of an armature turn (or coil) pass through the middle of the region between field poles, the current though it changes direction. This makes all the conductors under one pole carry current in one direction. As a consequence, the mmf due to the armature current is along the axis midway between the two adjacent poles, called the quadrature (or q) axis.

励磁绕组和电枢电路有各种接法，因而有不同的性能，这是直流电动机的显著优点。

除此之外，励磁可以使用两种不同的励磁绕组：并励和串励。并励绕组的匝数很多只有很小的励磁电流（大约是额定电流的5%）该绕组可以与电枢绕组并联，并因此而得名。串励绕组匝数很少，但流过的电流很大。该绕组与电枢绕组串联，并因此而得名。两种绕组可以同时存在，此时串励绕组绕在并励绕组之上。

  The field circuit and the armature circuit can be interconnected in various ways to provide a wide variety of performance characteristics-an outstanding advantage of DC motors. In addition, the field poles can be excited by two field windings, a shunt field winding and a series field winding. The shunt winding has a large number of turns and takes only s small current(less than 5% of the rated armature current). This winding can be connected across the armature(i. e., parallel with it), hence the name shunt winding. The series winding has fewer turns but carries a large current. It is connected in series with the armature, hence the name series winding. If both shunt and series winding are present, the series winding is wound on top of the shunt winding.

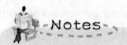

  1. stator 定子；rotor 转子
  2. field circuit 场电路，励磁回路；armature circuit 电枢回路
  3. 励磁绕组和电枢电路有各种接法，因而有不同的性能，这是直流电动机的显著优点。

  翻译这句时，有两个技巧，一是用动词不定式 to provide…characteristics 表示"因而有…性能"，二是用破折号，用于补充说明和评语。英文中破折号还可以表示插入、转折、代替括弧、省略等。

  e. g. The materials used—copper, stainless steel, concrete and glass—give the buildings a striking beauty. 这些使用的材料——铜、不锈钢、混凝土和玻璃等，使这些建筑更具非凡魅力。

Excercises

Task 1 Translate the following phrases and expressions into English.

涡流损耗	拉伸
非标件	冲压
电刷	旋压
时变磁场	运营成本

Task 2 Translate the following company profile into English.

阿诺（苏州）刀具有限公司成立于2002年，坐落在中新合作的苏州工业园区内，是国家高新技术企业。公司从事各类高品质精密金属切削刀具的制造和修磨服务。产品有硬质合金刀具和超硬刀具，如硬质合金钻头、铰刀、铣刀、刀片和PCD/CBN超硬刀具。公司拥有目前世界上最先进的刀具制造和测量设备：从德国进口的五轴联动的CNC刀具磨床共40多台,有目前市场上最先进的德国Zoller Genius 3刀具检测设备。公司通过了由德国TUV SUD认证的ISO9000/2008的质量认证体系。阿诺公司是我国刀具专业修磨行业的缔造者和领头羊,已在全国设立了10个刀具专业修磨中心,基本上覆盖了中国的精密机械加工集中地区。阿诺的高性能硬质合金钻头达到了世界先进水平,已在各机械加工领域批量替代进口。

作为中国精密切削刀具领域里最有影响力的企业之一,阿诺的主要客户分布在汽车、航空、模具、制冷、汽轮机等精密制造行业,其中汽车制造业的销售额大约占60%。客户中90%以上为在中国境内的外资、合资企业,大多为本领域里的高端客户。如汽车领域有大众Volkswagen、通用GM、福特FORD汽车等,航空领域有霍尼韦尔Honeywell、史密斯Smith、梅西埃Messier-Dowty、普美Primus等,制冷领域有特灵Trane、麦克维尔McQuay、LG等,汽轮机行业有东汽Dongfang Turbines、南汽Nanjing Turbines等,轴承行业有德国的舍弗勒Schaeffler,瑞典的斯凯孚SKF等,液压行业有力士乐Rexrodt、赫斯可Husco、萨澳Sauer等,钎具行业有宝长年Boart Long Year等行业巨头。

金属切削的整体解决、非标刀具的快速制造、刀具的专业修磨、刀具的外包管理都是阿诺的强项,一流的服务让阿诺成为客户自己的刀具车间。刀具是金属切削的牙齿,"做金属切削的好牙医!"是阿诺人的共同追求。

经营理念

"您的后院就是我们的前庭。阿诺公司为您提供的不仅是高品质的刀具,还有您真正需要的技术支持和技术服务。真诚希望我们能成为贵公司可以信赖的合作伙伴——犹如贵公司自己的刀具车间"。

A man becomes learned by asking questions
——不耻下问才能有学问

Chapter 5
Applying for a Job in an International Corporation

外资企业不但给中国创造了无限商机，也提供了无限多的就业机会。一般认为，要进入外资企业，英语水平是一个门槛。有很多人认为，能够到外资企业，尤其是知名的国际型企业就业，是对自身能力和素质的肯定和提高。外资企业可以提供优厚的薪水和再培训的机会，这是吸引人才的关键，但同时，要对外资企业工作的压力和快节奏的生活有心理准备。

作为应届毕业生，要想进入外资企业恐怕比较难，但是工作几年后，再进的机会就大很多。那么，申请进入外资企业需要大家熟悉外资企业的招聘流程、看懂招聘广告、会写英文申请信和简历，并且在英文面试中有良好的表现。本章就是从这几个方面给大家进行介绍。

5.1 Recruiting Process

The recruitment and selection is the major function of the human resource department and recruitment process is the first step towards creating the competitive strength and the strategic advantage for the organizations. Recruitment process involves a systematic procedure from sourcing the candidates to arranging and conducting the interviews and requires many resources and time. A general recruitment process is as follows:

(1) Identify vacancy
(2) Prepare job description and person specification
(3) Advertising the vacancy
(4) Managing the response
(5) Short-listing
(6) Arrange interviews
(7) Conducting interview and decision making

Chapter 5 Applying for a Job in an International Corporation

The recruitment process begins with the human resource department receiving requisitions for recruitment from any department of the company. These contain:
- Posts to be filled
- Number of persons
- Duties to be performed
- Qualifications required
- Preparing the job description and person specification.
- Locating and developing the sources of required number and type of employees(Advertising etc).
- Short-listing and identifying the prospective employee with required characteristics.
- Arranging the interviews with the selected candidates.
- Conducting the interview and decision making.

There are two kinds of interview. One is panel interview (= committee interview), as shown in Fig5.2. The other is Group interview (optional), as shown in Fig. 5.3.

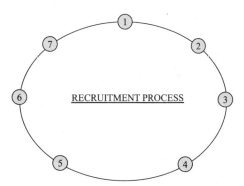

Fig. 5.1 Recruitment process

Fig. 5.2 Panel interview

Fig. 5.3 Group interview

5.2 Job Advertisement

5.2.1 A Job Advertisement from ABC Corporation

ABC Corporation is a world leader among NC machine manufacturer. Excellent product quality and innovative products and services have fueled our exceptional growth.

We have currently employed over 2,500 highly motivated and knowledgeable individuals worldwide. Covering all continents, ABC has branches in over 20 countries.

Through the subsidiary company, with headquarters in Shanghai, and branch offices in

Xi'an and Guangzhou, we have successfully developed our position in the market in China since 1990.

To further expand our strategic market position, we are seeking high caliber people to join us in the following positions.

- **Sales Engineer**
- Requirements:
- A bachelor degree of electromechanical engineering. A major in numerical control (NC) is preferred
- 2 – 3 years working experience in the relevant area
- Good communicative and interpersonal skills
- Willing to travel frequently and work under pressure
- A good command of spoken and written English
- Familiar with CAD/CAM
- **Assistant Engineer**
- Your tasks:
- CAD design and CAM product modeling
- NC programming and debugging
- NC equipment adjusting and maintaining
- Technical service and support for users
- Requirements:
- University or college in electromechanical engineering
- 2 or 3 years of working experience is preferred
- Familiar with CAD/CAM
- Good communicative skill, fluent spoken English
- Self - motivated, responsible and hard working
- Age below 35

5.2.2 Job Advertisement for a Product Design and Development Engineer

Responsibilities

- As the engineering sales, to collect market information, set - up the potential project propose
- During the potential project prophase develops, to leading the communication with customer, to clarify the customer request and concept
- Work out the customer request and concept's check list and description, to set - up the design and development base, provide the design propose
- According to the EDM system, to prepare the potential project prophase quotation and technical review material
- According to the customer request and concept, consideration on the balancing of the feasibility of the tooling, assembly, welding and testing, to work with headquarter design team to implement the product design and development, including the 2D and 3D, CAE

Chapter 5 Applying for a Job in an International Corporation

analysis.
- New project technical planning and controlling
- Based on the TS16949, to leading the DFMEA and design verification, to satisfy the customer request
- Responsible on the product design and development phase, engineering support of the new project's APQP phase.
- Completion of other tasks assigned by superiors

Requirement
- Engineering degree preferred.
- 5 years experience in automotive plastic product design and development, familiar with APQP.
- Manufacturing process knowledge, such as injection molding tooling, molding process, assembly, welding, and so on.
- Masterly working with CAD software(AutoCAD, UG, Ideas or Catia).
- Familiar with CAE software(Moldflow, FEA, NVH analysis, air flow and etc).
- Strong management/supervisory and people skills.
- Good communication ability with customer.
- Good leadership skills and understanding.
- Fluency in both spoken and written English.

5.2.3 HR Policy From Shenyang Machine Tools Co., Ltd

Remuneration System

Salary for an Intern RMB3650 per month for a graduate with a bachelor's degree from a higher education institution listed into the Project 985(salary RMB2500+housing subsidy RMB1000+Meal subsidy RMB150), RMB 5550 per month for a graduate with a master's degree from a higher education institution listed into the Project 985(salary RMB4000+housing subsidy RMB1400+Meal subsidy RMB150), RMB7450 per month for a graduate with a doctor's degree(salary RMB5500 + housing subsidy RMB1800 + Meal subsidy RMB150).

Salary for a Fixed Post

Basic compensation(post salary, working age salary)+Performance compensation(performance salary, overtime salary, project bonus, special bonus or penalty)

Welfare Treatment

Insurance The company is responsible for covering 5 insurances &housing fund for its employees.

Dining

The company provides a meal subsidy of RMB150 each month and provides employees with a good dining environment and various delicious breakfast, lunch and dinner.

Accommodations

Single employees can lodge into the University Students Mansion of SMTCL for free.

Travel

Employees can ride the company's commuting buses for free. The stops of commuting buses cover the whole Shengyang City.

Other

Birthday dinner for employees and delicate gift etc.

Training and Development

Training

We boast independent training organization.

The company attaches importance to providing employees with opportunities for trainings; and each year, the company invests over RMB20 million yuan in employee training every year.

The company jointly launches a master program in engineering with Jilin University and Dalian University of Technology and provides diversified development channels.

Diversity channel

- Technical channel(technician)→senior technical expert
- Management channel(lower management)→decision-making management
- Marketing channel(salesman)→Senior Sales Manager

Internal Selection

When there is a vacancy in the company, all the employees can participate in the internal selection for the job.

Backup Leader

Excellent employees have the opportunity to be listed as backup leaders of the company after passing relevant assessment.

Campus Recruitment

Here, you are going to:

- experience the heavy industrial history of Shengyang Machine Tool Co., Ltd.
- Contact the sole national high-end numerical control machine tool key laboratory in China
- work in an internationalized working environment
- be granted with an opportunity to take part in overseas training

What's more important, you are going to be one of Shengyang Machine Tool Co., Ltd., and share our great achievement.

5.2.4 Job Advertisement for Experienced Persons of Siemens

For Professionals

Even if you have many years of professional experience, it's still important to keep on being curious and to keep on looking for new challenges. Whether you want to develop yourself in a new direction or to move forward on your current career path, Siemens offers experienced professionals who dare to ask big questions a wide range of opportunities to continue their personal success stories-in their home countries or even abroad.

Siemens – Global powerhouse in electronics and electrical engineering

Siemens is a global powerhouse in electronics and electrical engineering, operating in the industry, energy and healthcare sectors. The company has around 405,000 employees working to develop and manufacture products, design and install complex systems and projects, and tailor a wide range of solutions for individual requirements. The company is the world's largest provider of environmental technologies from green products and solutions. Here, you will definitely find jobs where you can find your new role.

Personal development & Career Opportunities

After entering Siemens, there will be a lot of opportunities waiting for you for personal development and career opportunities. We have established the Siemens Management Institute where all our employees have the chance to broaden their knowledge, improve their skills, and further their careers. We have the annual performance evaluation process(PMP) to help evaluate individual employees'performance and potential across the entire organization by capturing the input of employees and managers.

Work Life Integration

As an attractive employer, we place great importance on our family-aware personnel policy——a policy that responds flexibly to the different life phases and the multifaceted needs of individual employees. In line with this policy we support our employees with an array of measures to help them mesh the reality of their jobs with the needs of their family. We provide an excellent work environment with flexible working conditions-regarding the work location as well as work times. The working hour models we offer include flex-time, job-sharing and sabbaticals. We also have an extensive offering regarding health, sports and leisure time all around the world.

5.3 Cover Letter

A cover letter, covering letter, motivation letter, motivational letter or a letter of motivation is a letter of introduction attached to, or accompanying another document such as a résumé or curriculum vitae.

For employment job seekers frequently send a cover letter along with their CV or employment application as a way of introducing themselves to potential employers and explaining their suitability for the desired position. Employers may look for individualized and thoughtfully written cover letters as one method of screening out applicants who are not sufficiently interested in their position or who lack necessary basic skills. Cover letters are typically divided into three categories:

- The application letter or invited cover letter which responds to a known job opening
- The prospecting letter or uninvited cover letter which inquires about possible positions
- The networking letter which requests information and assistance in the sender's job search

Format cover letters are generally one page at most in length, divided into a header, introduction, body, and closing.

Header. Cover letters use standard business letter style, with the sender's address and other information, the recipient's contact information, and the date sent after either the sender's or the recipient's address. Following that is an optional reference section (e.g. "RE: Internship Opportunity at Global Corporation") and an optional transmission note (e.g. "Via Email to jobs@example.net"). The final part of the header is a salutation (e.g. "Dear Hiring Managers").

Introduction. The introduction briefly states the specific position desired, and should be designed to catch the employer's immediate interest.

Body. The body highlights or amplifies on material in the resume or job application, and explains why the job seeker is interested in the job and would be of value to the employer. Also, matters discussed typically include skills, qualifications, and past experience. If there are any special things to note such as availability date, they may be included as well.

Closing. A closing sums up the letter and indicates the next step the applicant expects to take. It may indicate that the applicant intends to contact the employer, although many favor the more indirect approach of simply saying that the applicant will look forward to hearing from or speaking with the employer. After the closing is a valediction (e.g. "Sincerely"), and then a signature line. Optionally, the abbreviation "ENCL" may be used to indicate that there are enclosures.

Example

April 13, 2000
P. O. Box 36
BIIT University
Beijing, China 100000

Dear Sir/Madam:

Please consider me for your Sales Management Program. My background is one of selling ideas, concepts and programs, and of motivating myself and others to realize our potential.

Attitudes predict behavior-or so goes the saying in sales. If this holds true, I am sure to be as successful in sales management as I am in my college endeavors. My unceasing optimism, self-determination and ability to set goals have allowed me to achieve academic and personal objectives.

Because of my "can do" attitude, sales will provide the challenge and opportunity to continue my successful history of setting and achieving goals. Please allow me the opportunity to elaborate on how my background predicts sales success. I guarantee you'll be providing your corporation with an outstanding sales management. Thank you for your attention.

Sincerely,
Deng Yun

5.4　Resume

5.4.1　Introduction to Resume

A **résumé**, sometimes spelled **resumé** or **resume**, is a document used by individuals to present their background and skillsets. Résumés can be used for a variety of reasons but most often to secure new employment. A typical résumé contains a summary of relevant job experience and education. The résumé is usually one of the first items, along with a cover letter and sometimes job application packet, that a potential employer encounters regarding the job seeker and is typically used to screen applicants, often followed by an interview, when seeking employment. The résumé is comparable to a curriculum vitae (CV) in many countries, although in English Canada, the United States and Australia a résumé is substantially shorter than CV.

In many contexts, a résumé is short (usually one to three pages), and directs a reader's attention to the aspects of a person's background that are directly relevant to a particular position. Many résumés contain keywords that potential employers are looking for, make heavy use of active verbs, and display content in a flattering manner.

Since increasing numbers of job seekers and employers are using Internet-based job search engines to find and fill employment positions, longer résumés are needed for applicants to differentiate and distinguish themselves, and employers are becoming more accepting of résumés that are longer than two pages. Many professional résumé writers and human resources professionals believe that a résumé should be long enough so that it provides a concise, adequate, and accurate description of an applicant's employment history and skills. A résumé is a marketing tool in which the content should be adapted to suit each individual job application and/or applications aimed at a particular industry. The transmission of résumés directly to employers became increasingly popular as late as 2002. Job seekers were able to circumvent the job application process and reach employers through direct email contact and résumé blasting, a term meaning the mass distribution of résumés to increase personal visibility within the job market. However the mass distribution of résumés to employers can often have a negative effect on the applicant's chances of securing employment as the résumés tend not to be tailored for the specific positions the applicant is applying for. It is usually therefore more sensible to adjust the résumé for each position applied for.

The complexity and simplicity of various résumé formats tend to produce results varying from person to person, for the occupation, and to the industry. It is important to note that résumés or CV's used by medical professionals, professors, artists and people in other specialized fields may be comparatively longer. For example, an artist's résumé, typically excluding any non-art-related employment, may include extensive lists of solo and group exhibitions.

In a word, a resume is a summary of your personal background and your qualification for a job or enrolling at a school. The objective of resume is to get an INTERVIEW. It helps your potential employer or supervisor see at a glance whether you are suited for the job opening or qualified for a certain position. So it serves as a story foreshadowing. Good resume will give you the confidence in interview! So, the resume serves as story foreshadowing. Honesty is the most important. You should balance between "be yourself" and "show the right match".

How to create a resume?

- Step 1: use the right format to write down what you have done(academic, oversea, internship, extra-curriculum experience, personal achievement)
- Step 2: SUMMARIZE the key information
- Step 3: show the right MATCH between you and target company

Example for fresh graduate of Mechanical Engineering

Name: Zhang Bo
Sex: Male
Date of birth: July 20, 1989
Mobile phone: 131123456789
Email: abcd@126.com
HomePage: www.abcdefg.com

Education

Bachelor in mechanical and electrical engineering

Academic main courses

Mechanical design, electromechanics integrate, the electromechanical drive and control, control theory and project, Electrician electronics, CAD drawing, Principle of the microcomputer, etc

Computer abilities

Skilled in use of Autocad, pro-e, C, Office2007.

English skills

Have a good command of both spoken and written English. Past CET-6

Scholarships and Awards

2011——obtain the title of Excellence Member
2011——Obtained the first-class scholarship in 2011 academic years last term
2010——Obtained the second-class of Painting and Calligraphy of Freshman
2009——Obtained the first-class of college Dancing Compete

Social activities

Class Commissary of Studies for four years;
Joined the Study Part of Student Union and taking the post as the second president;
Organize the activities of the class, department and school grade many times;
The social activities temper my communication and team-work skills.

Chapter 5 Applying for a Job in an International Corporation

Practical experience

Participate in the production practice at China First Tractor Group Corporation in July 2012

Participate in the Hubei mechanical innovation design contest in April 2012

Participate in the drawing contest 1 at school in March of 2011

Participate in the metalworking practice at school was practised in May of 2010

1. Fresh graduate 应届生

e.g. Just as experience in Asia is coming to be seen as an essential career step in Western multinationals, the opportunities for recent graduates to gain such experience seem to be shrinking.

正如在亚洲工作的经验被看成是步入西方跨国公司的一种基本的职业生涯。应届生获得这样的经验的机会越来越少。

2. practical experience 实践经历，实习经历

e.g. Owing to that very practical experience, he develop his business and management philosophies.

从这种实践经历中，他摸索出了自己的经营和管理哲学。

3. class commissary in charge of studies 班级学习委员

commissary in charge of recreational activities/physical culture/labour 文娱/体育/劳动委员

4. temper vt. 锻炼，使回火

e.g. We should temper ourselves through manual labour. 我们应该通过劳动锻炼自己。

5. production practice 生产实习

e.g. In produce practice, we not only emphasize the operation ability but also attach great importance to the occupation character and morals quality.

在生产实习中，我们既强实际操作技能素质，又特别重视学生职业素质和道德品质。

5.4.2 Resume Tips for Engineers

Think Precision

Precision is paramount when it comes to engineering projects, and the same holds true for engineering resumes. Failing to proofread and correct all errors on the resume is a common mistake engineers make. It's imperative that you have a well-prepared, professional resume with no spelling or grammatical errors. Triple-check it and have other people go over it as well to make sure it's perfect.

Be Concise

During his career recruiting and hiring engineers, Andrew Naslund, HR coordinator for consulting firm Mazzetti & Associates in San Francisco, has observed a tendency among engineers to "go into information overload on their resumes." His advice? "Don't."

Ditch the Objective and Add a Summary

"Do not write an objective," Andrew Naslund says. Not only does it consume valuable space, but it can also hurt your candidacy. "I've seen hiring managers disregard otherwise solid candidates because their objective did not match the specifics of the position opening," he says but with this caveat: "If you are changing careers, then an objective is warranted. Otherwise, leave it out."

Replace the objective with a qualifications summary. Within a few hard-hitting sentences, your career summary should spotlight your most marketable qualifications. "The idea is to pique the interest of the hiring manager," Andrew Naslund says. Here's an example summary for a mechanical engineer:

Internationally experienced mechanical engineer with 15 years of experience and a strong background in Kaizen, ISO and automotive manufacturing. Qualifications include Six Sigma Black Belt, Advanced Pro-E license and PMP-certification.

Tailor the Resume to the Job Opportunity

"I strongly recommend adding personal touches to the resume every time you send it out," Naslund says. "If it's obvious you have mass-posted and haven't responded to me specifically, the resume will probably be trashed."

Customize each resume you send to the specific role and engineering specialty you are targeting. "If you see a Monster ad for a project engineer, for example, bring all of your project management experience to the forefront on your resume," Naslund says.

List Key Accomplishments

"Use bullet points to make your resume easier to read," Naslund says. When writing bulleted accomplishments, keep the text to a few key points and quantify the results so employers understand the significance of your work. Here are examples from various engineering disciplines:

Conducted process mapping studies to improve throughput by 36% and ensure compliance with customer specifications.

Regarded as one of consulting firm's most highly requested mechanical engineers, maintaining 89% or higher billable utilization for the past 4 years.

Co-developed material for cooling radiators that saved $300K/year.

Add a Project List

Depending on your engineering specialty and years of experience, you may find a dozen or more key projects should be included on your resume. When this causes your document to overflow onto a third page, a separate project list sheet is an effective solution.

"If you can get your vitals on a page, that's perfect," Naslund advises. "If you need two pages, that's OK. For any more than that, split the document and add a project list. List projects by employer or client, and give a short—even one—sentence—description of what you did. Most importantly, don't forget to include your project outcomes."

Be Honest

Your resume should be compelling but never misleading or deceptive. "Don't be lulled into thinking that embellishing your resume is OK," Naslund warns. "Never put anything

Chapter 5 Applying for a Job in an International Corporation

on your resume that you wouldn't tell your grandmother."An honest and well-crafted resume will facilitate your job search,and that would be one less problem to solve.

Resume Sample 2

Question:Could you find some advantages and correct it?

Name:Zhang Li

Nationality:China(Mainland)

Current Place:Guangzhou

Height/Weight:170cm/70kg

Marital Status:Single

Age:27 years

Preferred job title:

Mechanical engineer:Mechanical engineering

Project manager/administrator: Mechanical engineering, Quality management/test manager(QA/QC)

Manager:Mechanical engineering

Working life:5

Title:Middle title

Job type:Full time

Expected Start date:In two weeks

Expected salary:￥5,000~￥8,000

Preferred working place:Guangdong province

Work experience

Company's name:Coleman Guangzhou ＊＊＊＊ Company Ltd.

Begin and end date:Sept. 2009~Sept. 2012

Enterprise nature:Soly foreign funded enterprises

Industry:Comprehensive business

Job Title:CAD Designer

Job description:

According to ID requirement from foreign colleague,perform structure design or design improvement for burning appliance(Gas stove).

According to shipping requirement for accessories of burning appliance, design the blister package.

Prototype making at the initial stage of project development,provide the BOM and drawings to sourcing for quotation.

Cooperate with project engineer for the product manufacturing and improvement, cooperate with VE for product cost down design.

Company's name:MITAC International(ShunDe)Corp.

Begin and end date:Sept. 2006~Sept. 2009

Enterprise nature: Soly foreign funded enterprises

Industry: Computer industry

Job Title: Mechanical Engineer

Job description:

As a Mechanical Engineer, in charge of technical job of ODM, OEM, CM server/computer project of customers: Dell, Huawei, Intel, DotHill, BlueCoat, etc.

Approve all mechanical parts of product and do test.

To tooling part(plastic ejector and metal stamping): inspect and approve their cosmetic(burr, shrink/deform, flow trace/burn, silkscreen/painting, plated, etc) and dimension and modify drawing.

To purchased parts, issue drawing to suppliers to ask sample, inspect the dimension of sample and their related reports(FAI, RoHS COC, SGS).

Make sure best stability to product, do some mechanical tests(shock and rotational vibration, Sag&Bow, etc) and analyze the result.

Make sure project can run smoothly, cooperate with other departments for incoming material controling and trouble(design and assembly issues) shooting for product line, find solution and discuss with customer.

Provide design improvement and look for local source materials for customer to cost down.

Reasons for leaving:

Company's name: GuangZhou GuangRi Elevator Industry CO., Ltd

Begin and end date: June 2005~Sept. 2006

Enterprise nature: State-owned enterprises

Industry: Machine building & equipment

Job Title: Machine Design and Manufacture Engineer

Job description: Have been engaged in mechanical design and steel construction design of parking equipments for one year, which is main responsible for product design and diagram paper conversion. At the same time, I often participate the design and install equipments of engineering item. For example, The first tower type parking equipments item of our company: the intellective parking tower of Guangzhou industry and business bureau. In this process, I put forward a lot of project of declining the cost and made some non-standard design.

Educational Background

Name of School: ZHANJIANG Ocean University

Highest Degree: Bachelor Date of Graduation: 2005 - 06 - 01

Name of Major: Mechanical Design, manufacturing and automation

Education experience:

Sept. 2001 ~ June. 2005 ZHANJIANG Ocean University, Mechanical engineering Bachelor Degree

Language Ability

Foreign Language: English Level: excellent

Chapter 5   Applying for a Job in an International Corporation

Chinese level: excellent Cantonese Level: excellent

Relevant skills and abilities

Good English in reading, writing and speaking, usually discuss with foreign customer about the technologic issues and suggestion.

Sturdy foundation in mechanical part (plastic ejector and metal stamping) manufacturing and design.

Be skilled in several drawing softwares: Autocad, Pro/E, SolidWorks, Solidedge, Caxa and some office softwares (project)

C1 driver license.

Self-recommendation letter

With my strong academic background and related experience in mechanical technology, I feel I am hardworking, responsible and diligent in any project I undertake.

I am not a 100% talent, but I can do good job for your company with my 101% hardwork, this point was approved by my supervisor in last job and current job. If opportunity was given, I think your organization could benefit from my analytical and interpersonal skills.

Notes

1. intellective parking tower 智能停车塔
2. steel construction 钢结构
3. engineering item 工程项目
4. industry and business bureau 工商局
5. Middle title 中级职称

e. g. Graduate or above, Automobile, engineering and relevant major, middle title or have related certification.

大学本科(含)以上学历，汽车、机械等相关专业，中级职称或具有相关职业资格。

6. CM=Contract Manufacturer 合同制造商

OEM=Original Equipment Manufacturer 原始设备制造商，贴牌生产

CDM=Contract Design Manufacturer 合同设计制造商

ODM=Original Design Manufacturer 原始设计制造商

5.5　Job Interview

5.5.1　Introduction

A job interview is a process in which a potential employee is evaluated by an employer for prospective employment in their company, organization, or firm. During this process, the employer hopes to determine whether or not the applicant is suitable for the role.

A job interview typically precedes the hiring decision, and is used to evaluate the candidate. The interview is usually preceded by the evaluation of submitted résumés from interested candidates, then selecting a small number of candidates for interviews. Potential job interview opportunities also include networking events and career fairs. The job interview is considered one of the most useful tools for evaluating potential employees. It also demands significant resources from the employer, yet has been demonstrated to be notoriously unreliable in identifying the optimal person for the job. An interview also allows the candidate to assess the corporate culture and demands of the job.

Multiple rounds of job interviews may be used where there are many candidates or the job is particularly challenging or desirable. Earlier rounds may involve fewer staff from the employers and will typically be much shorter and less in-depth. A common initial interview form is the phone interview, a job interview conducted over the telephone. This is especially common when the candidates do not live near the employer and has the advantage of keeping costs low for both sides.

Once all candidates have been interviewed, the employer typically selects the most desirable candidate and begins the negotiation of a job offer.

A typical job interview has a single candidate meeting with between one and three persons representing the employer; the potential supervisor of the employee is usually involved in the interview process. A larger interview panel will often have a specialized human resources worker. While the meeting can be over in as little as 15 minutes, job interviews usually last less than two hours.

The bulk of the job interview will entail the interviewers asking the candidate questions about his or her job history, personality, work style and other factors relevant to the job. For instance, a common interview question is "What are your strengths and weaknesses?" The candidate will usually be given a chance to ask any questions at the end of the interview. These questions are strongly encouraged since they allow the interviewee to acquire more information about the job and the company, but they can also demonstrate the candidate's strong interest in them. When an interviewer asks about the weaknesses of a candidate, they are acknowledging the fact that they are not perfect. However, the interviewer is not really interested in their weaknesses but how they may make up for them. It also displays the skill of self-reflection and the pursuit for self-improvement.

Candidates for lower paid and lower skilled positions tend to have much simpler job interviews than do candidates for more senior positions. For instance, a lawyer's job interview will be much more demanding than that of a retail cashier. Most job interviews are formal; the larger the firm, the more formal and structured the interview will tend to be. Candidates generally dress slightly better than they would for work, with a suit (called an interview suit) being appropriate for a white-collar job interview.

5.5.2 Common Questions and Answers

Q: Can you sell yourself in two minutes? Go for it.

Chapter 5 Applying for a Job in an International Corporation

你能在两分钟内自我推荐吗？大胆试试吧！

A: With my qualifications and experience, I feel I am hardworking, responsible and diligent in any project I undertake. Your organization could benefit from my analytical and interpersonal skills.

依我的资格和经验，我觉得我对所从事的每一个项目都很努力、负责、勤勉。我的分析能力和与人相处的技巧，对贵单位必有价值。

Q: Give me a summary of your current job description.

对你目前的工作，能否做个概括的说明。

A: I have been working as a mechanical engineer for five years. To be specific, I do system analysis, trouble shooting and provide software support.

我干了五年的机械设计工程师。具体地说，我做机械设计，解决问题以及软件供应方面的支持。

Q: Why did you leave your last job?

你为什么离职呢？

A: Well, I am hoping to get an offer of a better position. If opportunity knocks, I will take it.

我希望能获得一份更好的工作，如果机会来临，我会抓住。

A: I feel I have reached the "glass ceiling" in my current job. I feel there is no opportunity for advancement.

我觉得目前的工作，已经达到顶峰，即没有升迁机会。

Q: How do you rate yourself as a professional?

你如何评估自己是位专业人员呢？

A: With my strong academic background, I am capable and competent.

凭借我良好的学术背景，我可以胜任自己的工作，而且我认为自己很有竞争力。

A: With my teaching experience, I am confident that I can relate to students very well.

依我的教学经验，我相信能与学生相处得很好。

Q: What contribution did you make to your current (previous) organization?

你对目前/从前的工作单位有何贡献？

A: I have finished three new projects, and I am sure I can apply my experience to this position.

我已经完成三个新项目，我相信我能将我的经验用在这份工作上。

Q: What do you think you are worth to us?

你怎么认为你对我们有价值呢？

A: I feel I can make some positive contributions to your company in the future.

我觉得我对贵公司能做些积极性的贡献。

Q: What make you think you would be a success in this position?

你如何知道你能胜任这份工作？

A: My graduate school training combined with my internship should qualify me for this particular job. I am sure I will be successful.

我在研究所的训练，加上实习工作，使我适合这份工作。我相信我能成功。

Q: Are you a multi-tasked individual? Do you work well under stress or pressure?

你是一位可以同时承担数项工作的人吗？你能承受工作上的压力吗？

A: Yes, I think so.

A: The trait is needed in my current(or previous) position and I know I can handle it well.

这种特点就是我目前（先前）工作所需要的，我知道我能应付自如。

Q: What is your strongest trait(s)?

你个性上最大的特点是什么？

A: Helpfulness and caring.

乐于助人和关心他人。

A: Adaptability and sense of humor.

适应能力和幽默感。

A: Cheerfulness and friendliness.

乐观和友爱。

Q: How would your friends or colleagues describe you?

你的朋友或同事怎样形容你？

(pause a few seconds)

（稍等几秒钟再答，表示慎重考虑。）

A: They say Mr. Chen is an honest, hardworking and responsible man who deeply cares for his family and friends.

他们说陈先生是位诚实、工作努力、负责任的人，他对家庭和朋友都很关心。

A: They say Mr. Chen is a friendly, sensitive, caring and determined person.

他们说陈先生是位很友好、敏感、关心他人和有决心的人。

Q: What personality traits do you admire?

你欣赏哪种性格的人？

A: I admire a person who is honest, flexible and easy-going.

诚实、不死板而且容易相处的人。

A: (I like) people who possess the "can do" spirit.

有"实际行动"的人。

Q: What leadership qualities did you develop as an administrative personnel?

作为行政人员，你有什么样的领导才能？

A: I feel that learning how to motivate people and to work together as a team will be the major goal of my leadership.

我觉得学习如何把人们的积极性调动起来，以及如何配合协同的团队精神，是我行政工作的主要目标。

A: I have refined my management style by using an open-door policy.

我以开放式的政策，改进我的行政管理方式。

Q: How do you normally handle criticism?

你通常如何处理别人的批评？

A: Silence is golden. Just don't say anything; otherwise the situation could become

Chapter 5 Applying for a Job in an International Corporation

worse. I do, however, accept constructive criticism.
　　沉默是金。不必说什么，否则情况更糟，不过我会接受建设性的批评。
　　A: When we cool off, we will discuss it later.
　　我会等大家冷静下来再讨论。
　　Q: What do you find frustrating in a work situation?
　　在工作中，什么事令你不高兴？
　　A: Sometimes, the narrow-minded people make me frustrated.
　　胸襟狭窄的人，有时使我泄气。
　　A: Minds that are not receptive to new ideas.
　　不能接受新思想的那些人。
　　Q: How do you handle your conflict with your colleagues in your work?
　　你如何处理与同事在工作中的意见不合？
　　A: I will try to present my ideas in a more clear and civilized manner in order to get my points across.
　　我要以更清楚文明的方式，提出我的看法，使对方了解我的观点。
　　Q: How do you handle your failure?
　　你怎样对待自己的失败？
　　A: None of us was born "perfect". I am sure I will be given a second chance to correct my mistake.
　　我们大家生来都不是十全十美的，我相信我有第二个机会改正我的错误。
　　Q: What provide you with a sense of accomplishment.
　　什么会让你有成就感？
　　A: Doing my best job for your company.
　　为贵公司竭力效劳。
　　A: Finishing a project to the best of my ability.
　　尽我所能，完成一个项目。
　　Q: If you had a lot of money to donate, where would you donate it to? Why?
　　假如你有很多钱可以捐赠，你会捐给什么单位？为什么？
　　A: I would donate it to the medical research because I want to do something to help others.
　　我会捐给医药研究，因为我要为他人做点事。
　　A: I prefer to donate it to educational institutions.
　　我乐意捐给教育机构。
　　Q: What is most important in your life right now?
　　眼下你生活中最重要的是什么？
　　A: To get a job in my field is most important to me.
　　对我来说，能在这个领域找到工作是最重要的。
　　A: To secure employment hopefully with your company.
　　希望能在贵公司任职对我来说最重要。
　　Q: What current issues concern you the most?

目前什么事是你最关心的？

A: The general state of our economy and the impact of China' entry to WTO on our industry.

目前中国经济的总体情况以及中国入世对我们行业的影响。

Q: How long would you like to stay with this company?

你会在本公司服务多久呢？

A: I will stay as long as I can continue to learn and to grow in my field.

只要我能在我的行业里继续学习和长进，我就会留在这里。

Q: Could you project what you would like to be doing five years from now?

你能预料五年后你会做什么吗？

A: As I have some administrative experience in my last job, I may use my organizational and planning skills in the future.

我在上一个工作中积累了一些行政经验，我将来也许要运用我组织和计划上的经验和技巧。

A: I hope to demonstrate my ability and talents in my field adequately.

我希望能充分展示我在这个行业的能力和智慧。

A: Perhaps, an opportunity at a management position would be exciting.

也许有机会，我将会从事管理工作。

Q: What range of pay-scale are you interested in?

你喜欢那一种薪水层次标准？

A: Money is important, but the responsibility that goes along with this job is what interests me the most.

薪水固然重要，但这工作伴随而来的责任更吸引我。

5.5.3　Interview Example

Dialogue Topical introduction: Applicant Wangjian is having a job interview with an interviewer in a personnel manager's office. The interviewer is Mike Anderson, personnel manager of a company.

Anderson: Come in, please. Good morning, I am Mike Anderson, personnel manager of our company.

Wang: How do you do? My name is Wangjian.

Anderson: Sit down and make yourself at home.

Wang: Thank you very much.

Anderson: As I know you have applied to work in our company, would you please introduce yourself?

Wang: I'm 22 years old and was born in Shanghai. I can speak and write English fluently as shown in the resume and know how to operate the computer and NC machines. I have been an assistant engineer for half a year in a famous company one year ago. So I am sure that I am quite efficient in technical work, like NC programming, operation, mainte-

Chapter 5 Applying for a Job in an International Corporation

nance and debugging.

Anderson: Ok, I would infer that you are an excellent student in your college. Could you tell me the courses you have learned in your college?

Wang: I have learned many courses, English, mathematics, engineering drawing, mechanical design, C - language program design, electric and electronics, and so on. Also, I have learned many specialized courses, such as machining processes and metal cutting, hydraulic drive, electromechanical control, NC machines and system, fault diagnostic and maintenance for NC machines, NC programming and operation, CAD/CAM, 3DMAX, Internet, electronic-commerce, economics, trade and so on.

Anderson: Why do you choose our company?

Wang: Your company is one of the largest NC machine manufacturers in East China. As you see in my resume, I specialized in CAD/CAM in college, so I expect to develop my capabilities in your company. On the other hand, the position for which I applied is quite challenging. That's the reason why I like to come to your company. I hope to display my talents fully here.

Anderson: If I accept you, how much do you expect to be paid?

Wang: At least RMB 2,500 a month.

Anderson: Oh, I know. Our company doesn't provide any housing. There are 8 regular hours a day. In general, it is from 8:30 a.m. to 5:00 p.m., extra work may be required sometimes with payment and someone need to be on duty on Saturday or Sunday without payment.

Wang: Ok. When can I get the reply about my application?

Anderson: I think you will know the final result within a week. It's my please to have a talk with you.

Excercises

Task 1 Translate the following into English

1. 相关领域2-3年的工作经验
2. 数控机床制造商
3. 领头羊
4. 高度敬业精神
5. 知识渊博的员工
6. 良好的英语说写能力
7. 良好的沟通技巧和人际关系
8. 寻觅高素质的人士加盟
9. 进一步拓展公司的战略市场
10. 工学学士学位
11. 熟悉CAD/CAM
12. 上进心,责任感

Task 2 Translate the following into Chinese

Position: Project Engineer

Position Objective: As core member and key interface in project execution team from technical aspect, overall responsible for project related any technical issue.

Principal Responsibilities:

1. As project technical interface with client, design institute, contractors, suppliers on project engineering aspect, including technical clarification, communication.

2. Interpret client/consultant's technical requirement and questions, clearly define and control on scope from technical aspect.

3. Prepare and attend kickoff meeting, vendor meeting with client, design institute, contractor, suppliers on technical aspect, prepare technical part of Meeting minutes.

4. Liaison with client, design institute on P&ID, GA, Foundation Plan, Piping GA & Isometrics and other drawing clarification and approval from client and design institute.

5. Have regular project technical meeting (conference call or on site) internally with global engineering, project, operation team in USA, India, France etc per project requirement.

6. Communicate with company internal domestic and oversea project & product engineering, Supply chain, manufacturing, quality on any technical issue resolution, including BOM, scope and drawing & document transmittal, clarification, management, quality issue root cause analysis, technical solutions etc,.

7. Work with field service representative on collecting, identifying, analysis, solution making with support from each function internally.

8. Coordinate with product engineering on specifications for procurement.

9. Evaluate impact on any external and internal change order from technical and work scope aspect.

10. Engineering drawings & document control.

11. Other tasks assigned by manager.

PROBLEM SOLVING:

1. Excellent interpersonal skill and strong communication abilities, both oral and written with internal and external customers.

2. Good team worker, inclusiveness.

3. Diligent and professional work attitude, Patient.

Knowledge/Formal Education/Experience:

1. At least hold a degree in Mechanical Engineering, major in compressor preferred.

2. Familiar with product, design, manufacturing of compressor packaging, reciprocating & centrifugal compressor, cylinder, lube oil console, vessel, and cooler etc.

3. A strong knowledge of general mechanical engineering, drafting, such as AutoCAD and UG NX, and PC process is necessary.

4. Fluency in English and Mandarin is essential.

5. Minimum 3 - 5 year working experience in compressor or relevant fluid control equipment industry.

> Books and friends should be few but good
> ——读书如交友,应求少而精

Chapter 6
Specifications and Manuals of Imported Machinery & Equipments

6.1 Introduction

随着我国加入WTO和制造业的蓬勃发展,机电产品进出口日趋旺盛,产品说明书翻译量大面广。因此,无论是在外资企业,还是在合资、国有企业,作为一个专业工程师,只有快速、准确地理解进口机械装备的英文说明书,才能够安装、使用和维护好进口设备,乃至在消化吸收的基础上,做出创新的设计。另外,参与国际竞争与合作,需要专业工程师参与制作成套设备,投标标书文件的制作、参加国际机床展等大型展会,也都要以熟悉进口装备的说明书作为基础。机械设备产品说明书和手册种类包括:Manual(指南手册)、Instruction book(说明书)、Specification(规格说明)、Brochure(手册)、Booklet(小册子)等,如图6.1所示。本章将围绕机械设备,特别是机床设备的说明书和规格说明,分析文体特点和实例讲解。

英语设备使用说明书属于科技英语范畴,它除了有科技英语的一般性文体特点外,还可以归纳出"三大四多"的特点,即:大量使用被动语态、大量使用非谓语动词结构、大量使用缩略语和符号;非人称句多、公式化语句多、省略语句多、祈使语句多。因此,译文要具有简练、严谨、明确、客观等特点。

 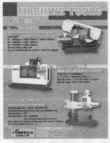  

(a) Brochure of lifts (b) specifications of machine tool (c) reading a broucher (d) a instruction book

Fig. 6.1 Manuals and specifications

6.2 Brochure of Moore Nanotech 350FG

1. Machine Features(Fig 6.2(a))

● PC based CNC motion controller with Windows operating system and 0.01 nanometer(0.0004μ") programming resolution;

● Thermally insensitive linear scale feedback system with 34 picometer(0.034 nanometer) resolution

(a) feature description

Fig 6.2 Specification of Moore Nanotech 350FG

Chapter 6　Specifications and Manuals of Imported Machinery & Equipments

(b) specifications

Fig 6.2(续)

- Allows raster flycutting and/or grinding of freeform surfaces, linear diffractive surfaces, and prismatic optical structures
- Allows increased swing capacity to 20"dia. (500mm) for off-axis and toric components
- Box-way hydrostatic oil bearing slides with 12"(300mm) of travel on Z, 14"(350mm) of travel on X, 6"(150mm) vertical travel on Y, and an adaptive air bearing counterbalance assembly on the vertical axis for optimal servo performance
- Dual linear motors on Y-Axis
- 10,000 rpm "heavy-duty" air bearing work spindle (with liquid cooling option) imbedded into the Y-Axis carriage to improve loop stiffness, reduce Abbe errors, and maintain symmetry
- Options include hydrostatic rotary B-Axis, C-Axis positioning control of the work spindle, Fast Tool Servo system, grinding & micro-milling attachments, optical tool set station, spraymist coolant system, vacuum chuck, micro-height adjust tool holders, Nano-CAM® 2D Aspheric Part Programming Software, on-machine measurement & Workpiece Error Compensation System (WECS), and air shower temperature control system.

2. Nanotech 350FG Specifications (Fig 6.2(b))

General	Description
System Configuration	Ultra-Precision three, four, or five axis CNC machining system for on-axis turning of aspheric and toroidal surfaces; slow slide-servo machining of optical freeform surface

(续)

General	Description
Workpiece size	500mm diameter×300mm long
Base Structure	Monolithic cast epoxy-granite, with integral coolant troughs
Vibration Isolation	Optimally located three point passive air isolation system
Control System	Delta Tau PC based CNC motion controller with 160MHz DSP, operating in a Windows environment, with color flat panel touch screen display and PC-Anywhere remote diagnostic software with modem. 256MB memory, AGP video, CD-RW/DVD Drive, and 80GB hard drive
Programming Resolution	1 nanometer linear/0.00001°rotary
Machining Performance	Material-High purity aluminum alloy. Form Accuracy(P-V): ≤0.15μm/75mm dia, 250mm convex sphere. Surface Finish(Ra): ≤3.0 nanometers
Work holding Spindle	Heavy Duty(Standard)
Type	Fully constrained Professional Instruments grove compensated air bearing
Liquid cooling (optional)	To maintain thermal stability and tool center repeatability, a closed loop chiller provides recirculating temperature controlled water to cooling channels located around the motor and bearing journals of the air bearing spindle. The chiller has an integral PID controller which maintains temperature control to ±0.5F
Mounting	Integrally mounted within the Y-axis carriage to increase loop stiffness and minimize thermal growth. Spindle cartridge resides in an athermal housing to further enhance thermal stability
Speed Range	50 to 10,000 rpm, bi-directional
Load Capacity(Radial)	36kg(80lbs.)@spindle nose
Axial Stiffness	140N/μm(800,000lbs./in.)
Radial Stiffness(at nose)	87N/μm(500,000lbs./in.)
Drive System	Frameless, Brushless DC motor
Motion Accuracy	Axial: ≤25nanometers; Radial: ≤25nanometers

Linear Axes	X	Z	Y(vertical)
Travel	350mm	300mm	150mm
Drive System	Brushless DC linear Motor	Brushless DC linear Motor	Dual Brushless DC linear Motor
Feedback Type	Laser holographic linear scale(athermally mounted)	Laser holographic linear scale(athermally mounted)	Laser holographic linear scale(athermally mounted)
Feedback Resolution	0.034 nanometer	0.034 nanometer	0.034 nanometer
Feed Rate(maximum)	1500mm/min	1500mm/min	1500mm/min
Straightness in Critical Direction	0.3μm over full travel	0.3μm over full travel	0.5μm over full travel 0.3μm(central)10mm
Hydrostatic Oil Supply	Compact, low flow, low pressure system with closed loop servo control and pressure accumulator to minimize pump plsation		

(续)

Optional Rotational Axes	B	C
Type	Oil Hydrostatic	Groove Compensated Air Bearing(liquid cooled)
Travel	360°(Bi-directional)	360°(Bi-directional)
Drive System	Brushless DC motor	Brushless DC motor
Axial Stiffness	875N/μm(5,000,000 lbs./in.)	140 N/μm(800,000 lbs./in.)
Radial Stiffness	260N/μm(1,500,000 lbs./in.)	87N/μm(500,000 lbs./in.)
Positioning Accuracy	≤±2.0 arc seconds(compensated)	≤±2.0 arc seconds(compensated)
Feedback Resolution	0.02 arc seconds	0.07 arc seconds
Maximum Speed (Positioning Mode)	50rpm	1,500rpm
Motion Accuracy	Axial:≤0.1μm; Radial:≤0.1μm	Axial:≤0.025μm; Radial:≤0.025μm

Utility Requirements	Air	Electrical	Floor Space
For optimal cutting results, facility thermal stability should be held within ±0.5℃(±0.1°F)	7.5 to 9 bar (110-130psi); 425 liters/min; Dry to 10℃ pressure dew point and prefiltered to 10μm	11kVA at the customer specified voltage from 220-480 VAC; 50/60Hz; 3Phase (26kVA with optional oil hydrostatic grinder)	1.93m wide×1.80m deep×2.06m high Approx. 3,180kg (Includes enclosure but not including peripheral equipment and control pendant)

6.3 Stylistic Characteristic of English Instruction Manuals for Machinery Equipment

1. 大量使用名词及名词化结构

设备使用说明书是随同设备一并附来的书面材料,用于指导设备的使用。内容以客观描述、介绍产品的安全使用、工作原理、技术参数、结构、安装、调试、操作、维护等为主,需要在上述各个部分里,提及产品各部件名称,还要在附图结构图、方框图、电路图、外形尺寸图等上说明各部分名称并附零件表等,整个说明过程大量使用名词,体现出如下特点:

(1) 大量使用名词短语及名词用作形容词。例如,hardware installation guide 硬件安装指南、conveyor guide rail 传输导轨、the main power indicator 主电源指示灯。

(2) 经常使用名词化结构(nominalization)。名词化结构是由名词化的词如动作名词、动词性名词、动名词或不定式加上各种修饰语构成,在句子中起名词的作用,被认为是科技英语的主要文体特点之一。机械设备说明书中,常采用名词化结构来替代从句或句子(祈使句除外),在其故障排除部分中更是密集使用,使句子结构变得简约、密集、凝练,风格上更显庄重。不过所采用的名词化的词与其他科技文体有所不同,以动作名词和动名词为主。表 6-1 给出了一些名词化结构的例子。

表 6-1 名词化结构的例子

Original sentence	Nominalization
If you operate and maintain arc welding equipment, you will run potential hazards.	Operation and maintenance of any arc welding equipment involves potential hazards.
When this switch is turned on, a compensation circuit is activated.	By turing this switch ON, a compensation circuit is activated.
It's difficult to establish an arc.	Difficulty in establishing an arc.

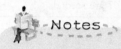

第一句分析:斜体部分短语属动作名词介词名词化结构。从深层结构来看,"of"前的动作名词与"of"之后的名词短语为动-宾关系。该名词化结构由条件状语从句简化、浓缩而来。

第二句分析:属介词动名词结构。用动名词对开启开关的动作进行名词化。该结构相当于时间状语从句。

第三句分析:属名词+介词+名词化结构。形容词 difficult 名词化,"to establish an arc"由不定式短语变为动名词。

2. 频繁使用技术术语和庄重语

(1) 频繁使用技术术语及行语。一般来说,机械设备与其他产品相比,技术含量较高。因此,说明书在描述中会频繁使用技术术语,包括跨行业的与行业专用的术语,从 6.2 节的例子中可以看出。例如,常用 electrode 而不用 welding rod 来表示"电焊条";常用"work"代替"workpiece"表示"工件"。

(2) 倾向于使用拉丁词源派生词与书面语词汇,举例如下。

常用	少用或不用	解释
application	use	应用
construction	structure, building	结构,建造
commission	experiment and adjust	调试
hazard	danger	危险
optional	choice(adj.)	任选的(供选购的)
prior to	before	…之前
terminate	end	结束,终止
assume	take	承担
vary(alter)	differ, change	与…不同,改变
dismantle(disassemble)	take apart	拆卸

3. 广泛采用祈使句和扩展的简单句

(1) 广泛采用祈使句。使用说明书属于"The D's-and-Don'ts-Style"("注意事项"文体),广泛使用祈使句是显著特点。例如,Turn off power. 关掉电源; Do not remove tabs. 不要去掉标签; Pull black lever toward you. 拉动黑色制动杆。

(2) 广泛使用扩展的简单句。机械设备说明书以介绍为主,一般不进行论述,因此,很少见冗长复杂的叠床架屋式的主从复合,特别是定语从句不多,这一点与专利说明书有较大不同。

6.4 Airfel Radiator

Please install your radiator before unpacking

1. Your panel radiator is manufactured in accordance with TS EN 442 standards by means of automation technology.

2. Max. operating pressure is 8 bar, max. operating temperature is 120℃.

3. This product is packed carefully to avoid any external influences.

4. Please do not drag or strike this product during transportation. During unpacking, please avoid contact of any sharp objects with the painted surface.

5. Mounting accessories are in the package. Please do not lose them.

6. Please have the installation performed by an authorized and competent specialist. Please respect the mounting dimensions mentioned in the manual.

7. Please open the radiator valve after startup of the heating installation.

8. Please check whether the radiator is heating or not. If not, please slightly open the air valve located on the upper right or left with a screwdriver. After the air is properly discharged, tighten the valve and check again if the radiator is heating (make sure that all valves are open).

9. To avoid corrosion problems, do not drain the water from the radiator. When the radiator is not in use, only close the inlet and outlet valves.

10. Never cover the radiator with any object or place anything on it. Do not step on the radiator.

11. Do not use or wet your radiator with water containing thermal, acidic or chemical additives. Do not clean it with detergents or chemical materials.

12. Use pressure control gauge in order to test your panel radiator directly with tap water before connecting to the boiler circuit.

6.5 HCX320A NC Low Speed Wire-cut EDM

HCX320A NC low speed wire-cut EDM machine is our newly developed product with mechanical, electrical and hydraulic in one structure on the base of absorbing the foreign technology of low speed wire cut machine.

1. Main Parameters

Size of workable surface/mm	660 * 420
Max. size of workpiece/mm	630 * 400 * 200
Max. weight of workpiece/kg	200
X, Y travel/mm	400 * 320
Z travel/mm	200
U, V travel/mm	35 * 35
Max. cutting taper/mm	±6°/100
Diameter range of electrode wire/mm	0.1~0.3
Max. feeding speed of electrode wire/(mm/sec)	240
Max. tension of electrode wire/N	19.6N(2.0kg·f)
Overall size of machine proper/mm	1610 * 1200 * 1910(without large cover)
	1935 * 2000 * 2080(with large cover)
Machine weight/kg	3000
CNC Power supply unit	MD25

Features of MD25 Pulse Power Unit
● Adopt Windows system, convenient and reliable for operation.
● Industry controlling computer, large capacity memory, 15″ color display.
● Achieved interface between disk and keyboard, transmit data to external by serial interface.
● Versatile parameter base of machining technology, convenient for operation and machining.
● Controllable tension and speed of running, water quality can also be tested.
● Four controllable, four coordinated axes; multi-cut, cutting of dissimilar shape and pitch compensation can be achieved.
● Real time display machining state, real time traces machining graphics.

2. Main performance parameters

Machining accuracy	0.01
Optimum surface roughness μm	Ra0.8
Max. Machining efficiency mm²/min	≥160
Max. Machining current A	20

6.6 Maintenance for a CNC Machine Tool

The following is a list of required regular maintenance for CNC machine tools. These required specifications must be followed in order to keep your machine in good working order and protect your warranty.

Daily
- Top off coolant level every eight hour shift(especially during heavy TSC usage).
- Check way lube lubrication tank level.
- Clean chips from way covers and bottom pan.
- Clean chips from tool changer.
- Wipe spindle taper with a clean cloth rag and apply light oil.

Weekly
- Check for proper operation of auto drain on filter regulator.
- On machines with the TSC option, clean the chip basket on the coolant tank.
- Remove the tank cover and remove any sediment inside the tank. Be careful to disconnect the coolant pump from the controller and POWER OFF the control before working on the coolant tank. Do this monthly for machines without the TSC option.
- Check air gauge/regulator for 85 psi.
- For machines with the TSC option, place a tab of grease on the V-flange of tools. Do this monthly for machines without the TSC option.
- Clean exterior surfaces with mild clean. Do not use solvents.
- Check the hydraulic counterbalance pressure according to the machine's specifications.
- Place a dab of grease on the outside edge of the fingers of the tool changer and run through all tools.

Monthly
- Check oil level in the gear box. Add oil until oil begins dripping from overflow tube at bottom of sump tank.
- Clean pads on bottom of pallets.
- Clean the locating pads on the A-axis and the load station. This requires removing the pallet.
- Inspect way covers for proper operation and lubricate with light oil, if necessary.

Six months
- Replace coolant and thoroughly clean the coolant tank.
- Check all hoses and lubrication lines for cracking.

Annually
- Replace the gear box oil. Drain the oil from the gear box, and slowly refill it with 2 quarts of Mobil DTE 25 oil.

● Check the oil filter and clean out residue at the bottom of filter.
Replace the air filter on the control box every 2 years.

Excercises

Task 1 Translate the following into English.

1. 性能指标。
2. 产品选型手册。
3. 启动 AGV 小车之前，请注意小车是否处于导引线中间。
4. X 轴和 Y 轴均由交流伺服电机控制，可实现两轴联动控制；Z 轴由步进电机控制，可实现开环控制。
5. 选用的力乐士内啮合齿轮泵 PGH 专用注塑机应用而特别优化，保证在各种转速条件下的高效、低泄漏和低噪声。

Task 2 Translate the following into Chinese.

1. Total solution for automation control of servo press, including special control system, DDR, electrical control cabinet, etc.
2. Increase the formability, precision and efficiency.
3. The power consumption has been reduced 60% compared to normal crank press machine in single running time with special control technique.
4. Real-time curve display function, convenient for commissioning and the state indicating.
5. Conform to DIN EN ISO 13849 – 1 and 692 (performance level e, category IV), CE approval.

> By reading we enrich the mind, by conversation we polish it
> ——读书使人充实,交谈使人精明

Chapter 7
On-site Communication and Interpretation

7.1 Introduction

全球化时代的工程师,都不可避免地要在现场使用英语进行简单的交流,有时候甚至要担任现场口译的工作(图 7.1)。

图 7.1 工程师现场英语交流

图 7.1(续)

另外，现场翻译工作的特点决定了工程技术人员现场翻译远比其他人员来得得心应手，适应性强，效果好。工程技术人员担任现场翻译比较容易适应，与双方对口技术人员有共同的兴趣，有利于促进双方的合作共事关系。因此，作为一个机械专业的本科生，应该掌握一些现场交流和翻译的英语技能。

要做好与国外技术人员的交流与现场翻译工作，应该注意以下五点：
(1) 熟悉合同及有关技术资料。
(2) 熟悉有关专业词汇。
(3) 熟悉引进设备和厂家的表达习惯。
(4) 注意常用的缩写和简称。
(5) 注意熟记现场交流的常用句子，并善于应变。

7.2 Technical Communication

7.2.1 Introduction to Technical Communication

Technical communication is a method of researching and creating information about technical processes or products directed to an audience through media. The information must be relevant to the intended audience. Technical communicators often work collaboratively to create products(deliverables)for various media,including paper,video,and the Internet. Deliverables include online help, user manuals, technical manuals, white papers, specifications, process and procedure manuals, industrial videos, reference cards, data sheets,journal articles,patents,training,business papers,technical reports,and forms and documents.

Technical domains can be of any kind,including the soft and hard sciences,high technology including computers and software,consumer electronics,and business processes and practices.

Technical communication jobs include the following:

Chapter 7 On-site Communication and Interpretation

Technical communication sometimes considered a professional task for which organizations either hire specialized employees, or outsource their needs to communication firms. For example, a professional writer may work with a company to produce a user manual. Other times, technical communication is regarded as a responsibility that technical professionals employ on a daily basis as they work to convey technical information to coworkers and clients. For example, a computer scientist may need to provide software documentation to fellow programmers or clients.

The process of developing information products in technical communication begins by ensuring that the nature of the audience and their need for information is clearly identified. From there the technical communicator researches and structures the content into a framework that can guide the detailed development. As the information product is created, the paramount goal is ensuring that the content can be clearly understood by the intended audience and provides the information that the audience needs in the most appropriate format. This process, known as the 'Writing Process', has been a central focus of writing theory since the 1970s, and some contemporary textbook authors have applied it to technical communication.

Technical communication is important to engineers mainly for the purpose of being professional and accurate. These reports supply specific information in a concise manner and are very clear in their meaning if done correctly.

The technical writing process can be divided into five steps:
- Determine purpose and audience
- Collect information
- Organize and outline information
- Write the first draft
- Revise and edit

7.2.2 100 Sentences for On-site Communication

1. Greetings and Talking

- I am very glad to meet you. Welcome to our corporation.
很高兴见到你，欢迎来到我们公司。
- I wish we shall have a friendly cooperation in coming days.
希望我们今后能友好共事（合作）。
- Allow me to introduce myself, my name is Wang Dawei.
请允许我自我介绍，我的名字叫王大伟。
- I am an engineer/a technician/a project manager.
我是工程师/技术员/项目经理。
- My technical specialty is manufacturing process.
我的技术专业是制造工艺。
- Which department do you belong to?

你属于哪个部门?

● Thank you for your direction/help.

感谢你的指导/帮助。

● I am very sorry. I can not speak English very well, but I can read document in English.

我很抱歉,我的英语说得不好,但我能看懂英文资料。

● What does this word mean?

这词是什么意思?

● Is my pronunciation correct?

我的发音对吗?

● Please tell me how to spell this English word.

请告诉我怎样拼写这个英文单词。

● I can follow you.

我能听懂你的话。

● I can not catch up with you.

我听不明白你的话。

2. Engineering Project

● A project execution is usually divided into some elementary phases, such as engineering design, procurement, transportation and field construction.

一个工程项目的实施通常可分为几个基本阶段:工程设计、采购、运输和现场施工。

● The contract number of this project is CJC78-8.

这个项目的合同号是 CJC78-8。

● This is the inquiry/commercial and technical proposal/approval/agreement/minutes/annex/technical appendix.

这是这个项目的询价书/商务和技术报价书/批准书/协议/会议记录/附加条件/技术附件。

● There are many information in the technical proposal, including process flow, process description, capacity of the plant, performance of the product.

技术报价书中有很多资料,包括工艺流程、工艺说明、生产能力、产品特性等。

● There are two units/installations in the contract plant.

在合同工厂内(界区范围内)有两个车间/两套装置。

● I am responsible for the technical/scheduling/inspection/quality control work of this project/area.

我负责这个项目/区域的技术/计划/检查/质量控制。

3. Planning and Scheduling

● We should work according to the overall schedule chart of the project.

我们应该按照这个工程项目的总进度表工作。

● The effective date of this contract will begin from June 1, 2010.

这个合同的有效期将从 2010 年 6 月 1 日开始。

● The basic/detailed process design will be issued before August.

Chapter 7   On-site Communication and Interpretation

基本的/详细的工艺设计资料将于 8 月前发出。
- This contract plant will start-up/put in commissioning on Nov. 13 this year.

这座合同工厂将于今年 11 月 13 日开车/投产。
- The date of acceptance of this plant will be Aug. 28, 2011.

这座工厂的交工验收期定在 2011 年 8 月 28 日。
- The plant is scheduled to be completed around 2013.

工厂计划于 2013 年前后建成。
- A crew of specialists will remain on the job until guarantees are met.

专家工作组将在现场一直工作到生产符合保证条件为止。
- We must take the plant through the test run and finally into commercial operation.

我们必须使工厂通过试运转并最终投入工业生产。
- Every month we shall establish construction schedule.

每个月我们都要制定建设进度计划。
- We shall also make the project schedule report every day.

我们也将每天提出项目进度报告。
- We have to change our plan for lack of materials/construction machinery/erection tools.

因缺少材料/施工机械/安装工具，我们只能改变计划。
- What is your suggestion about this schedule/three-week rolling plan?

你对这个计划进度/三周滚动计划有何建议？

4. Technical Documents and Drawings

- According to the technical standard/norm/rules of operation, the erection/alignment/testing work is now getting on.

安装/校准/试验工作正在根据技术标准/规范/操作规程进行。
- This is a plot plan/general layout/general arrangement/detail/flow sheet/assembly/isometric drawing.

这是一张平面布置图/总平面图/总布置图/细部图/流程图/装配图/空视图。
- That is a general/front/rear/side/left/right/top/vertical/bottom/elevation/auxiliary/cut-away/birds eye view.

那是全视/前视/后视/侧视/左视/右视/顶视/俯视/底视/立视/辅视/内部剖视/鸟瞰图。
- Is this a copy for reproduction?

这是一份底图吗？
- What is the edition of this drawing?

这张图纸是第几版？
- Is this a revised edition?

这是修订版吗？
- Are there any modifications/revision on the drawing?

这张图经过修改/修正吗？
- The information to be placed in each title block of a drawing includes drawing number,

drawing size, scale, weight, sheet number and number of sheets, drawing title, signatures of the drawer, checker and approver.

每张图纸的标题栏内容包括：图号、图纸尺寸、比例、重量、张号和张数、图标以及图纸的制图、校对、批准人的签字。

● We have not received this drawing/instruction book/operation manual, please help us to get it.

我们还未收到这张图纸/说明书/操作手册，请提供给我们。

● Please send us further information about this item.

请将有关这个项目的进一步资料送交我们。

● I want additional information on this.

我需要这方面的补充资料。

● Please explain the meaning of this abbreviation/mark/symbol on the drawing.

请解释图上这个缩写/标记/符号/的意思。

● We comply with and carry out the GB/ANSI/BS/AFNOR/JIS/DIN standard.

在这个工程中我们遵守并执行中国国家标准 GB/美国标准/英国标准/法国标准/日本标准/德国标准。

● Please make a sketch of this part on the paper.

请将这个零件的草图画在纸上。

● The copy is blurred. It is not very clear.

这个复件被弄模糊了，不太清晰。

● Please send us a technical liaison letter about it.

请给我们一份有关此事的技术联络笺。

● Please make a copy of this drawing.

请把这张图复印一份。

5. Project site

● Welcome to our construction site.

欢迎你到我们的工地来。

● Our job site is over there.

我们的施工线在那里。

● It is very simple and crude here. Don't mind, please.

这里很简陋，请勿介意。

● I am a site engineer/director/workshop head/chief of section/foreman/worker/staff member.

我是工地工程师/厂长/车间主任/班组长/领工/工人/职员。

● May I introduce our chief engineer to you.

请允许我向你介绍我们的总工程师。

● Mr. Wang is responsible for this task.

王先生负责这项工作任务。

● I am in charge of this section.

Chapter 7 On-site Communication and Interpretation

我负责这个工段。

● Here is our engineering office/drawing office/control room/laboratory/meeting room/rest room.

这里是我们的工程技术办公室/绘图室/调度室/实验室/会议室/休息室。

● The shift will start at half past seven a.m.

早班从七点半开始。

● We have flexible work hours during the summer.

我们在夏季采用弹性工作时间。

● Put on your safety helmet, please.

请戴上安全帽。

● Here is our machining shop/steel structure fabrication shop.

这里是我的机加工车间/钢结构预制车间。

● This way please. After you.

请走这边,您先请。

● Would you like to see this process/machine?

你要看看这个工艺过程/机器吗?

● The factory/workshop produces pipe fitting/spare parts/fasteners.

这个工厂/车间生产管件/配件/紧固件。

● Let me show you around and meet our workers.

让我带你到周围看一看,并见见我们的工人。

● We would like to know your opinion about our site work.

我们想听取你对我们现场工作的意见。

● Some training will fit them for the job.

经过培训,他们就能胜任这项工作。

● All has gone well with our site work plan.

一切均按照我们的现场工作计划进行。

6. Erection of the Equipment

● Erection of the equipment will be carried out according to the specifications and drawings.

设备安装将按照说明书和图纸进行。

● All site erection works will be performed by the Buyer under the technical instruction of the Seller.

所有的现场安装工作都应该在卖方的技术指导下由买方完成。

● What do you think of this erection work?

你认为这项安装工作如何?

● We are adjusting/installing/checking/aligning/leveling/purging the equipment.

我们正在调整/安装/检查/找正/找平/清洗这台设备。

● We can adjust the levelness of the machine by means of shim and screw jack.

我们可以用垫铁和螺旋千斤顶来调节机器的水平度。

● After seven days, the grouted mortar will have concreted, then we shall tighten the anchor bolts.

灌浆七天以后凝固，到时我们就将地脚螺栓拧紧。

● The alignment of the coupling should be performed by two dial gauges.

联轴器的找正对准应用两只千分表来进行。

● The maximum allowable misalignment of the coupling is 0.02mm.

联轴器找正的最大允许偏差为 0.02mm。

● How many radial/axial clearance are there in this bush/journal bearing/thrust bearing?

这个轴套/轴颈/轴承/止推轴承的径向/轴各间隙是多少？

● Does the bolt fit the nut?

这个螺栓与螺母相配吗？

● The bolt does not match the nut.

螺栓与螺母不配。

● We prefer welding to riveting.

我们认为焊接比铆接好。

● Do you know how to assemble/adjust this new machine?

你知道如何装配/调整这台新机器吗？

● I think that the on-site training will be necessary.

我认为现场培训是必要的。

7. Quality Control

● Total quality control(TQC)is a better quality control system.

全面质量管理(简称 TQC)是一种较好的质量管理体系。

● TQC over the project will be strengthened.

我们应该加强这个工程的全面质量管理。

● We possess skilled technician and complete measuring and test instruments used to ensure the quality of engineering.

我们拥有熟练的技术人员和齐全的检测仪器，可以确保工程质量。

● Field inspection work is handled/executed/directed by our inspection section.

现场检查工作由我们的检查科管理/实施/指导。

● Our site quality inspector will report to the project manager everyday.

我们的现场质量检查员每天会向工程项目经理汇报。

● I want to see the certificate of quality/manufacturer/inspection/shipment/material.

我要看看质量证书/制造厂证书/检查证明书/出口许可证书/材料合格证。

● We shall take the sample to test its physical properties/mechanical properties/tensile strength/yield point/percentage elongation/reduction of area/impact value/Brinell hardness.

我们将取样试验其物理性能/机械性能/抗张强度/屈服点/延伸率/断面收缩率/冲击值/布氏硬度。

● The weld passed the examination of radiographic test/ultrasonic inspection/magnetic testing.

这些焊缝通过射线透视检查/超声波探伤/磁力探伤。

● Are you a qualified nondestructive testing(NDT)person?

你是具有无损检测资格的人员吗?

● Let us go to the laboratory to check the radiographic films.

请到实验室去检查透视片子。

● This job will have to be done over again.

这项工作必须返工重做。

● The defect must be repaired at once.

缺陷必须立即修理。

● This problem of quality needs a further discussion.

这个质量方面的问题需要进一步研讨。

● The testing results fulfill quality requirement.

试验结果达到了质量要求。

● Check list/quality specification has been signed by the controller/inspector/checker.

检验单/质量说明书已由管理员/检查员/审核人签字。

● Is that ok/good/guaranteed/satisfied/passed?

那是正确的/好的/经担保的/令人满意的/合格的吗?

● We have received Certificate of Authorization for producing this product/electric vehicle.

我们具有这种产品/电动汽车生产的授权认可证书。

8. Test run and Start-up

● We shall put the machine to trial/test run after the erection work is finished.

这台机器的安装工作完成以后就将进行试车/试运转。

● We should start the installation according to the instruction and operation manual.

我们应该根据说明书和操作手册来开动这个装置。

● The test run is scheduled for next Monday.

试运行定于下周一进行。

● We have planned to finish the adjustment of the machine before Tuesday.

我们计划在星期二前完成机器的调试工作。

● Before initial start-up of the installation, we must check the equipment carefully.

在装置初次开动以前,我们必须仔细检查这些设备。

● The machine runs perfectly well, it has been operating with a continuous run of 72 hours.

这台机器运转很好,它至今已连续运转了72小时。

● The turbine had been running for 4 hours before carrying a full load.

透平在满载前已经运转了4个小时。

● We shall soon put the installation into commisioning test run/performance test.

我们将很快对这个装置进行投料试生产/性能考核。

● According to the schedule, the first batch process will be produced on Otc. 1 this year.

根据进度表，今年10月1日将首次批量生产。

9. Maintenance and Trouble-shooting

● The machine is out of order, will you see to it, please?

这台机器运转不好，请你去查看一下。

● I felt the machine shake seriously.

我感到这台机器振动严重。

● The machine parts went hot.

这台机器的零件发热。

● The noise of the machine is very loud.

这台机器的噪声很大。

● The machine is knocking badly.

这台机器撞击声厉害。

● If there arises any abnormal temperature, unusual noises and vibration, it is necessary to stop the machine and investigate the cause.

如果产生不正常的温升/异常噪声/振动，必须停车查明原因。

● You must turn off the switch when anything goes wrong with the motor.

如果电机出现异常，必须关掉开关。

● We shall select the suitable grease in accordance with the lubrication chart.

我们要根据润滑表来选用合适的油脂。

● What is the trouble with the machine?

这台机器有什么故障？

● I think the trouble lies here.

我认为故障在这里。

● It is necessary that we should repair it at once.

我们必须立即修理它。

7.2.3 Dialogue:Guide to Visit a Factory

A:Welcome to our factory.

B:Thank you. Yes,the surrounding is quite good.

A:Please wear this helmet for the tour.

B:This one seems a little small for me.

A:Here,try this one.

B:That's better

A:Come this way please.

B:Thank you.

A:This way.

B:After you.

A:The tour should last about one hour and a half.

B:I'm really looking forward to this.

Chapter 7 On-site Communication and Interpretation

A: We can start over here.
B: I'll just follow you.
A: Keep you outside the yellow line. Please stop me if you have any question.
B: OK.
A: Duck your heads as you go through the door there.
B: Thanks.
A: That's the end of the tour. See you.

7.3 Dialogue: Technical Instruction of Using Multimeter

Instructor: Nice to meet you. I am the instructor. My name is Lebron James. I'm responsible for CNC maintenance and application in this company. Welcome to our team.

Beginner: Nice to meet you, Mr. James.

Instructor: Today I will instruct you how to judge if the wiring in electrical circuits is properly connected with the aid of a multimeter. Have you ever used the multimeter?

Beginner: No.

Instructor: The multimeter is a versatile tool. If you want to do any electrical work, you have to use the multimeter.

Beginner: Oh, that's great. I am eager to know how.

Instructor: Ok, please take a closer look at the multimeter. Here, test leads. There are 2 test leads or probes. Generally, one is red and the other black. And this is the LCD display to show the readout. The first step is to turn the meter on. And the second step is to set the multimeter to Ohms with the selector. The third step is to get the test leads in contact with each other and observe the meter readout. If it becomes 0.0000, the meter is working.

Beginner: Oh, Yes, what shall we do next?

Instructor: The fourth step is to place one probe on each other end of a circuit. The fifth step is to observe the indicator. If the meter reads 1., then there is a break in the circuit. The last step is to turn the meter off. So, do you remember these steps? Now, it's your turn to have a try.

Beginner: ……(repeat the steps)

Instructor: Very good. You did a very good job.

7.4 Technical Translation

Technical translation is a type of specialized translation involving the translation of documents produced by technical writers (owner's manuals, user guides, etc.), or more specifically, texts which relate to technological subject areas or texts which deal with the practical application of scientific and technological information. While the presence of specialize-terminology is a feature of technical texts, specialized terminology alone is not sufficient for classifying a text as "technical" since numerous disciplines and subjects which are not "technical" possess what can be regarded as specialized terminology. Technical translation covers the translation of many kinds of specialized texts and requires a high level of subject knowledge and mastery of the relevant terminology and writing conventions.

The importance of consistent terminology in technical translation, for example in patents, as well as the highly formulaic and repetitive nature of technical writing makes computer-assisted translation using translation memories and terminology databases especially appropriate. In his book Technical Translation Jody Byrne argues that technical translation is closely related to technical communication and that it can benefit from research in this and other areas such as usability and cognitive psychology.

In addition to making texts with technical jargon accessible for a wider ranging audience, technical translation also involves linguistic features of translating technological texts from one language to another.

Translation as a whole is a balance of art and science influenced by both theory and practice. Having knowledge of both the linguistic features as well as the aesthetic features of translation applies directly to the field of technical translation.

Background

As a field, technical translation has been recognized, studied, and developed since the 1960's. Stemming from the field of translation studies, the field of technical translation traditionally emphasized much importance on the source language from which text is translated. However, over the years there has been a movement away from this traditional approach to a focus on the purpose of the translation and on the intended audience. This is perhaps because only 5 - 10% of items in a technical document are terminology, while the other 90 - 95% of the text is language, most likely in a natural style of the source language. Though technical translation is only one subset of the different types of professional translation, it is the largest subset as far as output is concerned. Currently, more than 90% of all professionally translated work is done by technical translators, highlighting the importance and significance of the field.

Methods and Practices

The role of the technical translator is to not only be a transmitter of information, but also to be a constructor of procedural discourse and knowledge through meaning, particularly because oftentimes, the technical translator may also take on the role of the technical writer. Research has demonstrated that technical communicators do, in fact, create new meaning as opposed to simply repackaging (198) old information. This emphasizes the important role that technical translators play in making meaning, whether they are doing technical translation in one language or in multiple languages.

Much like professionals in the field of technical communication, the technical translator must have a cross-curricular and multifaceted background. In addition to grasping theoretical and linguistic orientations for the actual translation process, an understanding of other subjects, such as cognitive psychology, usability engineering, and technical communication, is necessary for a successful technical translator. Additionally, most technical translators work within a specialized field such as medical or legal technical translation, which highlights the importance of an interdisciplinary background. Finally, the technical translators should also become familiar with the field of professional translation through training.

Technical translation requires a solid knowledge base of technological skills, particularly if the translator chooses to utilize computer - assisted translation(CAT) or machine translation(MT). Though some technical translators complete all translation without the use of CAT or MT, this is often with pieces that require more creativity in the document. Documents dealing with mechanics or engineering that contain frequently translated phrases and concepts are often translated using CAT or MT.

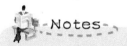
Notes

1. cross-curricular and multifaceted background 跨学科和多方面的背景
2. solid knowledge base 坚实的知识基础
  e. g. Therefore, we should make the educates of solid and wide knowledge base, and can't make them be earlier professioned. 为此，必须使受教育者具有坚实、宽广的知识基础，不能过早专业化。
3. computer-assisted translation(CAT) 计算机辅助翻译
   machine translation(MT) 机器翻译
4. usability and cognitive psychology 可用性和认知心理学

Excercises

Task 1 Translate the following into English.

1. 技术改造
2. 新建项目
3. 三周滚动计划
4. 试运转
5. 故障排除
6. 找平
7. 轴测图
8. 倒班
9. 安全帽
10. 设备大修
11. 授权证书
12. 设备安装
13. 为工人提供技术指导
14. 我认为有必要进一步讨论此事。

Task 2 Translate the following into Chinese.

1. On our most projects Critical Path Method(CPM) is used for scheduling.
2. Field erection work will begin in October this year and complete on June first next year.
3. Let us check the quantity of the parts(accessories) according to the packing list (shipping list).
4. What is the trouble with the machine?
5. You must turn off the switch when anything goes wrong with the motor.

Do nothing by halves
——凡事不可半途而废

Chapter 8
About Foreign Drawings

随着全球经济一体化的快速发展,中国和国际企业常有业务往来,外商传真发来的图纸都是英文标注,平时阅看有一定的困难。工程图纸(Fig. 8.1)的技术性很强,专业面广,因此阅读和翻译之前,应首先查找有关的专业书籍,一定要弄通所涉及机械的工作原理、零部件构造和标准,熟悉图纸的各种缩略表达形式,遇到疑难问题更应查证清楚,反复推敲。其次,工程图纸的语言比较简练、直观和明确,因此具有一定深度和广度的专业技术知识才能准确理解和把握。第三,工程图纸还有大量的缩略语,要在熟知缩略表达形式的基础上,通过不断的专业知识积累来解决。

(a) Drafter at work

(b) Copying technical drawings in 1973

(c) An isometric view of a four-cylinder inline crankshaft with pistons

(d) Cutaway drawing of a Nash 600

Fig. 8.1　Illustration of technical drawings

Chapter 8 About Foreign Drawings

8.1 Introduction to Technical Drawing

Technical drawing, also known as drafting or draughting, is the act and discipline of composing plans that visually communicate how something functions or has to be constructed. Drafting is the visual language of industry and engineering. A drafter, drafts person, or draughtsman is a person who makes a drawing (technical or otherwise). A professional drafter who makes technical drawings is sometimes called a drafting technician.

People who communicate with technical drawings, (those who design and those who are tradespeople), may use technical standards that define practical symbols, perspectives, units of measurement, notation systems, visual styles, or layout conventions. These enable a drafter to communicate more concisely by using a commonly-understood convention. Together, such conventions constitute a visual language, and help to ensure that the drawing is unambiguous and relatively easy to understand.

This need for unambiguous communication in the preparation of a functional document distinguishes technical drawing from the expressive drawing of the visual arts. Artistic drawings are subjectively interpreted; their meanings are multiply determined. Technical drawings are understood to have one intended meaning.

Methods

1) Sketching

Sketch is a quickly executed freehand drawing that is not intended as a finished work. In general, sketching is a quick way to record an idea for later use. Designer's sketches primarily serve as a way to try out different ideas and establish a composition before undertaking a more finished work, especially when the finished work is expensive and time consuming.

2) Manual or by instrument

The basic drafting procedure is to place a piece of paper (or other material) on a smooth surface with right-angle corners and straight sides—typically a drawing board. A sliding straightedge known as a T-square is then placed on one of the sides, allowing it to be slid across the side of the table, and over the surface of the paper.

"Parallel lines" can be drawn simply by moving the T-square and running a pencil or technical pen along the T-square's edge, but more typically the T-square is used as a tool to hold other devices such as set squares or triangles. In this case the drafter places one or more triangles of known angles on the T-square—which is itself at right angles to the edge of the table—and can then draw lines at any chosen angle to others on the page. Modern drafting tables (which have by now largely been replaced by CAD workstations) come equipped with a drafting machine that is supported on both sides of the table to slide over a large piece of paper. Because it is secured on both sides, lines drawn along the edge are guaranteed to be parallel.

In addition, the drafter uses several technical drawing tools to draw curves and circles.

Primary among these are the compasses, used for drawing simple arcs and circles, and the French curve, typically a piece of plastic with complex curves on it. A spline is a rubber coated articulated metal that can be manually bent to most curves.

Drafting templates assist the drafter with creating recurring objects in a drawing without having to reproduce the object from scratch every time. This is especially useful when using common symbols; i. e. in the context of stagecraft, a lighting designer will typically draw from the USITT standard library of lighting fixture symbols to indicate the position of a common fixture across multiple positions. Templates are sold commercially by a number of vendors, usually customized to a specific task, but it is also not uncommon for a drafter to create their own templates.

This basic drafting system requires an accurate table and constant attention to the positioning of the tools. A common error is to allow the triangles to push the top of the T-square down slightly, thereby throwing off all angles. Even tasks as simple as drawing two angled lines meeting at a point require a number of moves of the T-square and triangles, and in general drafting can be a time consuming process.

A solution to these problems was the introduction of the mechanical "drafting machine", an application of the pantograph(sometimes referred to incorrectly as a "pentagraph" in these situations) which allowed the drafter to have an accurate right angle at any point on the page quite quickly. These machines often included the ability to change the angle, thereby removing the need for the triangles as well.

In addition to the mastery of the mechanics of drawing lines, arcs and circles(and text) onto a piece of paper—with respect to the detailing of physical objects—the drafting effort requires a thorough understanding of geometry, trigonometry and spatial comprehension, and in all cases demands precision and accuracy, and attention to detail of high order.

Although drafting is sometimes accomplished by a project engineer, architect—or even by shop personnel such as a machinist—skilled drafters(and/or designers) usually accomplish the task and are always in demand to some level.

3) Computer aided design

Main article: Computer-aided design

Today, the mechanics of the drafting task have largely been automated and accelerated through the use of computer-aided design systems(CAD).

There are two types of computer-aided design systems used for the production of technical drawings two dimensions("2D") and three dimensions("3D").

2D CAD systems such as AutoCAD or MicroStation replace the paper drawing discipline. The lines, circles, arcs and curves are created within the software. It is down to the technical drawing skill of the user to produce the drawing. There is still much scope for error in the drawing when producing first and third angle orthographic projections, auxiliary projections and cross sections. A 2D CAD system is merely an electronic drawing board. Its greatest strength over direct to paper technical drawing is in the making of revisions. Whereas in a conventional hand drawn technical drawing, if a mistake is found, or a modification is required, a new drawing must be made from scratch. The 2D CAD system allows a copy of the original to be modified, saving considerable time. 2D CAD systems can be used to create plans for large projects such as buildings and aircraft but provide no way to check the various components will fit together.

3D CAD systems such as Autodesk Inventor or SolidWorks first produce the geometry of the part, the technical drawing comes from user defined views of the part. Any orthographic, projected and section views are created by the software. There is no scope for error in the production of these views. The main scope for error comes in setting the parameter of first or third angle projection, and displaying the relevant symbol on the technical drawing. 3D CAD allows individual parts to be assembled together to represent the final product. Buildings, Aircraft, ships and cars are modeled, assembled and checked in 3D before technical drawings are released for manufacture.

Both 2D and 3D CAD systems can be used to produce technical drawings for any discipline. The various disciplines; electrical, electronic, pneumatic, hydraulic, etc. , have industry recognized symbols to represent common components.

BS and ISO produce standards to show recommended practices but it is up to individuals to produce the drawings. There is no definitive standard for layout or style. The only standard across engineering workshop drawings is in the creation of orthographic projections and cross section views.

Drafting can represent two dimensions("2D")and three dimensions("3D")although the representation itself is always created in 2D(cf. Architectural model). Drafting is the integral communication of technical or engineering drawings and is the industrial arts sub-discipline that underlies all involved technical endeavors.

In representing complex, three-dimensional objects in two-dimensional drawings, the objects can be described by at least one view plus material thickness note, 2, 3 or as many views and sections that are required to show all features of object.

Technical illustrations

Technical illustration is the use of illustration to visually communicate information of a technical nature. Technical illustrations can be component technical drawings or diagrams. The aim of technical illustration is "to generate expressive images that effectively convey certain information via the visual channel to the human observer".

The main purpose of technical illustration is to describe or explain these items to a more or less nontechnical audience. The visual image should be accurate in terms of dimensions and proportions, and should provide "an overall impression of what an object is or does, to enhance the viewer's interest and understanding".

According to Viola(2005)"illustrative techniques are often designed in a way that even a person with no technical understanding clearly understands the piece of art. The use of varying line widths to emphasize mass, proximity, and scale helped to make a simple line drawing more understandable to the lay person. Cross hatching, stippling, and other low abstraction techniques gave greater depth and dimension to the subject matter".

Cutaway drawing of a Nash 600. A cutaway drawing is a technical illustration, in which surface elements a three-dimensional model are selectively removed, to make internal features visible, but without sacrificing the outer context entirely.

The purpose of a cutaway drawing is to "allow the viewer to have a look into an otherwise solid opaque object. Instead of letting the inner object shine through the surrounding surface, parts of outside object are simply removed. This produces a visual appearance as if someone had cutout a piece of the object or sliced it into parts. Cutaway illustrations avoid ambiguities with respect to spatial ordering, provide a sharp contrast between foreground and background objects, and facilitate a good understanding of spatial ordering".

The First-angle and Third-angle Projection Quadrants in descriptive geometry

Modern orthographic projection is derived from Gaspard Monge's descriptive geometry. Monge defined a reference system of two viewing planes, horizontal H ("ground") and vertical V ("backdrop"). These two planes intersect to partition 3D space into 4 quadrants (Fig. 8.2), which he labeled:

I: above H, in front of V
II: above H, behind V
III: below H, behind V
IV: below H, in front of V

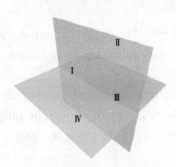

Fig. 8.2 Gaspard Monge's four quadrants and two planes

These quadrant labels are the same as used in 2D planar geometry, as seen from infinitely far to the "left", taking H and V to be the X-axis and Y-axis, respectively.

The 3D object of interest is then placed into either quadrant I or III (equivalently, the position of the intersection line between the two planes is shifted), obtaining first- and third-angle projections, respectively. Quadrants II and IV are also mathematically valid, but their use would result in one view "true" and the other view "flipped" by 180° through its vertical centerline, which is too confusing for technical drawings.

Monge's original formulation uses two planes only, and obtains the top and front views only. The addition of a third plane to show a side view (either left or right) is a modern extension. The terminology of quadrant is a mild anachronism, as a modern orthographic projection with three views corresponds more precisely to an octant of 3D space.

First-angle projection

In first-angle projection, the object is conceptually located in quadrant I, i.e. it floats above and before the viewing planes, the planes are opaque, and each view is pushed through the object onto the plane furthest from it. (Mnemonic: an "actor on a stage".) Extending to the 6-sided box, each view of the object is projected in the direction (sense) of sight of the object, onto the (opaque) interior walls of the box; that is, each view of the object is drawn on the opposite side of the box. A two-dimensional representation of the object is then created by "unfolding" the box, to view all of the interior walls. This produces two plans and four elevations. A simpler way to visualize this is to place the object on top of an upside-down bowl. Sliding the object down the right edge of the bowl reveals the right side view.

Third-angle projection

In third-angle projection, the object is conceptually located in quadrant III, i. e. it is positioned below and behind the viewing planes, the planes are transparent, and each view is pulled onto the plane closest to it. (Mnemonic: a "shark in a tank", esp. that is sunken into the floor.) Using the 6-sided viewing box, each view of the object is projected opposite to the direction(sense) of sight, onto the (transparent) exterior walls of the box; that is, each view of the object is drawn on the same side of the box. The box is then unfolded to view all of its exterior walls. A simpler way to visualize this is to place the object in the bottom of a bowl. Sliding the object up the right edge of the bowl reveals the right side view.

Here is the construction of third angle projections of the same object as above. Note that the individual views are the same, just arranged differently.

Additional information

First-angle projection is as if the object were sitting on the paper and, from the "face" (front) view, it is rolled to the right to show the left side or rolled up to show its bottom. It is standard throughout Europe(excluding the UK) and Asia. First-angle projection used to be common in the UK, and may still be seen on historical design drawings, but has now fallen into disuse in favour of third-angle projection.

Third-angle is as if the object were a box to be unfolded. If we unfold the box so that the front view is in the center of the two arms, then the top view is above it, the bottom view is below it, the left view is to the left, and the right view is to the right. It is standard in the United Kingdom(BS 8888:2006 specifies it as the default projection system), USA (ASME Y14.3-2003 specifies it as the default projection system), Canada, and Australia.

Both first-angle and third-angle projections result in the same 6 views; the difference between them is the arrangement of these views around the box.

A great deal of confusion has ensued in drafting rooms and engineering departments when drawings are transferred from one convention to another. On engineering drawings, the projection angle is denoted by an international symbol consisting of a truncated cone, respectively for first-angle(FR) and third-angle(US), as shown in Fig. 8.3.

Fig. 8.3 Convention placement

Bill of Materials

A. The bill of material table shall be attached to the top of the title block.

B. The bill of material table shall show part numbers in increasing order from bottom to top.

C. The bill of material table format shall consist of, from left to right: item number, quantity, part name, part description.

D. Text in the bill of material shall be placed on a layer with thin continuous lines.

E. The description in the bill of material for a non-standard part shall be the drawing number corresponding to the detail drawing of the part. Standard parts shall be described with a manufacturer name and catalog number or common description.

F. The parts called out in an assembly drawing with balloons shall be identified with numbers. The font shall be the same as used in the dimension text. The part numbers shall be centered horizontally and vertically in the balloons. The plotted text size and balloon diameter shall vary according to the drawing paper size(see table below).

Paper Size		Balloon Diameter	Text Size
Inch	ISO		
A	A4	11mm(.44")	3mm(.125")
B	A3		
C and larger	A2 and larger	13mm(.50")	5mm(.19")

G. The balloons, leaders, and part numbers in the balloons shall be placed on a layer with thin continuous lines.

H. The bill of material, balloons, leaders, and all related text shall be placed in Paper Space.

I. Balloons shall be attached to leaders radially. Balloons shall not have landings.

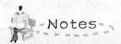

Notes

Artistic drawings   艺术画
quadrants   象限
descriptive geometry   画法几何
Axonometric projection   轴测投影
Cutaway drawing   剖面图
drafting technician   绘图员
Gaspard Monge, 蒙日(1746-1818), 法国人, 数学家, 创立了画法几何技术

8.2 Methods of Reading Foreign Mechanical Blueprints

8.2.1 Key Terms on Foreign Drawing

1. Title block

Scale   绘图比例

Chapter 8　About Foreign Drawings

ITEM No.　设备号/货号
STYLE No.　型号
DRG. No.　图纸序号
REVISION No.　修订号，版本号
DESIGNED & DRAWN/DRAWN BY/DWN　设计与制图签名处
DATE　日期
MATERIAL/MAT'L/MAT　材料
DESCRIPTION　说明
APPROVED /APPD　批准签字
CHECKED/CKD　审核签字
TRACED/TCD　描图签字
Heat Tr　热处理

2. Project relationship

View　视图
Local views　局部视图
Inclined view　斜视图
Half sectional view　半剖视图
Local sectional view　局部剖视图
Cross-section　断面图
Local enlarged view/DETAIL　局部放大图(Fig. 8.4)

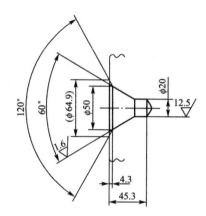

Fig. 8.4　Detail of center

3. Dimensioning 尺寸标注

英文图纸中尺寸常以英寸为单位，1英寸＝25.4mm。若以mm为单位，则常在标题栏处注明有metric。

(1) 圆弧标注。

1.25R：表示半径为1.25英寸；

Chord：弦长；arc：弧长；angle：角度；

1.50SPHERE：表示球面半径为1.50；

.75 TRUE R：表示真实的半径为0.75（所标注的投影图上可能变形）。

(2) 直径标注。

.88DIA：表示直径为0.88；

ϕ30TYP 5：相当于5×ϕ30，TYP＝TYPICAL。

(3) 孔的标注。

.375THRU.875CDRILL.19DEEP　ϕ.375通孔；ϕ.875埋头锥孔，深度0.19；

Through - hole 通孔；CounterBore 埋头孔；

10－M20×1.5JIS, P.C.D ϕ285.7 10－M20×1.5JIS 螺纹，分布圆ϕ285.7；

Pitch Circle Diameter 节圆直径，均匀分布圆直径。

(4) 螺纹孔的标注。

MAJOR DIA：螺纹大径；MINOR DIA 螺纹小径；PITCH　螺纹中径；

PITCH/P 螺距；CREST 牙顶；ROOT 牙底；DEPTH OF THREAD 牙槽深；

ANGLE OF THREAD 牙型角；HELIX ANGLE 螺纹升角；LEAD/L 导程。

(5) 键槽的标注。

KEYWAY 孔上键槽；KEYSEAT 轴上键槽；WIDE 槽宽；DEEP/DP 槽深；Lg 长；Woodruf 半圆键槽

(6) 退刀槽的标注。

NECK 退刀槽；UNDER CUT 切深；WIDE 宽度；DEEP/DP 槽深。

(7) 其他：TAPER 锥度；CHAM 倒角。

4. Abbreviation

U.O.S=unless otherwise specified 除非特别指明/其余；
ID=inner diameter 内径；
IN=inch 英寸；
ISO=International Standard Organization 国际标准化组织；
ANSI=American National Standards Institute 美国国家标准学会；
BS=British Standards 英国标准；
JIS=Japanese Industrial Standards 日本工业标准；
NF=Normes Francaise 法国标准；
DIN=Deutsche Industrie Norm 德国标准；
AS=Australian Standard 澳大利亚标准；
CSA=Canadian Standards Association 加拿大标准。

5. Technical requirement

SHARP CORNERS PERMISSBLE(MUST BE BURR FREE)
允许锐角转角（必须去除毛刺）；
SURFACE FINISH/ROUGHNESS 表面光洁度/粗糙度；
TOLERANCES UNLESS OTHERWISE SPECIFIED 未注公差；
ANGULAR TOLERANCE 角度公差；
DIMS TOLERANCE ±0.1 尺寸公差为±0.1；
SURFACE FINISH 12.5 UNLESS STATED 未标注光洁度12.5；
HRC 30~35 洛氏硬度30~35；
BURR SHARP EDGES 锐边倒钝；
CASTING TO BE AGED 时效处理铸件；
BRINELL HARDNESS/BHN 布氏硬度；
FREE OF SCALE & RUST 不得有氧化皮和锈蚀；
UNLESS OTHERWISE SPECIFIED DRAFT ANGLE 5° 未注明拔模斜度5°；
CAST TO BE FREE OF EXCESSIVE FLASH 铸件不得有过多毛边；
TURNING 车削；DRILLING 钻削；MILLING 铣削；
BORING 镗削；BROACHING 拉削；PLANING/SHAPING 刨削；
SLOTTING 插削；TAPPING 攻丝；REAMING 铰孔；
LAPPING 抛光；POLISHING 研磨；CHAMFERING 倒角；
Deburring 去毛刺；BLACKENING 发黑；NORMALIZING 正火；

ANNEALING 退火；QUENCHING 淬火；TEMPERING 回火；
AGEING 时效；CARBURIZING ['kɑːbjuraizin] 渗碳；
NITRIDING ['naitraidin] 渗氮；SHOT BLASTING 喷丸；
SAND BLASTING 喷砂；PAINTING 喷漆；
PLATEING 电镀；BUFFING 抛光。

8.2.2 Example of Title Block

每幅图样都应有标题栏，内容包括企业名称、零部件名称、图样编号和页数、比例、材料、件数、投影标记、所属部件或零件的相关图号、图样发放日期、设计者、校对者、审核者的签名、图上未注明的公差和表面粗糙度要求等。

A SHAMBLES PTY LTD(Fig. 8.5)　　（公司名称）SHAMBLES 有限公司
JACK BODY　　　　　　　　　　　（零件名称）千斤顶体
Dwg No：17544　　　　　　　　　　（图号）：17544
Sheet 1 of 4　　　　　　　　　　　第 1 页（共 4 页）
Size：A4　　　　　　　　　　　　　图幅：A4
Scale：1：2　　　　　　　　　　　　比例：1：2
Drn. A. B. 5,4,96　　　　　　　　　绘图者：A. B. 96 年 4 月 5 日（美国为 5 月 4 日）
Ckd. J. M. 6,4,96　　　　　　　　　校对者：J. M. 96 年 4 月 6 日
Appd. F. N. 4,8,96　　　　　　　　批准者：F. N. 96 年 4 月 8 日

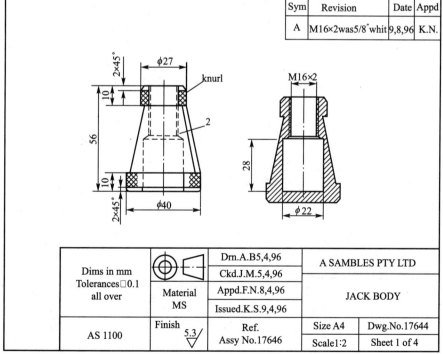

Fig. 8.5　jack body

Issued. K. S. 9,4,96	发放者:K.S.96年4月9日
Ref. Assy. No. 17646	参考部件图号:17646
Material:MS	材料:低碳钢
Finish	表面光洁度
Dims in mm	尺寸以毫米为单位
Tolerances±0.1 all over	全部尺寸公差为±0.1
AS 1100	澳大利亚制图标准

8.2.3 Example of Transformation From The First-angle to The Third-angle

在我国，因为国家标准是用第1角投影，过去制图教科书上绝大部分篇幅谈的都是第1角投影，对第3角投影只作非常简单的介绍，或甚至没有提及，有些工程人员对第3角投影没有多少概念，这就容易出错。但生产任务又很紧，来不及重新培训，这时就需要有人能将第3角投影的图形转换成第1角投影图，以便立即开始加工而不会出错。

另一种情况是，和来自英、美、日、德等国家的客户商谈时，如果把我国的第1角投影图样给他们看，他们也会感到不习惯，沟通有困难，在此情况下，也有必要事先将我们的第1角投影图转换成第3角投影图，如图8.6所示。

再有一种情况是，当搜集资料时，会有两种投影图的资料，此时也有必要将其中一种投影图转换成另一种。

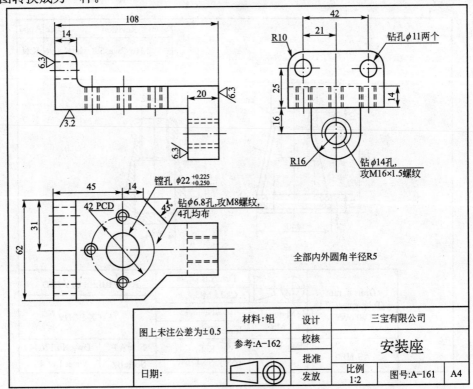

(a) Chinese drawing(first-angle)

Fig. 8.6 Projection transformation

Chapter 8 About Foreign Drawings

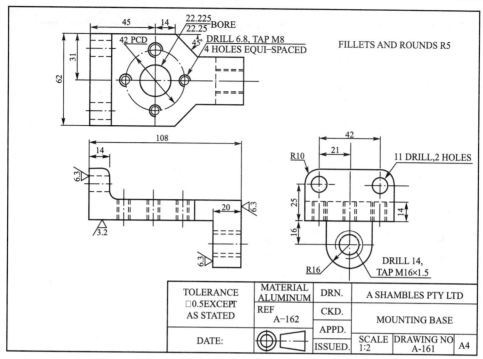

(b) third-angle projection

Fig. 8.6 Projection transformation（续）

8.3 Reading and Discussion

8.3.1 ASME_Y14.5M-1994

Common Symbols

Shown below are the most common symbols that are used with geometric tolerancing and other related dimensional requirements on engineering drawings. Note the comparison with the ISO standards. Most of the symbology is identical. There are a few symbols that are used in the ASME Y 14.5,1994 standard that are being proposed for the ISO standards. The symbols marked with an "x" are new or revised from the previous Y14.5M,1982 standard.

SYMBOL	Y14.5M	ISO
FEATURE CONTROL FRAME	⊕ ∅.030Ⓜ A B C	⊕ ∅.030Ⓜ A B C
DIAMETER	∅	∅
SPERICAL DIAMETER	s∅	s∅
AT MAXIMUM MATERIAL CONDITION	Ⓜ	Ⓜ
AT LEAST MATERIAL CONDITION	Ⓛ	Ⓛ

(续)

SYMBOL	Y14.5M	ISO
REGARDLESS FEATURE SIZES	NONE	NONE
PROJECTED TOLERANCE ZONE	Ⓟ	Ⓟ
FREE STATE	Ⓕ	Ⓕ
TANGENT PLANE\	Ⓣ	Ⓣ
STATISTICAL TOLERANCE	⟨ST⟩	NONE
RADIUS	R	R
CONTROLLED RADIUS	CR	NONE
SPHERICAL RADIUS/	SR	SR
BASIC DIMENSION (theoretically exact dimension in ISO)	50	50
DATUM FEATURE	* ▰▰B	* ▰▰B or ▰▰
DATUM TARGET	⌀8/A1 ⌀8/A1 — φ8	⌀8/A1 ⌀8/A1 — φ8
TARGET POINT/	×	×
DIMENSION ORIGIN	⊕→	⊕→
REFERENCE DIMENDION/	(50)	(50)
NUMBER OF PLACES	8x	8x
COUNTERBORE/SPOTFACE	⌴	⌴
COUNTERSINK	∨	∨
DEPTH/DEEP	↧	↧
SQUARE	□	□
ALL AROUND	⊙⟋	NONE
DIMENSION NOT TO SCALE	150	150
ARC LENGTH/	⌒150	⌒150
BETWEEN	↔	NONE
SLOPE	◁	◁
CONICAL TAPER/	▷	▷
ENVELOPE PRINCIPLE	None(implied)	Ⓔ

注：* 可能填实也可能不填实。

8.3.2 Turning and Lathe

Please read Fig. 8.7(a)~(c), and discuss the following questions:

(1) Describe the types of machining operations that can be performed on a lathe.

(2) What is the difference between feed rob and lead screw?

(3) What are the ways in a lathe?

(4) Describe the differences between boring a workpiece on a lathe an boring it on a boring mill.

(5) Explain the functions of different angles on a single-point lathe cutting tool.

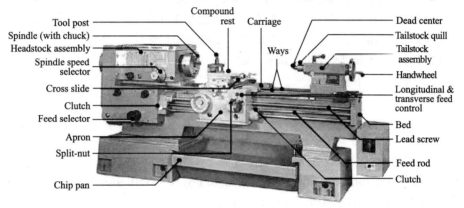

(a) components of a lathe

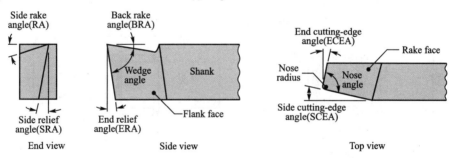

(b) designations for a right-hand cutting tool

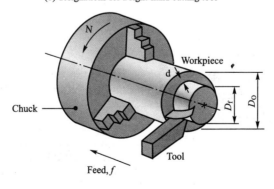

(c) schematic illustration of the basic turing operation

Fig. 8.7 Lathe and turing

Exercises

Task1 Translate the following into Chinese

1. Must conform to die CAST A-13 aluminum
2. title block
3. SECT A-A 4×SIZE
4. TOLERANCE EXCEPT WHERE OTHERWISE STATED±0.125
5. SURFACE FINISH 3.2 UNLESS STATED
6. DOTTED LINES INDICATED MAX FINISH 1"/8
7. FORGING MUST BE ANNEALED TO BE BELOW 203 BRINELL HARDNESS
8. CAST TO BE FREE OF EXCESSIVE FLASH

Task2 Translate the following into English

1. 未注明铸造拔模斜度2°
2. 圆弧必须光滑且与平面相切
3. 钻1"通孔
4. 铰孔1"/4
5. 攻美国固定特种螺纹M1",每英寸牙数14,精度等级为二级

Task3 Read the following drawings(Fig. 8.8. Fig. 8.9)and answer questions.

(1) What are the largest overall dimensions?

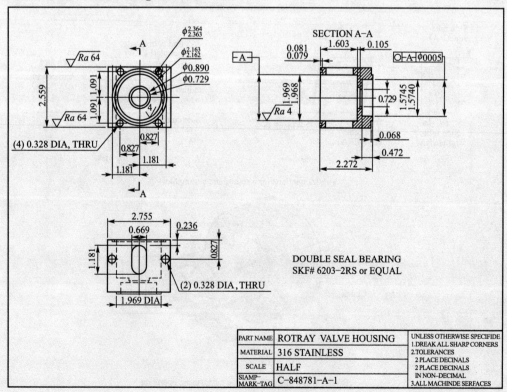

Fig. 8.8 Rotary valve housing

(2) Does it conform to metric system or British system? Why?
(3) Which size requirement is the most accurate?
(4) Are there position tolerance requirements?
(5) Is it the first-angle or third-angle projection? Why?

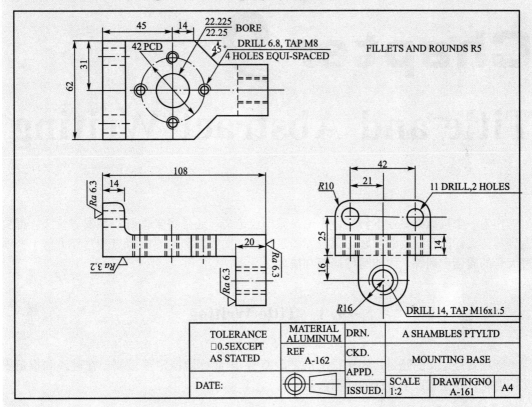

Fig. 8.9 Mounting bracket

Ideal is the beacon.
——理想是指路明灯

Chapter 9
Title and Abstract Writing

作为一个机械类专业本科生，无论是做毕业论文，还是将来提升职称发表论文，都要遇到写英文标题和摘要的问题。只有弄清楚科技论文标题和摘要的特点和写作方法，并通过大量的阅读和训练，才能写好标题和摘要。

9.1 Title Writing

标题就是论文的题目，好比论文的"眼睛"，因此标题拟定很重要。在翻译和拟定中文标题时，要注意以下方面的问题。

1. 求美七原则（中英文科技论文通用）

(1) 留有余地，求低调。
诸如"…研究，…学，…论，…系统，…规律，…机理"字样，要慎用。

(2) 删繁就简，求简洁。
诸如"关于…的研究，关于…的调查，关于…的探讨，关于…的报告"等字样，拟题时尽量规避为好。

(3) 便于检索，求特指。
拟定标题时，通常提倡用特指性而非泛指性词语。泛指性标题笼统、概念易模糊，不利于文献检索。

(4) 修辞结构，求合理。
科技论文标题，习惯用以名词或名词性词组为中心的偏正词组形式表达，尽可能不用动宾结构形式。最好遵从标题用语习惯和简洁性原则。

(5) 详略得当，求通顺。
针对滥用虚词或虚词位置不当或堆砌实词或漏掉实词等现象，在不违背语法修辞的前提下，如果标题名不用某词（字）也通顺，就尽量不用；如果舍去某词（字）便不通顺，就留用。

Chapter 9　Title and Abstract Writing

（6）结构相似，求工整。

这是针对小标题（层次标题）而言。同一层次标题应尽可能用排比修辞手法，即词组（一般词组）结构相同（或相近），意义相关，语气一致。

（7）干净明晰，非重复。

针对机械重复上级标题字面内容的现象，作者拟定各级小标题和编辑审读加工时，应遵从简洁原则，去掉重复内容。

2. 标题中尽量不用赘词冗语

e.g.

《失效分析》中几个学术问题的探讨
Discussion on Several Academic Problems in the Book Failure Analysis(×)
Several Questions in Failure Analysis(√)
解决人工智能语言问题的方法论原则
Methodological Principles of Solving Linguistic Problems Relating to Artificial Intelligence(×)
Methodological Principles of Solving Linguistic Problems of AI(√)

3. 标题中尽量多用关键词语

e.g.

An Investigation of a Heat Pipe Cooling System for Use in Turning on a Lathe(√)
Wear evaluation of a self-propelled rotary tool when machining titanium alloy IMI 318(√)
A review of machine vision sensors for tool condition monitoring(√)
3D measurement of crater wear by phase shifting method(√)
Assessment and visualisation of machine tool wear using computer vision(√)
Driver current analysis for sensorless tool breakage monitoring of CNC milling machines(√)

4. 根据需要拟定主、副标题，用冒号隔开，使主标题不至于过长

e.g.

Why Is Chinese Modal Logic Different from Its Western Counterpart(×)
中国模态逻辑为何不同于它的西方对应物
Chinese and Western Modal Logic: The Difference and Its Cause(√)
中西模态逻辑的差异及其成因

5. 英文标题大小写的3种格式

（1）全部字母大写。

EVALUATION OF SURFACE ROUGHNESS BY VISION SYSTEM

(2) 每个词的首字母大写,但 3 个或 4 个字母以下的冠词、连词、介词全部小写。
Evaluation of Surface Roughness Using a Image Processing and Machine Vision System
(3) 题名第 1 个词的首字母大写,其余字母均小写(专用缩写除外)。
Shape control properties of VC mills(VC 辊平整机板形调控性能)
A study on the use of single mesh size abrasives in abrasive waterjet machining

9.2 Abstract Writing

An abstract is a brief summary of a research article, thesis, review, conference proceeding or any in-depth analysis of a particular subject or discipline, and is often used to help the reader quickly ascertain the paper's purpose. When used, an abstract always appears at the beginning of a manuscript or typescript, acting as the point-of-entry for any given academic paper or patent application. Abstracting and indexing services for various academic disciplines are aimed at compiling a body of literature for that particular subject.

Academic literature uses the abstract to succinctly communicate complex research. An abstract may act as a stand-alone entity instead of a full paper. As such, an abstract is used by many organizations as the basis for selecting research that is proposed for presentation in the form of a poster, platform/oral presentation or workshop presentation at an academic conference. Most literature database search engines index only abstracts rather than providing the entire text of the paper. Full texts of scientific papers must often be purchased because of copyright and/or publisher fees and therefore the abstract is a significant selling point for the reprint or electronic form of the full text.

An academic abstract typically outlines four elements relevant to the completed work:
- The research focus(i.e. statement of the problem(s)/research issue(s) addressed);
- The research methods used(experimental research, case studies, questionnaires, etc.);
- The results/findings of the research; and
- The main conclusions and recommendations

It may also contain brief references, although some publications' standard style omits references from the abstract, reserving them for the article body(which, by definition, treats the same topics but in more depth).

Abstract length varies by discipline and publisher requirements. Typical length ranges from 100 to 500 words, but very rarely more than a page and occasionally just a few words.

Steps: purpose(background)—methods—results—conclusions.
- Write after finishing most of manuscript
- <200 words or <18 lines
- Start with "why" (2-3 sentences)
- Followed by "In this study,…" (what was done; 2-3 sentences)
- Followed by results(2-3 sentences): include numbers!
- Followed by conclusions

Chapter 9 Title and Abstract Writing

- End with "significance"
- Emphasize uniqueness, impact
- Spelling check!

An Example:

An automated flank wear measurement of microdrills using machine vision

FROM: Journal of Materials Processing Technology 180(2006)328-335

Abstract

The objective of this study is to develop an automated flank wear measurement scheme using vision system for a microdrill. The images of worn-out microdrills were captured after the hole-drilling tests on a 10-layered printed circuit board(PCB). The models were evaluated and validated based on the acquired image with a computer-based acquisition system. Edge detection was employed to extract the boundary with a pair of edge points, including both raising and falling edges, to compute the height of the cutting plane. The flank wear area, average flank wear height, and maximum wear height are computed by using this approach to evaluate the tool life. Experimental results show that the proposed scheme is reliable and effective for the automated flank wear measurement of microdrill in PCB production.

1. 此例回答了如下四个问题：

（1）回答为什么做？（研究目的）

The objective of this study is to develop an automated flank wear measurement scheme using vision system for a microdrill.

（2）回答做了什么？（研究工作范围）

（3）回答怎样做的？（实验要点）

（2）（3）常结合在一起写。

The images of worn-out microdrills were captured after the hole-drilling tests on a 10-layered printed circuit board(PCB). The models were evaluated and validated based on the acquired image with a computer-based acquisition system. Edge detection was employed to extract the boundary with a pair of edge points, including both raising and falling edges, to compute the height of the cutting plane. The flank wear area, average flank wear height, and maximum wear height are computed by using this approach to evaluate the tool life.

（4）回答结果如何？（主要结论）

Experimental results show that the proposed scheme is reliable and effective for the automated frank wear measurement of microdrill in PCB production.

2. 写作要点

（1）简明扼要。

（2）严格、全面的表达中文摘要的内容。

（3）符合英文专业术语规范。

（4）符合英文的表达习惯。

（5）用词力求简单，尽量用短词代替长词。

（6）时态：①叙述研究过程，多采用一般过去时；②在采用一般过去时叙述研究过程当中提及在此过程之前发生的事，宜采用过去完成时；③说明某课题现已取得的成果，宜采用现在完成时;④摘要开头表示本文所"报告"或"描述"的内容,以及摘要结尾表示作者所"认为"的观点和"建议"的做法时,可采用一般现在时。

(7)语态:①在多数情况下可采用被动语态;②在某些情况下,特别是表达作者或有关专家的观点时,又常用主动语态,其优点是鲜明有力。

(8)造句技巧:

① 熟悉英文摘要的常用句型:

ⅰ 表示研究目的,常用在摘要之首

In order to……This paper describes……The purpose of this study is……

ⅱ 表示研究的对象与方法

The curative effect of certain drug was observed/detected/studied…

ⅲ 表示研究的结果。

[The result showed/It proved/The authors found] that……

ⅳ 表示结论、观点或建议。

The authors [suggest/conclude/consider] that…

② 尽量采用-ing分词和-ed分词作定语,少用关系代词which,who等引导的定语从句。

9.3 Reading Materials

9.3.1 A Robust Design Approach to Determination of Tolerances of Mechanical Products

From:CIRP Annals-Manufacturing Technology 59(2010)195-198

Abstract

Tolerance specifications of design parameters influence both functional performance and manufacturing cost of products. Product functional performance is usually affected by uncertainties of design parameters,robust design can make product functional performance insensitive to those uncertainties. Based on the robust design method and the cost-tolerance models,a mathematical model has been developed for describing the relationships among functional performance,manufacturing costs,design parameters and tolerances. A new robust optimization method has also been developed to determine tolerances and design parameters simultaneously. This new approach has been used for determining design parameters and tolerances of a coating head of printing machinery.

Keywords:

Product design;Robust design;Tolerance design

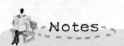

Specifications 规格

e. g. Please mark item No. ,Specifications and tolerance for order.

订货时候请注明产品编号、规格和公差。

9.3.2 High-speed Machining of Cast Iron and Alloy Steels for Die and Mold Manufacturing

Abstract

This paper gives a brief overview of HSC technology and presents current progress in high performance machining of cast iron and alloy steels used in die and mold manufacturing. This work covers: (a) theoretical and experimental studies of tool failure and tool life in high-speed milling of hard materials, (b) optimization of CNC programs by adjusting spindle RPM and feed rate (program OPTIMILL) to maintain nearly constant chip load in machining sculptured surfaces, and (c) prediction of chip flow, stresses and temperatures in the cutting tool as well as residual stresses in the machine surface layer. Experimental studies are conducted using a 4-axis high-speed milling machine. Tool materials evaluated include carbides, coated carbides, and PCBN. Workpiece materials investigated include II-13 at 46 HRC, P-20 at 20±40 HRC and cast iron.

Keywords: HSC technology; CNC programs; Cast iron

9.3.3 An Overview of Power Electronics in Electric Vehicles

From: IEEE Transactions on Industrial Electronics, Vol. 44, No. 1, February 1997

Abstract

In response to concerns about energy cost, energy dependence, and environmental damage, a rekindling of interest in electric vehicles (EV's) has been obvious. Based on the "California rules" on zero emission vehicles in the United States, as well as similar tightened air pollution regulation in Europe, Asia, and much of the rest of the world, the market size of EV's will be enormous. Thus, the development of power electronics technology for EV's will take an accelerated pace to fulfill the market needs. This paper reviews the current status of multidisciplinary technologies in EV's. Various challenges of power electronics technology for EV propulsion, battery charging, and power accessories are explored.

Index Terms: Electric vehicles, power electronics.

9.3.4 A Tool Planning Approach Considering Cycle Time Constraints and Demand Uncertainty

From: Int J Adv Manuf Technol (2005) 26:565 – 571

Abstract

The tool planning problem is to determine how many tools should be allocated to each tool group to meet some objectives. Recent studies aim to solve the problem for the cases of uncertain demand. Yet, most of them do not involve cycle time constraints. Cycle time, a key performance index in particular in semiconductor foundry, should not be ignored. The uncertain demand is modeled as a collection of scenarios. Each scenario, with an occurrence probability, represents the aggregate demand volume under a given product mix ratio. A genetic algorithm embedded with a queuing analysis is developed to solve the problem. Experiments indicate that the proposed solution outperforms that obtained by considering only a particular scenario.

Propulsion 推进力，推进
genetic algorithm 遗传算法
power accessories 电源附件
tool planning 刀具规划
electric vehicle 电动汽车
battery charging 电池充电

Exercises

Task 1 Translate the following abstracts into Chinese.

Abstract: A novel proposal is presented in this paper for reducing the thermal inaccuracy of turning on a lathe by removing the portion of the heat generated during the cutting process which is transferred to the carbide cutting insert by installing a heat pipe in the toolholder. The ability of the heat pipe to affect the temperature of the carbide cutting insert and the elongation of the toolholder is inferred from the response of thermocouples and strain gauges mounted on the toolholder to the heat generated during various cutting conditions. The results of the experimental investigation have proved the feasibility of the concept and recommendations have been made for continuing the research and improving the performance of the system.

Task 2 Translate the following abstracts into English.

1. 自回转车刀结构优化设计与制造

摘要：阐述自回转车刀的优点和使用中存在的一些问题。刀片回转不均匀是实际应用中面临的难题之一，解决刀片回转不均匀问题的关键在于优化设计刀片回转轴与轴承、刀片内孔之间的配合间隙。通过优化设计其结构参数以及采用合理的加工工艺，改善自回转车刀刀片的回转均匀性。通过切削试验证明，经过优化设计后的自回转车刀在实际生产中具有良好的使用性能。此外，还讨论了自回转车刀刀体与刀片制造的加工工艺问题。

关键词：自回转车刀；圆刀片；回转均匀性；优化设计

2. 基于最优控制理论的储能飞轮转子形状优化设计研究

摘要：为克服飞轮转子形状优化时一般优化方法效率低的缺点，在分析角速度对转子形状影响的基础上，将转子角速度划分为低速、中速和高速三个阶段，采用最优控制理论，直接得到实心和空心飞轮转子的最优形状解析表达式。通过比较实心和空心转子低速、中速和高速情况下的最优形状，揭示飞轮转子最优形状随角速度变化的规律。研究结果表明，低角速度下，转子的最优形状沿半径方向"内薄外厚"；高角速度下，"内厚外薄"；中等角速度下，"两端厚中间薄"。低角速度情况下，实心和空心转子的最优形状相同；但中、高速情况下，实心转子的最优形状中包含等应力弧段，而空心转子的最优形状中不包含等应力弧段。由于实心转子的最优形状中包含有等应力弧段，实心转子的储能性能更优于空心转子。

关键词：飞轮转子；形状优化；最优控制

A burden of one's choice is not felt

——爱挑的担子不嫌重

Chapter 10
Attending Professional Exhibition and Conference

会展是制造产业中一个关键的环节，每一个企业都需要宣传，都要有展览，会展这个环节是制造产业链中高附加值的环节，它能为制造产业带来巨大的利润和财富。

参加国际展会或高水平技术研讨会，对于企业而言，可以宣传产品，对于工程师个人而言，可以开阔视野、广交朋友、发现新的工作机会，因此，是非常有意义的。如今，在上海、深圳、北京等国际大都市，国际展会已很具规模，成为我国城市经济中的一种新经济现象。对于中国制造商而言，参加诸如汉诺威国际机床展，无疑是最好的展示我国制造水平的机会。因此，作为一个机械类专业的本科生，了解一些参加国际制造展会或学术会议的基本知识是非常有必要的。

10.1 Professional Exhibitions

10.1.1 Introduction to Four Largest Manufacturing Shows

IMTS(Chicago)

The International Manufacturing Technology Show(IMTS), first held in Cleveland, Ohio in 1927. It is the largest manufacturing technology trade show in North America.

The six-day show is held in even-numbered years at Chicago's McCormick Place and draws attendees and exhibitors from the U. S. and some 40 other nations. The 2010 show registered 82,411 attendees and 1,728 exhibitors across 4 buildings and 1,137,375 square feet(105,665.6 m2)of exhibit space.

In addition to being an exhibition for suppliers of machinery and other manufacturing technology, since 2004 IMTS has sponsored the Emerging Technology Center, where new developments from both academia and industry are showcased. IMTS 2010, for example, focused on Cloud computing and the MTConnect communication standard.

The show is managed by the Association for Manufacturing Technology(AMT). An agreement between the AMT and the CECIMO(European Machine Tool Industry Association), which organizes the European-based EMO trade show for the metal working industry, coordinates the IMTS and the EMO such that every even-numbered year the IMTS is held in Chicago, and every odd-numbered year the EMO is held in Europe.

EMO(Hannover)

Exposition Mondiale de la Machine Outil (English: Machine Tool World Exposition), or "EMO" is a bi-annual European trade show for the metal working industry. It occurs every odd-numbered year, with a cycle that finds it at the Hanover fairground in Hannover, Germany for 2 shows, then the FieraMilano exhibition center in Milan, Italy for 1 show.

The show covers the spectrum of metalworking technologies, such as cutting, splitting, milling, and forming machine tools, manufacturing systems, precision tools, automated material flow, computer technology, industrial electronics, and accessories.

EMO is an initiative of, and under the auspices of, the Comité de coopération des industries de la machine-outil, or CECIMO(European Machine Tool Industry Association). The Verein Deutscher Werkzeugmaschinenfabriken(English: German Machine Tool Builders' Association), or VDW, is responsible for the organization of the trade show when in Hanover, while UCIMU, the Association of Italian Manufacturers of Machine Tools, Robots, Automation Systems and ancillary products(NC, tools, components, accessories) manages the Milan show.

The premier machine tool trade show for the whole of Asia

You can establish new business contacts with companies representing various industries in Asia and look for new and upcoming business opportunities, including cooperation and joint ventures with Japanese suppliers.

JIMTOF

JIMTOF is the abbrication of Japan International Machine Tool Fair. It was founded in 1962 and was held in Tokyo and in Osaka. It is not only a platform for state-of-the-art technologies, but also a global business meeting platform. In 2011, a total of over 100,000 visitors attend JIMTOF, including about 8,000 overseas visitors from 71 countries and regions. The number of attendees at recent JIMTOF events from China, Taiwan, South Korea, and other East Asian countries, where brisk economic growth is driving demand for capital investment, has been increasing.

CIMT

CIMT, as shown in Fig. 10.1, is one of the four most important machine tool exhibitions in the world. Engineers and managers from all parts of the world flock to Beijing, Where they get abreast of the last manufacturing technology and promote their new products. Also, some people may find job opportunities.

Chapter 10 Attending Professional Exhibition and Conference

Fig. 10.1   At CIMT

芝加哥国际机床展(IMTS)、汉诺威国际机床展(EMO)、日本国际机床展(JIMTOF)和中国国际机床展(CIMT),并称为四大国际机床名展。

10.1.2 At CIMT

Brown is a Franch customer. Li is a sales engineer of a domestic manufacture.

Outside the hall

Li:Welcome to the China International Machine Tool Show. The opening ceremonies have just begin.

Brown:Yes,the scene is grand and lively.

Li:Look at those large balloons in the air with welcoming slogans on them.

Brown:They are very impressive indeed. There seems to be a big turnout.

Li:Exactly. The registration is around 45000 visitors so far,from all parts of the world and the number is expected to increase over the next two or three days.

Brown:I'm lucky to have this opportunity.

Li:You are right. The show has been very important to China's machine tool industry. There are about 1,000 new machine tools on display. Delegations representing many different countries or regions are participating in this CMIT.

Brown:Fantastic! Do you have such a big event every year?

Li:Actually,it has been held in China every 2 years ever since 1989. And the show has been recognized as one of the top four marketing activities in the world's machine tool sector.

Brown:I'm sure to come next time.

Li:You are welcome!

Inside the hall

Brown:Look! The exhibits are spectacular.

Li:Sure. This is the exhibition hall 8A. It's divided into four sections. Here on display are some new domestic machine tools. Many of them have caught up with the technical levels of similar products made abroad. Let me show you around.

Brown:It's very kind of you! Oh,that's a big simultananeous five-axis CNC machine.

Li: Yes. This new machine reaches the advanced world level. It is suitable for the aviation industry.

Brown: I see. Is this a boring-milling machine?

Li: That's right. It is highly recommended in the world because it is economical, easy to operate and outstanding in performance.

Brown: That sounds interesting. But the size is a bit small.

Li: It is specially designed to handle small pieces, and it is stable and efficient. The bigger one is also available. Over there, you see.

Brown: Is that a gantry five face machining center?

Li: Yes. With travels of approximately 150″×246″, it can accommodate your large work pieces.

Brown: What's the unit price?

Li: Here is our price list and this is the catalogue.

In the negotiation booth

Brown: We have studied your catalogue and we have great interest in your boring-milling machine. But your price appears a little high.

Li: What quantity are you looking to order?

Brown: We plan to order 15 units, provided the price is right.

Li: To be frank, this machine was out of stock for a while because the demand exceeded the supply. The list price remains unchanged. But because of the large order size, and because we would like to establish a long-term relationship with you, we are prepared to offer you a reduced unit price of $20000 FOB Shanghai. That's our bottom price.

Brown: It seems acceptable. What is your lead time?

Li: Twelve weeks. The goods can be ready by August.

Brown: Well, we expect to use them this October. Time is too tight. We need to transit the goods at Singapore since there is no direct vessel from Shanghai to Lagos. Could you get the good ready for shipment by mid July?

Li: July is OK.

Brown: When can we sign the contract?

Li: Tomorrow afternoon.

Brown: See you tomorrow then.

Li: See you tomorrow.

10.2 Academic Conference

10.2.1 Introduction

An academic conference or symposium is a conference for researchers(not always academics) to present and discuss their work. Together with academic or scientific journals, conferences provide an important channel for exchange of information between researchers.

Conferences are usually composed of various presentations. They tend to be short and concise, with a time span of about 10 to 30 minutes; presentations are usually followed by a discussion. The work may be bundled in written form as academic papers and published as the conference proceedings. Usually a conference will include keynote speakers (often, scholars of some standing, but sometimes individuals from outside academia), as shown in Fig. 10.2(a). The keynote lecture is often longer, lasting sometimes up to an hour and a half, particularly if there are several keynote speakers on a panel.

In addition to presentations, conferences also feature panel discussions, round tables on various issues and workshops.

Prospective presenters are usually asked to submit a short abstract of their presentation, which will be reviewed before the presentation is accepted for the meeting. Some disciplines require presenters to submit a paper of about 6 - 15 pages, which is peer reviewed by members of the program committee or referees chosen by them.

In some disciplines, such as English and other languages, it is common for presenters to read from a prepared script. In other disciplines such as the sciences, presenters usually base their talk around a visual presentation that displays key figures and research results.

A large meeting will usually be called a conference, while a smaller is termed a workshop. They might be single track or multiple track, where the former has only one session at a time, while a multiple track meeting has several parallel sessions with speakers in separate rooms speaking at the same time.

At some conferences, social or entertainment activities such as tours and receptions can be part of the program. Business meetings for learned societies or interest groups can also be part of the conference activities.

The larger the conference, the more likely it is that academic publishing houses may set up displays, as shown in Fig. 10.2(b). Large conferences also may have a career and job search and interview activities.

(a) keynote speech

(b) display and discussion

Fg. 10.2　At academic conference

10.2.2　Opening Remarks on Simulated Conference

Distinguished guests, distinguished delegates, ladies and gentlemen, and all the friends:

At this special time of wonderful March, in this grand hall of the beautiful campus, Our respectable guests are here getting together. Jointly sponsored by Chinese Mechanical Engineering Society, undertaken by Modern Manufacturing Institute of ABC university at Shanghai, the first International Conference on High Speed Machining, will be open. Now, First of all, please allow me to give our hearty welcome to all of you present, and thank you, for your friendly coming. We feel so proud, and appreciated as well to be the host of the event.

It is a great honor for us to have all you here to attend this conference, of which the theme is the academic exchange about the advanced technologies on HSM. Here I'd be delighted to introduce our conventioneers in brief. Apart from our faculty and students, Most of the delegates and guests are prestigious experts and scientists, who are related in these fields from all over the world. With many significant achievements, they are the most dynamic leaders in the movements of the science and technology.

As the host, I would like to take this opportunity to give you a general introduction about our school. ABC university was founded in 1960 and was designated in 1978 as one of the key institutions of higher learning in China. The university consists of 24 departments or colleges, 12 scientific research institutions and one international training center. The university, covering an area of 140 hectares with a floor space of 420000 square meters, boasts 42 basic and special laboratories such as Key Laboratory of Material Processing. With a total collection of over 1170000 books, the library was listed as one of the most completed literature libraries in China in terms of mechanical manufacturing.

For this conference, we are following the agenda here. The meeting is supposed to last for three days, and to be separated into two parts. To begin with, we'll invite some representatives from our guests to give lectures about their latest researches and reports on the issue, and then we will have some symposiums. During the conference we are pleased to be your guide to this city. If anything needed, don't hesitate to contact us. We believe by our collaboration we are sure to make this gathering a consummation. And finally I wish you an unforgettable and prefect experience here.

Thanks!

10.2.3 TIPS for Academic Speech

1. No, nos in public speaking 演讲切忌

Talking too rapidly 语速太快
Speaking in a monotone 声音单调
Using too high a vocal pitch 声音尖细
Talking and not saying much "谈"得太多,说得太少
Presenting without enough emotion or passion 感情不充分
Talking down to the audience 对观众采取一种居高临下的姿态
Using too many "big" words 夸张的词语使用得太多

Chapter 10 Attending Professional Exhibition and Conference

Using abstractions without giving concrete examples 使用抽象概念而不给出事例加以说明

Using unfamiliar technical jargon 使用别人不熟悉的技术术语

Using slang or profanity 使用俚语或粗俗语

Disorganized and rambling performance 演讲无组织,散乱无序

Indirect communication i. e. beating around the bush 说话绕弯子,不切中主题

2. How to communicate with the audience 怎样与听众交流

A message worth communicating 要有值得交流的观点

Gain the listeners' attention: capture their interest and build their trust 引起听众的注意:抓住他们的兴趣并赢得信任

Emphasize understanding 重视理解

Obtain their feedback 获得反馈

Watch your emotional tone 注意声调要有感情

Persuade the audience 说服听众

3. How to gain confidence 怎样变得自信

Smile and glance at the audience 微笑并看着观众

Start very slowly, with your shoulders back and your chin up 开始发言时要慢一点,身体保持昂首挺胸的姿态

Open your speech by saying something very frankly 开场白说一些真诚话

Wear your very best clothes 穿上自己最好的衣服

Say something positive to yourself 对自己说一些积极的话

4. Four objectives of the speech 演讲的四个目标

To offer information 提供信息

To entertain the audience 使听众感到乐趣

To touch emotions 动之以情

To move to action 使听众行动起来

5. How to organize the speech 怎样组织演讲

To have a structure: such as first, second, third; geographically, north, south, east, west; compare and contrasts; our side versus their side; negative and positive

要有一个结构:可以分一二三点;可以从地理上分东南西北;比较与对比;我方与他方;正面与反面

To label the materials such as jokes, funny anecdotes, favorite sayings, interesting statistics

将材料归类整理,如笑话、趣事、名人名言、有趣的数据

To use notecards 使用卡片

6. How to use cards 怎样使用卡片

Number your cards on the top right 在卡片的右上角标上数字

Write a complete sentence on both your first and last card 在第一张和最后一张上写上完整的句子

Write up to five key words on other cards 其他卡片上最多只能写五个关键词

Use color to mark the words you want to emphasize 用颜色来标记你想强调的词

Remind yourself at a particular sport to check the time 在某一处提醒自己查看时间

7. How to cope with brownout 如何对付忘词

Just smile and go to the next card. Not the one in front of you, but to the next following. Look at the first word on it. This will be the point from which you will now continue. Of course you missed part of your speech. But nobody will notice it. They will blame themselves for not following your thoughts.

只需要微微一笑,继续下一张卡片上的内容,不是摆在你目前的那张卡片,而是下一张。看一下卡片上的第一个单词,这就是你要继续的要点。当然你会遗漏一部分内容,但是没有人会注意到这一点。听众只会责怪自己没有跟上你的思路

8. How to begin 如何开头

To tell a story(about yourself) 讲个(自己的)故事

To acknowledge the occasion of the gathering 对大家能够聚在一起表示感谢

To pay the listeners a compliment 称赞一下听众

To quote 引用名人名言

To use unusual statistics 使用一些不平常的数据

To ask the audience a challenging question 问观众一个挑战性的问题

To show a video or a slide 播放录像带或看幻灯片

9. How to close 如何结尾

To repeat your opening 重复你的开头

To summarize your presentation 概括你的演讲

To close with an anecdote 以趣事结尾

To end with a call to action 以号召行动结尾

To ask a rhetorical question 以反问结尾

To make a statement 以一个陈述句结尾

To show an outline of your presentation 展示演讲大纲

10.3 Useful Sentences for Professional Speech

1. Opening

- I'm here today to…
- My purpose today is to…
- My goal for this presentation is to…

Chapter 10　Attending Professional Exhibition and Conference

- The aim of this presentation is to…
- The reason why I'm here today is to…

2. Show the core content

- Today/this morning/this afternoon I would like to talk to you some of our work in the field of ABC.
- Today I will be speaking mostly about ABC, but I will also cover DEF later on.
- My topic today is about ABC.
- My topic today will deal with one of the most serious problems we are facing today.
- What I would like to do today is to review the present situation of ABC to point out what I think are the areas of difficulty and to indicate where ABC studies will be going in the next few years.

3. Statement order

- I will first discuss ABC, and then touch on DEF, and finally describe GHI.
- I would like to divide my talk this afternoon into three parts. 1)…, 2)…and 3)…
- I would like to give this talk in three parts. The first part deals with ABC. The second part concerns DEF, and the last part related to GHI.

4. Comparison

- There are important differences between A and B
- There are great distinctions between A and B
- There are obvious contrasts between A and B
- We can see discrepancies between A and B
- We find great differences between A and B

5. Excuse for error

- I'm sorry for the delay; it will only take a moment to flip the slide
- I apologize for the technical difficulties
- Please pardon the error
- I'm sorry for the inconvenience
- I hope you will excuse the delay
- The first figure, excuse me, the first curve shows

6. Conclusions

- I appreciate the opportunity to speak to you. I invite you to ask some questions.
- Thank you for having me here today. I'm sure some of you have questions.
- It's been a pleasure speaking with you. At this time, I'd be happy to answer your questions.
- Thanks for being here today. Any questions?

Words

turnout n. 出席者,到场人数
slogan n. 标语口号
delegation n. 代表团,展团
exhibit n. 展品,展示会
register 注册,登记
spectacular 壮观的
negotiation 谈判
catalogue 产品样本,目录
order n. & v. 订货,订购
booth n. 展位,摊位
workshop(小的)研讨会

accommodate vt. 能容纳,使适应
promote vt. 推销,宣传
conventioneer 与会者,参会代表
field(研究)领域
designate vt. 指定,定名
hectares 公顷
agenda 议程
symposium(专题的)研讨会
conference(大型的)会议,研讨会
meeting(一般的)会议

Phrases

opening ceremony 开幕式
participate in 参加
flock to 涌向,成群地走向
exhibition hall 展馆,展厅
domestic machine tool 国产机床
prestigious experts 知名专家,资深专家
simultaneous five-axis CNC machine 五轴联动数控机床
dynamic leaders 有活力的领导者
gather a consummation 获得圆满成功

out of stock 脱销
sign the contract 签订合同
unit price 单价
boring-milling machine 镗铣床
delegates and guests 代表和嘉宾
high speed machining 高速加工
negotiation booth 谈判展位,写上展位
oral presentation 口头陈述,口头报告

Exercises

Task 1 Translate the following into English.

1. 龙门加工中心/五面加工中心/卧式加工中心。
2. 我想在报告的开头首先对组织者邀请我参加这次大会表示感谢。
3. 我很高兴今天有机会来这里参加中国机械工程学会2012年年会。
4. 我打算做的报告分三个部分:第一部分关于激光加工的现状,第二部分关于激光加工的关键技术,第三部分是本人的最新的研究结果。
5. 我想再用几页幻灯片详谈说明这一情况。

Task 2 Translate the following sentences into Chinese.

1. I'm afraid I won't have time to cover everything about green manufacturing.
2. I don't know the answer to this problem, but I do know the question is really important.

3. My talk this afternoon would not be complete without a brief mention of machine vision.

4. We cannot proceed any further without receiving your thoughts with respect to the manner of payment.

5. Today I would like to talk to you some of our work in the field of rapid prototyping.

A good beginning makes a good ending
——善始者善终

Appendix I
Reference Translation of Reading Materials

1.4.1 麻省理工学院机械工程系介绍

麻省理工学院(MIT)的机械工程系的历史和 MIT 的历史一样悠久，其对整个学校和社会的影响可以从该系的发展与世界上发生的大事和技术进步始终同步这一点充分体现出来。

机械工程系的诞生可以追溯到美国 1865 年的南北战争时期。该系最早的发展重点包括用于交通和固定用途的动力工程和蒸汽机方面的广泛的培养计划。到 19 世纪 70 年代中期，随着北美工业革命的发展，机械工程系已经声名鹊起。该系创新地运用了实验技术，给学生充分的机会，将亲手操作的实验方法应用到解决当时的工程实际问题中。

那时的学科专业充分反映了当时工业界的伟大成就，包括航海工程、机车、纺织和造船等。1893 年，由于其独立的课程体系，航海工程从机械工程分开并保持独立，直到 2005 年，作为海洋科学与工程专业重新合并到机械工程。从 20 世纪之交到第一次世界大战爆发，蒸汽轮机、发动机设计、制冷及航空工程等专业设置为美国后来的技术发展奠定了基础。

在两次世界大战之间的一段时间里，汽车工程是机械工程系最热门的专业。创办于 1929 年的斯隆汽车实验室后来成为世界一流的汽车研究中心。二战后，该系的研究重点开始从军事应用开始从军事应用（目前仍然是全系整体培养计划的重要构成部分）逐步转向提高"生活质量"方面的应用，如生物医学工程、能源和环境工程、公共事业等。

质量、运动、力、能量、设计、制造——这些构成了机械工程领域的要素。今天，机械工程系荟萃了各种各样的优秀人才，包括 400 名本科生、500 名研究生和 75 名教师，不少教师是国家级研究院所和著名专业协会的成员。

机械工程系每年的科研经费达 3500 万美元，其研究项目包括机械、产品设计、能源工程、纳米工程、海洋工程、控制技术、机器人和生物工程等多个领域，而且还可以和本系及 MIT 其他院校的很多有关工程和科学学科进行充分的合作与交流。

这种广泛的研究领域十分重视各种多学科创新项目的研究，包括用主动控制优化燃烧过程、外星探索用的迷你型机器人设计、无人水下交通工具的研制、质子交换薄膜燃料电池的抗老化技术、人类肝组织生理模型的建立，以及在两维基片上制造三维是纳米结构等。

1.4.2 吴贤铭研究中心的历史

1987 年，吴贤铭教授接受了来自 James Duderstadt 博士的邀请（后来的密歇根工程院院长），去重建其制造研究方案。虽然吴教授已经 63 岁了，他将此次邀请看做宝贵的机会，在美国的制造"心脏"去展示他的制造科学与工程方法带来的利益。

从 20 世纪 60 年代开始，吴贤铭教授努力地工作，以提升制造科学的水平。他是第一个将先进的统计技术和分析用到制造研究和实践的人。他是将计算机技术用于精密加工的先驱，采用的是误差补偿的方法而不是采用精密机械。另外，吴教授在行业中积极探索和强调行业关联性，而他团队的研究人员和学生在这方面所进行的研究在学术上都取得卓越成效。

由于吴贤铭教授的艰苦的工作和创新方法，到 1992 年 10 月他的突然逝世之前，该制造中心已经成为备受尊敬的制造工厂研究团队。他坚持用现实的假定来理解真实工业问题，并发展了通用的和工业相关理论方法，重建了密歇根大学与当地工业的信誉。他强调的学术卓越，通过向最佳学习，激励创新理念，以及设置高标准，使得这个团队以制造工程研究员教育的杰出中心，获得了卓越的信誉。为对他教授表达敬意，这个中心于 1992 年被命名为吴贤铭制造研究中心。

1.4.3 工程师的角色

机械工程师研究、发展、设计、制造和测试工具、发动机、机器，以及其他机械装置。他们从事于电力设备，例如发电机、内燃机、蒸汽和燃气轮机、飞机和火箭发动机等有关的工作。工程师也研究发用电机器，例如：冰箱、空调、制造机器人、机床、材料处理系统以及工业生产设备。机械工程师要和各种产品与机器打交道，涉及汽车、飞机和喷气式飞机的发动机、计算机硬盘、微机械电子加速度传感器（用于汽车气囊）、加热与通风系统、重型建筑设备、手机、人工髋关节植入体、机器人制造系统、人工替代心脏瓣膜、星球探测与通讯飞船、深海探测船以及爆炸物探测装置等。由于参与到从概念到最终生产的产品生命周期的几乎每一个阶段，工程师往往像设计师一样去指定组件、尺寸、材料和加工工艺。专攻制造的机械工程师关注的是日常的硬件的生产和保持持续的质量。在另一方面，研发工程师工作时间更长，负责展示新的产品和技术。工程管理者，例如，组织复杂的技术工艺和为公司识别新的客户、市场和产品。

机械工程是传统工程学科的第二大领域，也许是最通用的。1998 年，美国有将近 220000 人受雇于机械工程师职业，占所有工程师的 15%。这个学科非常接近于工业（126000）、航空（53000）、石油（12000）、核工程（12000）等技术领域，这些历史上都是作为机械工程的一个分支分离出去的。机械与航空工业的工程师占到工程师总数的 28%。机械工程中常常遇到的其他专业，包括汽车、设计和制造工程。机械工程常被视为传统工程学科中最广泛和最灵活的学科，但是，存在很多的机会使得机械工程专门化到一个特定的行业或技术。例如，在航空工业中，工程师会进一步关注某一核心技术，也许是喷气式发动机的推进与飞机控制。工程师的贡献最终要由他们所设计与制造的产品能否正常发挥其应有的功能来评价。

通过科技推进社会的愿望推动了机械工程的发展。为了确认机械工程的主要的成就，美国机械工程师协会（ASME）在千年之交对其会员进行了调研。这里总结的被誉为现代制造技术里程碑的机械工程"十大"成就包括：(1)汽车，(2)阿波罗计划，(3)发电，(4)农业机械化，(5)飞机，(6)大规模生产集成电路，(7)空调和制冷，(8)计算机辅助工程技术，(9)生物工程，(10)规范和标准。

2.5.1 嵌入式热管冷却的干切削的有限元分析和实验研究

1. 引言

机械加工是工业中的一种重要的制造工艺。机械加工的目的就是为了产生一个具有特定形状和合格表面光洁度的表面，并且阻止刀具的磨损和已加工部分的热变形。切削刃处的热动力学行为消耗了加工的主要能量。研究表明，至少99%的能量输入会通过切屑变形和切屑与工件之间的摩擦转变为热。切削时，切屑所滑过刀具的界面通常是最热的区域。实际温度受到工件材料、切削速度、进给量、切削深度、刀具形状、切削液和其他因素的强烈影响。在高压和高温的状态下，由于切屑和刀具相互作用，刀具将产生磨损。因此，通常会使用切削液。在切削液的作用中，最重要的是冷却和润滑作用，因为这两种作用直接与热量产生和刀具磨损有关。但是，使用切削液也会带来对环境、健康和安全等的不良后果。

在切削过程中，已经有多种方法被用来预测切削温度。Tay 和 Usui 分别用有限元和有限差分的方法来确定分布在刀具、切削和工件中的切削能量的比例。Radulescu 和 Kapoor 提出了一种分析模型，用来预测连续和断续三维切削过程的温度场。该分析预测了刀具中的仅以切削力为输入的依赖时间的热通量。Stephenson 等人在 Radulescu 和 Kapoor 的断续切削温度模型的基础上，提出了一种计算轮廓车削中的刀具温度的方法。另外，该模型采用了环境绝热的条件，以简化输入要求和减少计算时间。

热管是一种被动的传热装置，它有很高的热传导率。通过对合适的液体的先蒸发后冷凝作用，热管可以将热量从一端输送到另一端。在热管中，流体的循环是靠毛细力维持的。热管在很多场合被用于冷却，包括：电子、压铸成型、注塑成型、热量回收、飞机除冰、电池冷却，以及加工温度的控制。本文的研究旨在帮助从根本上理解新的嵌入式热管新技术在金属切削过程中的散热作用，即如何能够有效地带走刀具和切屑表面的热量从而减少刀具磨损和延长刀具寿命。本文提出了一个不同于前人的干切削的有限元模型，因为采用了更加实际的带有嵌入式热管的用于切削过程的刀具设计。由于热管冷却系统的使用可以减少或消除切削液的使用，因此由切削液引起的环境污染问题和皮肤接触和微粒吸入等人体健康问题也能够有效减少。

2. 切削过程中热的产生

在加工过程中，机械能通过切屑的塑性变形和刀具-工件之间的摩擦而转化为热。图1显示了热量在刀具、切屑和工件中的耗散。绝大部分有关加工过程中稳态温度预测分析方法都是建立在适用于于正交切削的 Merchant 的模型基础上的，该模型给出了根据测量的切削力、刀-屑接触长度、切屑厚度比。从 Radulescu 和 Kapoor 的模型，以及 Stephenson 和 Ali 的方法可以看出，受力依赖于切削参数和工件形状。该模型能够预测受力的实际大小或它们所依赖的材料类型和切削条件。

2.5.2 自回转刀具在硬车削条件下的刀具磨损及切屑形成

1. 引言

以车代磨加工淬硬钢是一种经济的生产高质量的加工表面的方法。在过去的几年里，采用干切削代替磨削淬硬钢和其他难加工材料，已经产生了显著的工业效益。例如，汽车差速器侧齿轮的干式硬车削是这项技术在工业上的一个成功的应用。这种技术减少了加工时间和特定的切削能量，并消除了在传统加工操作中对切削液的使用所造成的对健康和环境产生的危害。虽然关于硬车削有大量的文献，对刀具磨损及其对加工表面的物理性质的影响的控制是一项主要的技术挑战。理解切屑形成机理对于深入了解加工过程的基本原理是必不可少的。在硬车削中观察到锯齿切屑形成过程，是一些研究人员感兴趣的主题。

研究者们提出了几种排屑机理模型。一些研究者采用绝热剪切理论解释了锯齿型切屑的形成机理。然而，其他一些研究者把切屑形态性质归因于其裂纹扩展。最近使用急停机制的研究证实，锯齿形切屑是由循环裂纹扩展引起的。

采用硬车削产生表面完整性是另一个重要研究课题。控制加工引起的残余应力是这种技术广泛应用于工业的一个重要方面。硬车削的刀具材料要求具有较高的耐磨性和能够承受特殊的切削力和加工过程产生的较高温度。此外，至少需要三倍于工件硬度的压痕硬度。因为刀具磨损和切削刃的塑性变形会影响已加工表面的质量和完整性，常采用陶瓷刀具和 PCBN 刀具来进行硬切削。

虽然在早期的研究中，不同材料制成的回转刀具已经显示出了优越的耐磨性，能够延长刀具寿命，其在硬切削中的性能仅仅使用倾斜旋转立方氮化硼刀具研究过。另外，在公开的文献中并没有建立回转刀具在切削过程的温度特征模型的尝试。

本文试图评估由不同材料制成的回转刀具在硬切削条件下的切削性能。另外，提出了一种温度模型来描述这种回转刀具的传热特性和自冷却特性。

2. 实验过程

我们开展了一个综合测试过程，来评估在硬切削条件下回转刀具的切削性能。干硬车削试验在 10 马力的数控车床上进行。采用的材料是经过热处理 AISI 4340 钢棒料（54-56HRC），直径为 75mm 或 100mm，长度为 200mm。该试验采用硬质合金和 TiN 涂层硬质合金刀片。采用的切削速度为 100mm，130 和 270m/min，进给量为 0.2mm/转，切削深度为 0.1mm 和 0.2mm，圆形刀片的直径为 25.4mm。刀具磨损的测量将在 4 个不同地点大约等距的位置进行，沿着刀片的周长，采用刀具制造商的显微镜。取这些测量值的平均值来获得刀具磨损值。收集了不同的切削条件下的切屑，然后这些切屑安装在环氧树脂中，经研磨、抛光和采用 1.5%硝酸浸蚀液进行刻蚀。通过光学显微镜被检查和拍摄这些切屑的横截面。利用光学和电子扫描电子显微镜(SEM)来分析所收集的切屑，并分析刀具失效模式。利用光学转速表测量了刀具的转速。

3. 回转刀具的基本特性

在一个开拓性工作中，Shaw 等提出了一种以圆盘形的车刀围绕其中心旋转的研究。

刀具围绕其中心连续转动，考虑到了刀片整个圆周的使用。由于刀具的转动，使得切削刃的新部分处于切削状态，因此，后刀面磨损将更好的地分布在整个切削刃。在滑动轴承情况下，刀具的回转运动以高切口速度为运载流体给工具点提供了一种方式。此外，这种回转刀具提供了一个自我冷却功能，通过这种功能其中的热量不断从切削区被带走。

回转刀具有两种形式：驱动式或自力推进式。驱动式刀具的回转运动是由一个独立的外部能量源驱动的。自力推进式刀具的回转运动是由刀具和切屑的相互作用产生的。驱动式刀具与切削速度可能是正交或斜交的，然而自回转式刀具要求切削刃与切削速度是斜交的。驱动刀具旋转速度与工艺参数是相互独立的。自回转刀具的旋转速度是切削速度、工件和旋转的切削刃速度矢量之间夹角的函数。一般来说，驱动旋转刀具提供更多的旋转速度控制。图1显示了一个典型的在旋转刀具使用时的机械加工工艺设置和在中旋转刀具的主要运动情况。

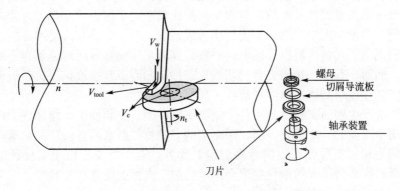

图1 在切削过程中的典型的回转刀具

在采用旋转刀具进行切削加工中，定义了三个主要运动，即工件的旋转速度(N_{WP})、刀具的旋转速度(N_{tool})和刀具切入工件的进给量(f)。由于刀具的旋转运动，产生的切屑将沿着刀具的前刀面被带出。因此，在正交切削加工情况下，切屑速度与切削刃的法向产生偏斜。

Venuvinod 和 Rubenstein 对采用用旋转刀具加工过程中的切屑形成进行了详细的运动学分析。Armarego 等也开展了基础实验和理论研究也有提出。其他研究者员研究了在用回转刀具加工时刀-屑界面处流体膜的形成，并已经得出使用旋转刀具是提供连续的刀-屑界面处流体膜的唯一方法的结论。的确，这为在第二变形区域形成接近零摩擦铺平了道路。最近，Kishawy 等在端铣加工中采用了自回转刀具。与其他传统工具进行了性能比较，自回转刀具显示出优越的性能并延长了刀具寿命。

2.5.3 中华人民共和国专利法实施细则

第十八条 发明或者实用新型专利申请的说明书应当写明发明或者实用新型的名称，该名称应当与请求书中的名称一致。说明书应当包括下列内容：

（一）技术领域：写明要求保护的技术方案所属的技术领域；

（二）背景技术：写明对发明或者实用新型的理解、检索、审查有用的背景技术；有可能的，并引证反映这些背景技术的文件；

（三）发明内容：写明发明或者实用新型所要解决的技术问题以及解决其技术问题采

用的技术方案,并对照现有技术写明发明或者实用新型的有益效果;

(四)附图说明:说明书有附图的,对各幅附图作简略说明;

(五)具体实施方式:详细写明申请人认为实现发明或者实用新型的优选方式;必要时,举例说明;有附图的,对照附图。

发明或者实用新型专利申请人应当按照前款规定的方式和顺序撰写说明书,并在说明书每一部分前面写明标题,除非其发明或者实用新型的性质用其他方式或者顺序撰写能节约说明书的篇幅并使他人能够准确理解其发明或者实用新型。

发明或者实用新型说明书应当用词规范、语句清楚,并不得使用"如权利要求……所述的……"一类的引用语,也不得使用商业性宣传用语。

发明专利申请包含一个或者多个核苷酸或者氨基酸序列的,说明书应当包括符合国务院专利行政部门规定的序列表。

申请人应当将该序列表作为说明书的一个单独部分提交,并按照国务院专利行政部门的规定提交该序列表的计算机可读形式的副本。

第十九条 发明或者实用新型的几幅附图可以绘在一张图纸上,并按照"图1,图2,……"顺序编号排列。

附图的大小及清晰度,应当保证在该图缩小到三分之二时仍能清晰地分辨出图中的各个细节。

发明或者实用新型说明书文字部分中未提及的附图标记不得在附图中出现,附图中未出现的附图标记不得在说明书文字部分中提及。

申请文件中表示同一组成部分的附图标记应当一致。

附图中除必需的词语外,不应当含有其他注释。

第二十条 权利要求书应当说明发明或者实用新型的技术特征,清楚、简要地表述请求保护的范围。

权利要求书有几项权利要求的,应当用阿拉伯数字顺序编号。

权利要求书中使用的科技术语应当与说明书中使用的科技术语一致,可以有化学式或者数学式,但是不得有插图。

除绝对必要的外,不得使用"如说明书……部分所述"或者"如图……所示"的用语。

权利要求中的技术特征可以引用说明书附图中相应的标记,该标记应当放在相应的技术特征后并置于括号内,便于理解权利要求。

附图标记不得解释为对权利要求的限制。

第二十一条 权利要求书应当有独立权利要求,也可以有从属权利要求。

独立权利要求应当从整体上反映发明或者实用新型的技术方案,记载解决技术问题的必要技术特征。

从属权利要求应当用附加的技术特征,对引用的权利要求作进一步限定。

第二十二条 发明或者实用新型的独立权利要求应当包括前序部分和特征部分,按照下列规定撰写:

(一)前序部分:写明要求保护的发明或者实用新型技术方案的主题名称和发明或者实用新型主题与最接近的现有技术共有的必要技术特征;

(二)特征部分:使用"其特征是……"或者类似的用语,写明发明或者实用新型区别于最接近的现有技术的技术特征。

这些特征和前序部分写明的特征合在一起，限定发明或者实用新型要求保护的范围。

发明或者实用新型的性质不适于用前款方式表达的，独立权利要求可以用其他方式撰写。

一项发明或者实用新型应当只有一个独立权利要求，并写在同一发明或者实用新型的从属权利要求之前。

3.6.1 切削加工性

一种材料的切削加工性通常从四个方面来定义：
（1）已切削部分的表面光洁度和表面完整性。
（2）刀具的寿命。
（3）切削力和切削的功率需求。
（4）切屑控制。

由上述可知，好的切削加工性指的是好的表面光洁度和完整性，长的刀具寿命，低切削力和功率需求。至于切屑控制，细长而卷曲的切屑，如果没有及时清理，就会在切削区缠绕，严重影响切削工序。

由于切削工序的复杂性，因此很难建立一个定量确定一种材料切削加工性的关系式。在制造厂里，刀具寿命和表面粗糙度通常被认为是切削加工性中最重要的影响因素。尽管切削性能指数使用的并不多，但基本的切削性能指数在下面的材料中仍然被使用。

1. 钢的切削加工性

因为钢是最重要的工程材料之一，所以它的切削加工性已经被广泛地研究过。通过加入铅和硫磺，可以使钢的切削加工性得到大幅度地提高。从而得到了所谓的高速切削钢。

1）二次硫化钢和二次磷化钢

硫在钢中形成硫化锰夹杂物（第二相粒子），这些夹杂物在第一剪切区形成应力集中元。其结果是使切屑容易断开而变小，从而改善了切削加工性。这些夹杂物的大小、形状、分布和集中程度显著的影响切削加工性。化学元素如碲和硒，其化学性质与硫类似，在二次硫化钢中起杂质改性作用。

钢中的磷有两个主要的作用。第一它加强铁素体，增加硬度。越硬的钢，就会对切屑的形成和表面光洁度越有利。需要注意的是软钢是很难加工的，因为软钢加工容易产生积屑瘤而且表面光洁度差。第二个作用是硬度增加会引起短切屑的形成而不是连续细长的切屑的形成，因此提高切削加工性。

2）铅钢

钢中高含量的铅在硫化锰杂质尖端析出。在非二次硫化钢中，铅呈细小而分散的颗粒。铅在铁、铜、铝和它们的合金中是不能溶解的。由于它的低抗剪强度，铅在切削时充当固体润滑剂，被涂在刀具和切屑的分界处。这一特性已经被证实——在切削加工铅钢时，在刀具横向表面的切屑上有高浓度的铅存在。

当温度足够高时——例如，在高的切削速度和进刀速度下——铅在刀具前直接熔化，并且充当液体润滑剂。除了这个作用外，铅还可以降低第一剪切区中的剪应力，减小切削

Appendix Ⅰ　Reference Translation of Reading Materials

力和降低功率消耗。铅能用于各种型号的钢,例如10XX,11XX,12XX,41XX等等。铅钢由型号中第二和第三数码中的字母L识别(例如,10L45)。(需要注意的是在不锈钢中,字母L指的是低碳,这是提高不锈钢耐腐蚀性的先决条件)。

然而,因为铅是众所周知的毒素和污染物,因此在钢的使用中存在着严重的环境隐患(在钢产品中每年大约有4500吨的铅消耗)。于是,消除铅在钢中使用是一个必然的趋势(无铅钢)。铋和锡现正作为最可能替代钢中铅的物质而被人们所研究。

3) 脱氧钙钢

一个重要的发展是脱氧钙钢,在脱氧钙钢中可以形成硅酸钙的氧化物片。这些片状物,可以减小第二剪切区中的应力,降低刀具和切屑分界处的摩擦和磨损。温度也相应地降低。于是,这种钢产生更小的月牙洼磨损,特别是在高速切削时更是如此。

4) 不锈钢

通常奥氏体钢很难进行切削加工。振动可能是一个问题,这必需要求机床有足够的刚度。然而,铁素体不锈钢有很好的切削加工性。马氏体钢易磨蚀,易于形成积屑瘤,并且要求刀具材料有高的热硬性和耐月牙洼磨损性。经沉淀硬化的不锈钢强度高、磨蚀性强,因此要求刀具材料硬度高而耐磨。

5) 钢中其他元素对切削加工性能的影响

钢中铝和硅元素的存在总是有害的,因为这些元素结合氧会生成氧化铝和硅酸盐,而氧化铝和硅酸盐硬度高且具有磨蚀性。这些化合物会加快刀具磨损,降低切削加工性。因此生产和使用净化钢是非常必要的。

根据它们的构成,碳和锰在钢的切削加工性方面有各种不同的影响。低碳钢(少于0.15%的碳)容易形成积屑瘤而使毛坯的表面光洁度很低。铸钢的切削加工性和锻钢的大致相同,但铸钢更容易磨蚀。工具钢和模具钢很难用于切削加工,通常是在切削加工之前进行退火处理。大多数钢的切削加工性在冷加工后都有所提高,冷加工能使材料变硬而减少积屑瘤的形成。

其他合金元素,例如镍、铬、钼和钒,能改善钢的特性,而通常会钢减小切削加工性。硼的影响可以忽视。气态元素比如氢和氮在钢的特性方面有特别有害的影响。氧已经被证明了在硫化锰夹杂物的纵横比方面有很强的影响。含氧量越高,纵横比越低且切削加工性越好。

在选择各种元素以改善切削加工性时,我们应该考虑这些元素对已加工零件在使用中的性能和强度的不利影响。例如,当温度升高时,铅会使钢变脆(液态金属的脆化,热缩性),尽管其在室温下对机械性能没有影响。

由于硫化铁的构成,硫元素能严重地降低钢的热加工性,除非有足够的锰元素来防止这种结构的形成。在室温下,二次硫化钢的机械性能取决于变形的硫化锰夹杂物的定位(各向异性)。二次磷化钢具有更小的延展性,被单独生成来提高切削加工性。

2. 其他不同金属的切削加工性

尽管越软的材料更易于生成积屑瘤而导致很差的表面光洁度,但铝通常很容易进行切削加工。这需要高的切削速度,高的前角和后角。铸铝合金和高含量硅的锻铝合金可能具有磨蚀性,它们要求刀具材料硬度更高。在加工铝材料的工件时尺寸公差控制可能会是一个难题,这是因为它具有高热膨胀系数和相对较低的弹性模数。

铍和铸铁相似。由于它更具磨蚀性和毒性，于是它需要在可控环境下进行加工。

灰铸铁通常是可进行切削加工的，但也有磨蚀性。铸件中的游离碳化物降低它们的切削加工性，容易导致刀具破裂或裂口，因此它需要具有强韧性的刀具。在刀具具有足够硬度的情况下球墨铸铁和可锻铸铁是可加工的。

钴基合金有磨蚀性和高度的加工硬化性。这要求刀具必须锋利而且具有耐蚀性，并且在加工时进给速度要低。

铸铜合金是很容易进行切削加工的，与此相反的是锻铜因为容易产生积屑瘤而很难进行切削加工。黄铜易进行切削加工，特别是在添加了一定量铅的情况下更容易。而青铜比黄铜更难进行切削加工。

镁是很容易加工的，加工后的镁件具有很好的表面光洁性而且使加工零件的刀具寿命更长。然而，因为镁极易氧化而燃烧（这种元素易燃），因此我们应该要特别小心地使用它。

钼有很好的延展性和加工硬化性，因此加工后它的表面光洁性很差。所以锋利的刀具是很很有必要的。

镍基合金具有加工硬化性和磨蚀性，且在高温下非常坚硬。它的切削加工性和不锈钢相似。

钽具有非常好的加工硬化性，延展性和柔性。加工后零件的表面光洁性很差且刀具磨损非常大。

钛和钛的合金导热系数很低（的确，是所有金属中最低的），因此在加工时会引起明显的温度升高和还会产生积屑瘤。它们是很难进行切削加工的。

钨易脆，坚硬，且具有磨蚀性，因此尽管它的性能在高温下能大幅提高，但它的切削加工性仍很低。

锆切削加工性很好。然而，因为有爆炸和起火的危险，锆在加工时要求切削液冷却性能非常好。

5.2.1　ABC 公司招聘广告

ABC 仪器设备英文说明书的文体特征及其翻译是世界数控机床制造商的领头羊，优质而富有创新的新产品和服务使本公司得以超常的成长。

公司目前在世界范围内拥有 2500 名具有高度敬业精神和知识渊博的员工。ABC 公司遍及各大洲，在 20 多个国家拥有分支机构。

自 1990 年以来，通过总部在上海的子公司和西安、广州的办事处，我们已成功地立足于中国市场。

为进一步拓展公司的战略市场，我们正在寻觅高素质的人士加盟，具体职位如下：

销售工程师

要求：

- 机电工程学士，数控专业优先
- 相关领域两至三年工作经验
- 良好的沟通技巧和人际关系
- 愿意经常出差和承受工作压力
- 良好的英语说写能力

- 熟悉 CAD，CAM
- 助理工程师
- 任务：
- CAD 产品设计和 CAM 产品加工
- 数控编程和调试
- 数控设备调整和维护
- 用户技术服务支持
- 要求：
- 机电工程本科或高职
- 两至三年的工作经验者优先
- 熟悉 CAD，CAM
- 良好的沟通技巧，英语口语流利
- 上进心、责任感和勤奋
- 35 岁以下

5.2.3 沈阳机床人力资源政策

薪酬制度

实习工资：985 院校本科生 3650 元/月（工资 2500 元＋购房补贴 1000 元＋饭补 150 元），985 院校硕士生 5550 元/月（工资 4000 元＋购房补贴 1400 元＋饭补 150 元），博士生 7450 元/月（工资 5500 元＋购房补贴 1800 元＋饭补 150 元）。

定岗工资：

基础薪酬（岗位级别工资、司龄工资）＋绩效薪酬（绩效工资、加班工资、项目奖、特殊奖罚）。

福利待遇

保险：公司为员工缴纳五险一金。

就餐：

公司每月为员工提供饭补 150 元，同时为员工提供了优美的就餐环境和丰富可口的早、中、晚餐。

住宿：单身员工可以免费入住沈阳机床大学生公寓。

交通：员工可以免费乘坐公司通勤车，通勤站点遍及沈阳市内。

其他：

员工生日餐及精美礼品，等等。

培训发展

培训：

我们拥有独立的培训机构。

企业注重为员工提供培训机会，每年公司投入培训经费两千余万元。

与吉林大学、大连理工大学合办工程硕士班，与东北大学合办 MBA 班等等。

多元化发展通道：

(1) 技术通道（技术人员）→高级技术专家

(2) 管理通道（基层管理）→决策管理

（3）营销通道（业务员）→资深销售经理

内部竞聘：公司内部岗位空缺时，所有员工都可以参与竞聘。

后备干部：表现优异的员工，通过考核后列为公司后备干部。

校园招聘

在这里，您将：
- 体验沈阳机床厚重的工业历史
- 接触中国唯一国家高档数控机床重点实验室
- 进入国际化的工作环境
- 有机会参加海外培训

更重要的是，您将成为沈阳机床的一员，共享沈阳机床登峰的不凡荣耀。

5.2.4　西门子公司针对有工作经验人士的招聘广告

有经验人士

你已有几年或多年的专业工作经验，但接受新的挑战仍是十分重要的。你希望尝试一些新的东西——新的挑战、更大的责任，或者在现有的职业发展道路再进一步。西门子能够提供众多机会，帮助你在本土或世界各地实现自己的事业目标。我们能够为积极进取、富有才华的员工提供岗位轮换和海外工作机会。

一家企业，多个行业

西门子是电工电子行业的全球巨头。我们的业务主要集中在工业、能源和医疗领域。公司拥有大约40.5万名员工，主要从事产品的开发及生产、复杂系统和项目的设计及安装，并为客户个性化的需求提供广泛的解决方案。西门子成立160多年来，以其卓越的技术成就、不懈的创新追求、出众的品质、令人信赖的可靠性和广泛的国际性在业界独树一帜。西门子公司也是世界上最大的环保技术供应商，提供众多绿色产品和解决方案。在这里，你一定能够找到你感兴趣的领域。

个人发展和职业发展的良机

一旦你进入西门子，就有许多机会等待着你。西门子设有专业的培训机构"西门子管理学院"，为员工提供持续培训的机会，帮助员工提高业务水平和自身能力。西门子通过每年的绩效考评流程（PMP），对每位员工的工作成绩进行测评，同时经理跟员工也会坐在一起沟通，根据员工的个人能力，发展愿望设定其下一步职业发展的目标，并确立具体的发展/培训计划和发展措施。

工作和生活的平衡

作为一家有吸引力的公司，西门子非常重视员工在工作的同时兼顾家庭生活。为此，我们将帮助你在工作和生活之间取得最佳平衡。我们为员工提供优良的工作环境和灵活工作安排，包括灵活的工作地点和工作时间。具体取决于当地情况和法律要求，其中包括弹性工时，远程办公和休年假等。另外，我们也为员工的健康、运动和休闲提供广泛的支持。

6.2　Moore Nanotech 350FG 超精密自由形面复合加工车床说明书

机床特性：
- 基于PC的数控加工运动控制器，Windows操作系统，编程分辨率为0.01nm；

- 热稳定线性标尺反馈系统，分辨率为 0.034nm；
- 飞刀车削或磨削加工自由形面、线性衍射表面和棱柱形光学器件；
- 偏摆加工直径为 500mm 的非对称复曲面光学器件；
- 箱式静压油支持导轨，行程为：Z 向 300mm，X 向 350mm，Y 向（垂直）向 150mm；Y 轴采用自适应空气轴承平衡装配，以保证优良的伺服控制性能；
- Y 轴配有双向直线电机；
- 转速为 10000 转/分的"重型"空气轴承支撑的液冷式工作主轴嵌入安装在 Y 轴的滑座内，以提高环路刚度，减小阿贝误差，维持结构对称性。
- 还有以下其他功能可任选：液压旋转 B 轴、工作主轴的 C 轴定位控制、快速刀具伺服控制系统、磨削和微铣削附件、光学对刀装置、喷雾冷却液、真空卡盘、刀架高度微调装置、非球面光学器件加工编程软件（APPS）、在线测量和工件误差补偿系统（WECS），以及空气簇射温度控制系统等。

Nanotech 350FG 机床规格

各系统概述	详细说明
系统配置	超精密多轴（3，4，5 轴）慢速伺服控制系统，同轴车削加工光学自由曲面（非球面或环形表面）
工件尺寸	工件尺寸 ϕ500mm×300mm 长
基础结构	基座为整体环氧树脂花岗岩浇注，集中式冷却液槽
隔振	三点优化定位结构的被动式控制隔振系统
控制系统	采用美国 Delta Tau 公司生产的基于 PC 的数控运动控制器，160MHz 数字信号处理器，Windows 操作系统，彩色平板触摸屏显示器，带调制解调器的 PC-Anywhere 远程诊断软件，256MB 内存。高级图形端口视频，可重写光盘 DVD 驱动和 80G 硬盘驱动。
编程分辨率	直线运动：1nm，旋转运动：0.0001°
加工性能	工件材料：高纯度铝合金 形状精度（峰谷值）$\leqslant$0.15μm/75mm（直径） 表面光洁度（Ra）$\leqslant$3.0μm

工件夹紧主轴	重型（标准）
轴承类型	充分约束沟槽补偿式空气轴承
液冷式（可选）	为保证其热稳定性，采用闭环冷却装置提供循环冷却水到主轴马达和空气轴承颈部的冷却流道。冷却装置采用 PID 控制器，可控制温度在±0.5F 左右。
安装方式	整体安装在 Y 轴滑座中，以提高结构环路刚度和减少发热。主轴滑座在不发热支座中，以进一步改善热稳定性
转速范围	50～10000rpm，双向
承载能力（径向）	主轴端部的承载能力为 36kg（80lbs.）

(续)

工件夹紧主轴	重型（标准）		
轴向刚度	140N/μm(800000lbs./in.)		
径向刚度（轴端位置）	87N/μm(500000lbs./in.)		
驱动系统	无框架无电刷直流电机		
运动精度	轴向≤25nm；径向≤25nm		

线性轴	X	Z	Y（垂直方向）
行程	350mm	300mm	150mm
驱动系统	无刷直流直线电机	无刷直流直线电机	双向无刷直流直线电机
反馈类型	激光全息线性（无热安装）	激光全息线性（无热安装）	激光全息线性（无热安装）
反馈分辨率	0.034nm	0.034nm	0.034nm
进给率（最大）	1500mm/min	1500mm/min	1500mm/min
敏感方向上的直线度	全行程 0.3μm	全行程 0.3μm	全行程 0.5μm，（中部）10mm 范围内 0.3μm
静压供油	结构紧凑，小流量，低压，闭环伺服控制，采用储压器减小		

可选旋转轴	B	C
类型	静压供油	沟槽补偿空气轴承（液冷）
旋转范围	360°（双向）	360°（双向）
驱动系统	无刷直流电机	无刷直流电机
轴向刚度	875N/μm(5000000lbs./in.)	140N/μm(800000lbs./in.)
径向刚度	260N/μm(1500000lbs./in.)	87N/μm(500000lbs./in.)
定位精度	（补偿后）≤2.0 弧秒	（补偿后）≤±2.0 弧秒
反馈分辨率	0.02 弧秒	0.07 弧秒
最大转速（定位模式）	50rpm	1500rpm
运动精度	轴向≤0.1μm；径向≤0.1μm	轴向≤0.025μm；径向≤0.025μm

设备安装要求条件	（压缩）空气参数	电气条件	场地要求
为了保证最佳切削效果，该设备的热稳定性应保持在±0.5℃(±0.1℉)	气压：7.5 to 9 bar(110-130psi)；流量：425liters/min；干燥到压力露点为10℃，过滤颗粒尺寸为10μm	11kVA 电压 220—480VAC；频率 50/60Hz；三相（若选用液压驱动磨削头，需用 26kVA 供电）	宽×深×高：1.93m×1.80m×2.06m 总重约3180kg（包括包装但不包括辅助设备和悬挂式控制操纵盒）

6.3 Airfel 散热器

请您在不打开包装前安装散热器。
1. 板式散热器利用符合 TS EN 442 标准的自动化技术生产制造。
2. 最大工作压强 8bar，最高工作温度为 120℃。
3. 产品是考虑到会有来自外界影响的情况下进行包装的。
4. 运输过程中请注意避免拖拉、碰撞。在拆包装过程中，请避免使用刀具接触散热器表面。
5. 安装附件都在包装内，请勿丢失。
6. 请由授权的专业管钳工作人员进行安装。请注意安装手册中的安装尺寸。
7. 中央供暖装置启动后再打开散热器阀。
8. 请您检查散热器是否加热。如果未加热，用放气阀扳手或者螺丝刀轻轻打开右侧或者左侧上部的放气阀，放气后再关上。如果没有其他问题，请等待加热。
9. 为了避免生锈，请不要将散热器内的水放出。不使用时请将出入阀扳到关闭位置。
10. 散热器上面不要放置任何物体。请勿重压。
11. 不要使用地下热水，加了酸或者化学剂的水。不要把散热器弄湿。切勿使用的清洁剂和化学品擦拭。
12. 将板式散热器与燃气采暖热水炉和中央加热锅炉连接前，请使用压力控制阀直接用自来水调试。

6.5 HCX320A 低速数控线切割机床

● 采用 Windows 操作系统，人机操作方便可靠。
● 工业控制计算机，大容量存储器，彩色 15″显示器。
● 可以实现磁盘、键盘接口，串行接口与外界的数据传输。
● 丰富的加工工艺参数库给操作加工带来更多的方便。
● 可控制走丝张力、速度，检测水质状态
● 四轴控制四轴联动，可实现多次切割、异形切割及螺距补偿。
● 加工状态实时显示，加工图形实时跟踪。

主要参数：
工作台面尺寸
加工工件最大尺寸
加工工件最大重量
X，Y 坐标行程
Z 向移动行程
U，V 轴移动行程
最大切割锥度
电极丝直径范围
电极丝最大进给速度
电极丝最大张紧力

主机外形尺寸
主机重量
配用电源柜
主要性能指标：
加工精度 mm
最佳表面粗糙度
最大加工效率
最大加工电流

6.6 某数控机床的维护

以下是某数控机床的常规维护事项，为了使机床工作正常，保护维修权利，用户必须遵守这些必要的规范。

每日保养
- 每 8 小时倒班应加满冷却液（尤其在大量使用主轴中心孔冷却液时）
- 检查导轨润滑油箱液位。
- 清理导轨防护罩和底板上的铁屑。
- 清理换刀装置上的铁屑。
- 用干净的布毯清洁主轴锥孔，并涂上轻油。

每周保养
- 检查过滤调节器自动排出口是否正常工作。
- 对于带主轴中心孔冷却的机床，清理冷却箱上的铁屑收集盘。
- 卸下冷却箱盖子，清除其中的沉淀物。注意要关闭冷却液泵，处理冷却箱前要切断数控系统电源。
- 检查气压表/调节器为 85 磅/平方英寸。
- 根据机床规格检查液压平衡压力。
- 涂少量油脂于换刀装置机械手的外边沿，并对全部刀具都用机械手换一遍。

每月保养
- 检查齿轮箱中的油位。将油加到油开始从废油罐底部的溢流管滴出为止。
- 清理托盘底部的衬垫。
- 清理 A 轴和上料工位上的定位垫。此项操作需卸下托盘。
- 检查导轨防护罩是否正常运行，必要时用轻油润滑。

每半年保养
- 更换冷却液，彻底清洗冷却箱。
- 检查所有软管和润滑管路是否破裂。

每一年保养
- 更换齿轮箱润滑油。从齿轮箱中将油排尽，慢慢注入 2 夸脱（1.9L）的美孚 DTE25 润滑油。
- 检查润滑油过滤器，清除过滤器底部的残余物。

每两年保养
- 更换控制箱上的空气过滤器。

Appendix II
Terms of College Campus

综合性大学　comprehensive university
理工科大学　university of science & engineering
本科院校　undergraduate college
教育部直属高校　colleges and universities directly under the Ministry of Education
全国重点大学　national key university
地方高校　Local university
中专　secondary specialized school
技校　technical school
博士生　Ph. D candidate/Ph. D student
硕士生　master student
在职研究生　on-the-job postgraduate
应届毕业生　this year's graduates
本科生　undergraduate
高职生　students from higher vocational schools
中专生　secondary specialized school student
技校生　technical school student
毕业证　diploma/graduation certificate
学位证　Degree Certificate
复合型人才　compound talents
应用型人才　applicative talents
技能型人才　Skilled Talents
素质教育　quality education
教学质量　teaching quality
办学特色　Characteristics of schooling
产学研合作　industry-university-research cooperation
协同创新　collaborative innovation；
学科交叉(跨学科)　interdisciplinary
人才培养模式　personnel training mode
培养目标　training target
培养方案　training program
课程体系　curriculum
学业评价　academic assessment
教学方法改革　teaching method reform
启发式教学　heuristic teaching　英音：［hjuə'rıstık］美音：［hju'rıstık］
参与式教学　participating teaching
研究性学习　investigative learning
探究性学习　inquiry Learning；
科研项目　Scientific Research Project
国家"863"高技术研究项目　"863"National High-tech Research and Development Program
国家"973"基础研究项目　"973"National Basic Research Program
国家杰出青年基金　National Science Fund for Distinguished Young Scholars
国家自然基金　NSFC; National Natural Science Foundation of China
湖北省自然基金　Hubei province natural fund
博士基金　Fund for doctoral dissertation

基础研究	basic research
应用基础研究	applied basic research
院士	academician
中国工程院院士	CAE(Chinese Academy of Engineering)academicians
中国科学院院士	CAS(Chinese Academy of Sciences)academicians
长江学者	Cheung Kong Scholar
长江特聘教授	Specially hired Cheung Kong Professor
长江讲座教授	Cheung Kong Chair Professor
学科带头人	Academic leader
博导	Doctoral advisor
硕导	postgraduate's tutors
教授	Professor
副教授	Vice Professor
讲师	Lecturer
助教	Teaching Assistant
留学生（海归）	Returned Overseas Chinese Student
本科/硕士毕业论文	Thesis
博士论文	Dissertation
开题报告	Opening report
毕业实习	Graduation field work
毕业答辩	Oral defense for one's thesis（dissertation）
毕业设计	graduation project
课程设计	curricular project
课程表	curriculum schedule
课程设置	curriculum provision
课件	courseware
必修课	required(compulsory)course
选修课	elective(optional)course
辅修课	minor course
基础课	basic course
专业课	specialized course
主修	major
辅修	minor
闭卷考试	close-book examination
开卷考试	open-book examination
成绩单	academic record
考试成绩	examination scores
排名次序	ranking position
三好学生	"three good" student
奖学金	scholarship
助学金	grant-in-aid
一等奖	first-grade award;fist prize
考研	take part in the entrance exams for graduate school
班主任	class advisor
班长	class monitor
学习委员	class committee member in charge of learning affairs
学生会学习部长	head of learning depart of Student Union
学生会主席	Chair of Student Union
机械创新大赛	Mechanical innovation contest
英语演讲竞赛	The English speech contest
数学建模竞赛	Mathematical Contest in Modeling
电子创新大赛	Electronic innovation contest
3D设计大赛	3D design competition
全国大学生挑战杯	The national college students' the challenge cup
智能车大赛	Intelligent car competition
工程训练大赛	Engineering training contest
主动的，活跃的	active
适应性强的	adaptable
有进取心的	aggressive
有雄心壮志的	ambitious
和蔼可亲的	amiable
友好的	amicable
有理解力的	apprehensive
有志气的	aspiring
能干的	capable
谨慎的	chary
办理仔细的	careful
正直的	candid
自信的	confident
能胜任的	competent

有合作精神的　cooperative
富创造力的　creative
有奉献精神的　dedicated
可靠的　dependable
老练的　diplomatic
守纪律的　disciplined
尽职的　dutiful
博学的　erudite
高效的　efficient
精力充沛的　energetic
善于表达　expressivity
守信的　faithful
直率的　frank
有幽默感的　humorous
公正的　impartial
有主见的　independent

勤奋的　industrious
有独创性的　ingenious
目的明确的　motivated
理解力强的　intelligent
条理分明的　logical
谦虚的　modest
一丝不苟的　precise
严守时刻的　punctual
负责的　responsible
意志坚强的　purposeful
踏实的　steady
明白事理的　sensible
性情温和的　sweet-tempered
稳健的　temperate
孜孜不倦的　tireless

Appendix III
Terms of Mechanical Engineering

III.1 Drawing

数学模型　mathematical model
画法几何　descriptive geometry
机械制图　Mechanical drawing
投影　projection
视图　view
剖视图　profile chart
点画线　chain dotted line
粗线　bold line
截面　section
标准件　standard component
零件图　part drawing
装配图　assembly drawing
尺寸标注　size marking
技术要求　technical requirements
比例尺　scale
表面粗糙度　surface roughness
参数化设计　parameterization design, PD
公差　tolerance
配合　fits
基本尺寸　basic size
偏差　deviation
上/下偏差　upper/lower deviation
配合/间隙配合/过盈配合/过渡配合　fit/clearance fit/interference fit/transition fits
单/双边公差　unilateral/bilateral tolerance
标准/精度公差　(standard/precision tolerance)
基准/特征/点/线/平面/轴线　(datum/feature/point/line/plane/axis)
最大/小材料状态　(M/LMC = maximum/least material condition)
理论尺寸　theoretical size
基本尺寸　basic dimension
基轴制/基孔制　basic shaft system/basic hole system
直径/半径　diameter/radius
直线度　straightness
平面度　flatness
圆度　circularity
圆柱度　cylindricity
线轮廓度　profile of a line
面轮廓度　profile of a surface

Appendix Ⅲ   Terms of Mechanical Engineering

定向公差   orientation tolerance
平行度   parallelism
垂直度   perpendicularity
倾斜度(角度)   angularity
位置度   position
对称度   symmetry
同轴度(同心度)   concentricity
圆跳动   circular runout
全跳动   total runout
坐标尺寸   coordinate dimensioning
几何尺寸   geometric dimensioning
拔模斜度   draft angle
分型线   parting line
外圆角/内圆角拔模斜度   rounds/fillets draft
肋材和尖角   rib and corner
顶/测/端视图   (top/side/end view)

Ⅲ.2   Mechanics

强度/屈服强度   strength, yielding strength
刚度   rigidity
内力   internal force
位移   displacement
截面/横截面   section/cross section
疲劳极限   fatigue limit
断裂   fracture
塑性变形/弹性变形   plastic distortion/elastic distortion
安全系数   safety factor; factor of safety
载荷/静载荷/动载荷   load/dead/live load
挠曲   flexure
弯曲力矩   bending moment
扭矩   torque/torsion moment
应力/拉应力/压应力/正应力/应力极限/屈服应力   Stress/tensile stress/compressive stress/normal stress/ultimate stress/yielding stress
应变/拉应变/压应变/正应变   Strain/tensile strain/compressive strain/normal strain
许用应力/载荷   allowable stress/load
安全因子   safety factor,
可靠性   reliability
残余应力   residual stress
塑性材料   Plastic/ductile material,
脆性材料   brittleness material
准则/强度准则/刚度准则   Criterion, strength criterion, rigidity criterion
载荷   load
载荷—变形曲线   load—deformation curve
载荷—变形图   load—deformation diagram
惯性力   inertia force
惯性力矩   moment of inertia, shaking moment
惯性力平衡   balance of shaking force
惯性力完全平衡   full balance of shaking force
惯性力部分平衡   partial balance of shaking force
摩擦角/力   friction angle/force
摩擦学设计   tribology design, TD
摩擦阻力   frictional resistance
摩擦力矩   friction moment
摩擦系数   coefficient of friction
应力幅   stress amplitude
应力集中   stress concentration
应力集中系数   factor of stress concentration
应力图   stress diagram
应力-应变图   stress-strain diagram
约束   constraint
约束条件   constraint condition
约束反力   constraining force
合成弯矩   resultant bending moment
合力   resultant force
合力矩   resultant moment of force
计算力矩   factored moment; calculation moment

计算弯矩　calculated bending moment
交变应力　repeated stress
交变载荷　repeated fluctuating load
力矩　moment
力平衡　equilibrium
力偶　couple
力偶矩　moment of couple
力　force
作用力　applied force
静力　static force
静平衡　static balance
静载荷　static load
动力学　dynamics
动密封　kinematical seal
动能　dynamic energy
动力粘度　dynamic viscosity
动力润滑　dynamic lubrication
动平衡　dynamic balance
动平衡机　dynamic balancing machine
动态特性　dynamic characteristics
动态分析设计　dynamic analysis design
动压力　dynamic reaction
动载荷　dynamic load
工作载荷　external loads
垂直载荷、法向载荷　normal load
速度　velocity
速度不均匀（波动）系数　coefficient of speed fluctuation
速度波动　speed fluctuation
速度曲线　velocity diagram
速度瞬心　instantaneous center of velocity
等效力　equivalent force
等效力矩　equivalent moment of force
等效量　equivalent
等效质量　equivalent mass
等效转动惯量　equivalent moment of inertia
等效动力学模型　dynamically equivalent model
角加速度　angular acceleration
角速度　angular velocity
角速比　angular velocity ratio

Ⅲ.3　Mechanism design

机械原理　theory of machines and mechanisms
方案设计、概念设计　concept design, CD
子机构　sub-mechanism
自锁　self-locking
自锁条件　condition of self-locking
自由度　degree of freedom, mobility
分度线　reference line; standard pitch line
分度圆　reference circle; standard(cutting) pitch circle
分度圆柱导程角　lead angle at reference cylinder
分度圆柱螺旋角　helix angle at reference cylinder
分度圆锥　reference cone; standard pitch cone
分析法　analytical method
封闭差动轮系　planetary differential
复合铰链　compound hinge
复合式组合　compound combining
复合轮系　compound(or combined) gear train
总效率　combined efficiency; overall efficiency
组合机构　combined mechanism
机械创新设计　mechanical creation design, MCD
机械系统设计　mechanical system design, MSD
机械动力分析　dynamic analysis of machinery
机械动力设计　dynamic design of machinery
机械动力学　dynamics of machinery
机械的现代设计　modern machine design

机构	mechanism
机构分析	analysis of mechanism
机构平衡	balance of mechanism
机构学	mechanism
机构运动设计	kinematic design of mechanism
机构运动简图	kinematic sketch of mechanism
机构综合	synthesis of mechanism
机构组成	constitution of mechanism
空间机构	spatial mechanism
空间连杆机构	spatial linkage
空间凸轮机构	spatial cam
基础机构	fundamental mechanism
渐开螺旋面	involute helicoid
渐开线	involute
渐开线齿廓	involute profile
渐开线齿轮	involute gear
渐开线发生线	generating line of involute
渐开线方程	involute equation
渐开线函数	involute function
渐开线蜗杆	involute worm
渐开线压力角	pressure angle of involute
简谐运动	simple harmonic motion
低副	lower pair
高副	higher pair
等加等减速运动规律	parabolic motion; constant acceleration and deceleration motion
等速运动规律	uniform motion; constant velocity motion
复式螺旋机构	Compound screw mechanism
复杂机构	complex mechanism
加速度	acceleration
加速度分析	acceleration analysis
加速度曲线	acceleration diagram
尖点	pointing; cusp
尖底从动件	knife-edge follower
间隙	backlash
间歇运动机构	intermittent motion mechanism
基圆	base circle
基圆半径	radius of base circle
基圆齿距	base pitch
基圆压力角	pressure angle of base circle
基圆柱	base cylinder
基圆锥	base cone
齿轮机构	gear
槽轮	Geneva wheel
槽轮机构	Geneva mechanism; Maltese cross
从动件	driven link, follower
从动件平底宽度	width of flat-face
从动件停歇	follower dwell
从动件运动规律	follower motion
节点	pitch point
节距	circular pitch; pitch of teeth
节线	pitch line
节圆	pitch circle
节圆齿厚	thickness on pitch circle
节圆直径	pitch diameter
节圆锥	pitch cone
节圆锥角	pitch cone angle
传动比	transmission ratio, speed ratio
传动装置	gearing; transmission gear
传动系统	driven system
传动角	transmission angle
四杆机构	four-bar linkage
双摇杆机构	double rocker mechanism
双转块机构	Oldham coupling
双滑块机构	double-slider mechanism, ellipsograph
双曲柄机构	double crank mechanism
曲柄导杆机构	crank shaper (guide-bar) mechanism
曲柄滑块机构	slider-crank (or crank-slider) mechanism
曲柄摇杆机构	crank-rocker mechanism
曲柄存在条件	Grashoff's law
曲柄	crank
原动件	driving link
运动倒置	kinematic inversion

运动方案设计	kinematic precept design
运动分析	kinematic analysis
运动副	kinematic pair
运动构件	moving link
运动简图	kinematic sketch
运动链	kinematic chain
气动机构	pneumatic mechanism
平面凸轮机构	planar cam mechanism
平面机构	planar mechanism
平面连杆机构	planar linkage
平面凸轮	planar cam
偏置曲柄滑块机构	offset slider-crank mechanism
闭链机构	closed chain mechanism
不完全齿轮机构	intermittent gearing
差动轮系	differential gear train
差动螺旋机构	differential screw mechanism
齿轮齿条机构	pinion and rack
齿式棘轮机构	tooth ratchet mechanism
串联式组合机构	series combined mechanism
对心滚子从动件	radial (or in-line) roller follower
对心直动从动件	radial (or in-line) translating follower
对心移动从动件	radial reciprocating follower
对心曲柄滑块机构	in-line slider-crank (or crank-slider) mechanism
六杆机构	six-bar linkage
力封闭型凸轮机构	force-drive (or force-closed) cam mechanism
连杆	connecting rod, coupler
连杆机构	linkage
连杆曲线	coupler-curve
连心线	line of centers
挠性机构	mechanism with flexible elements
其他常用机构	other mechanism in common use
阿基米德蜗杆	Archimedes worm
常用机构	conventional mechanism; mechanism in common use
并联式组合	combination in parallel
并联机构	parallel mechanism
并联组合机构	parallel combined mechanism
并行设计	concurred design, CD
图解法	graphical method
创新	innovation; creation
创新设计	creation design
急回机构	quick-return mechanism
急回特性	quick-return characteristics
急回系数	advance-to return-time ratio
急摆杆	oscillating bar
摆动从动件	oscillating follower
摆动从动件凸轮机构	cam with oscillating follower
摆动导杆机构	oscillating guide-bar mechanism
摆线齿轮	cycloidal gear
摆线齿形	cycloidal tooth profile
摆线运动规律	cycloidal motion
摆线针轮	cycloidal-pin wheel
回运动	quick-return motion
定轴轮系	ordinary gear train; gear train with fixed axes
机械平衡	balance of machinery
机械设计	machine design; mechanical design
机械特性	mechanical behavior
机械调速	mechanical speed governors
机械效率	mechanical efficiency
机械运转不均匀系数	coefficient of speed fluctuation
机械无级变速	mechanical stepless speed changes
转动导杆机构	whitworth mechanism
转动副	revolute (turning) pair
开链机构	open chain mechanism
形封闭凸轮机构	positive-drive (or form-closed) cam mechanism
工作机构	operation mechanism
棘轮机构	ratchet mechanism
棘爪	pawl

螺旋机构　screw mechanism
微动螺旋机构　differential screw mechanism
输出机构　output mechanism
替代机构　equivalent mechanism
凸轮倒置机构　inverse cam mechanism
凸轮机构　cam, cam mechanism
蜗杆传动机构　worm gearing
蜗杆蜗轮机构　worm and worm gear
蜗杆形凸轮步进机构　worm cam interval mechanism
原始机构　original mechanism
圆柱式凸轮步进运动机构　barrel(cylindric)cam
圆锥齿轮机构　bevel gears
正切机构　tangent mechanism
正弦机构　sine generator, scotch yoke
肘形机构　toggle mechanism
驱动器，执行机构　actuator

Ⅲ.4　Machine elements

键　key
键槽　keyway
齿轮　gear
惰轮　idle gear
标准齿轮　standard gear
变位齿轮　modified gear
标准直齿轮　standard spur gear
非标准齿轮　nonstandard gear
非圆齿轮　non-circular gear
齿槽　tooth space
齿槽宽　space width
齿侧间隙　backlash
齿顶高　addendum
齿顶圆　addendum circle
齿根高　dedendum
齿根圆　dedendum circle
齿厚　tooth thickness
齿距　circular pitch
齿宽　face width
齿廓　tooth profile
齿廓曲线　tooth curve
齿轮变速箱　speed-changing gear boxes
齿轮轮坯　gear blank
齿条　rack
齿条传动　rack gear
齿数　tooth number
齿数比　gear ratio
齿形链、无声链　silent chain
齿形系数　form factor
根切　undercutting
传动轴　transmission shaft
从动带轮　driven pulley
从动轮　driven gear
粗牙螺纹　coarse thread
大齿轮　gear wheel
带传动　belt driving
带轮　belt pulley
带式制动器　band brake
滚动轴承　rolling bearing
滚动轴承代号　rolling bearing identification code
滚针轴承　needle roller bearing
滚子轴承　roller bearing
单列轴承　single row bearing
单向推力轴承　single-direction thrust bearing
磁流体轴承　magnetic fluid bearing
多列轴承　multi-row bearing
单万向联轴节　single universal joint
当量齿轮　equivalent spur gear; virtual gear
等效构件　equivalent link
底座　chassis
渐开线花键　involute spline

（疲劳）点蚀	pitting
垫圈	gasket
垫片密封	gasket seal
碟形弹簧	belleville spring
端面参数	transverse parameters
端面压力角	transverse pressure angle
多楔带	poly V-belt
额定寿命	rating life
额定载荷	load rating
法面	normal plane
法面参数	normal parameters
法面齿距	normal circular pitch
法面模数	normal module
法面压力角	normal pressure angle
法向齿距	normal pitch
法向齿廓	normal tooth profile
法向直廓蜗杆	straight sided normal worm
刚性联轴器	rigid coupling
高速带	high speed belt
公称直径	nominal diameter
工况系数	application factor
工作循环图	working cycle diagram
工作空间	working space
公法线	common normal line
构件	link
固定构件	fixed link; frame
滚道	raceway
滚动体	rolling element
滚子链	roller chain
滚子链联轴器	double roller chain coupling
滚珠丝杆	ball screw
滚柱式单向超越离合器	roller clutch
含油轴承	oil bearing
互换性齿轮	interchangeable gears
花键	spline
滑键、导键	feather key
滑动轴承	sliding bearing
滑块	slider
环面蜗杆	toroid helicoids worm
环形弹簧	annular spring
缓冲装置	shocks; shock-absorber
机架	frame, fixed link
棘轮	ratchet
减速比	reduction ratio
减速齿轮、减速装置	reduction gear
减速器	speed reducer
减摩性	anti-friction quality
交叉带传动	cross-belt drive
交错轴斜齿轮	crossed helical gears
角接触球轴承	angular contact ball bearing
角接触推力轴承	angular contact thrust bearing
角接触向心轴承	angular contact radial bearing
角接触轴承	angular contact bearing
铰链、枢纽	hinge
阶梯轴	multi-diameter shaft
结构	structure
结构设计	structural design
解析设计	analytical design
紧固件	fastener
径节	diametral pitch
径向	radial direction
径向当量动载荷	dynamic equivalent radial load
径向当量静载荷	static equivalent radial load
径向基本额定动载荷	basic dynamic radial load rating
径向基本额定静载荷	basic static radial load rating
径向接触轴承	radial contact bearing
径向平面	radial plane
径向游隙	radial internal clearance
径向载荷	radial load
径向载荷系数	radial load factor
径向间隙	clearance
静密封	static seal
局部自由度	passive degree of freedom
矩形螺纹	square threaded form

Appendix Ⅲ   Terms of Mechanical Engineering

锯齿形螺纹   buttress thread form
矩形牙嵌式离合器   square-jaw positive-contact clutch
抗压强度   compression strength
开式链   open kinematic chain
可靠性   reliability
可靠性设计   reliability design, RD
空气弹簧   air spring
空间运动副   spatial kinematic pair
空间运动链   spatial kinematic chain
空转   idle
宽度系列   width series
框图   block diagram
离心力   centrifugal force
离心应力   centrifugal stress
离合器   clutch
离心密封   centrifugal seal
理论廓线   pitch curve
理论啮合线   theoretical line of action
隶属度   membership
链   chain
链传动装置   chain gearing
链轮   sprocket; sprocket-wheel; sprocket gear; chain wheel
联组V带   tight-up V belt
联轴器   coupling; shaft coupling
二维凸轮   two-dimensional cam
轮坯   blank
轮系   gear train
螺杆   screw
螺距   thread pitch
螺母   screw nut
螺旋锥齿轮   helical bevel gear
螺钉   screws
螺栓   bolts
螺纹导程   lead
螺纹效率   screw efficiency
螺旋传动   power screw
螺旋密封   spiral seal
螺纹   thread (of a screw)
螺旋副   helical pair
螺旋角   helix angle
螺旋线   helix, helical line
脉动无级变速   pulsating stepless speed changes
脉动循环应力   fluctuating circulating stress
脉动载荷   fluctuating load
铆钉   rivet
迷宫密封   labyrinth seal
密封   seal
密封带   seal belt
密封胶   seal gum
密封元件   potted component
密封装置   sealing arrangement
模数   module
磨损   abrasion; wear; scratching
末端执行器   end-effector
目标函数   objective function
耐腐蚀性   corrosion resistance
耐磨性   wear resistance
挠性转子   flexible rotor
内齿轮   internal gear
内齿圈   ring gear
内力   internal force
内圈   inner ring
啮出   engaging-out
啮合   engagement, mesh, gearing
啮合点   contact points
啮合角   working pressure angle
啮合线   line of action
啮合线长度   length of line of action
啮入   engaging-in
凝固点   freezing point; solidifying point
扭转应力   torsion stress
扭矩   moment of torque
扭簧   helical torsion spring
O形密封圈密封   O ring seal
盘形凸轮   disk cam
盘形转子   disk-like rotor
抛物线运动   parabolic motion
疲劳极限   fatigue limit

疲劳强度	fatigue strength	润滑装置	lubrication device
偏置式	offset	润滑	lubrication
偏(心)距	offset distance	三角形花键	serration spline
偏心率	eccentricity ratio	三角形螺纹	V thread screw
偏心质量	eccentric mass	三维凸轮	three-dimensional cam
偏距圆	offset circle	砂轮越程槽	grinding wheel groove
偏心盘	eccentric	少齿差行星传动	planetary drive with small teeth difference
偏置滚子从动件	offset roller follower	设计方法学	design methodology
偏置尖底从动件	offset knife-edge follower	设计变量	design variable
平带	flat belt	设计约束	design constraints
平带传动	flat belt driving	深沟球轴承	deep groove ball bearing
平底从动件	flat-face follower	升程	rise
平面副	planar pair, flat pair	升距	lift
平面运动副	planar kinematic pair	实际廓线	cam profile
平面轴斜齿轮	parallel helical gears	十字滑块联轴器	double slider coupling; Oldham's coupling
普通平键	parallel key	输出功	output work
启动力矩	starting torque	输出构件	output link
起始啮合点	initial contact, beginning of contact	输出力矩	output torque
气体轴承	gas bearing	输出轴	output shaft
千斤顶	jack	双头螺柱	studs
嵌入键	sunk key	双万向联轴节	constant-velocity(or double)universal joint
切齿深度	depth of cut	双列轴承	double row bearing
曲齿锥齿轮	spiral bevel gear	双向推力轴承	double-direction thrust bearing
曲面从动件	curved-shoe follower	松边	slack-side
曲轴	crank shaft	瞬心	instantaneous center
驱动力	driving force	死点	dead point
驱动力矩	driving moment(torque)	塔轮	step pulley
全齿高	whole depth	弹性滑动	elasticity sliding motion
权重集	weight sets	弹性联轴器	elastic coupling; flexible coupling
球面滚子	convex roller	弹性套柱销联轴器	rubber-cushioned sleeve bearing coupling
球轴承	ball bearing	套筒	sleeve
球面副	spheric pair	梯形螺纹	acme thread form
球面渐开线	spherical involute	特殊运动链	special kinematic chain
球面运动	spherical motion	特性	characteristics
球销副	sphere-pin pair		
热平衡	heat balance; thermal equilibrium		
人字齿轮	herringbone gear		
冗余自由度	redundant degree of freedom		
润滑油膜	lubricant film		

Appendix Ⅲ　Terms of Mechanical Engineering

调节　modulation, regulation
调心滚子轴承　self-aligning roller bearing
调心球轴承　self-aligning ball bearing
调心轴承　self-aligning bearing
调速　speed governing
调速电动机　adjustable speed motors
调速系统　speed control system
调压调速　variable voltage control
调速器　regulator, governor
铁磁流体密封　ferrofluid seal
同步带　synchronous belt
同步带传动　synchronous belt drive
凸的,凸面体　convex
凸轮　cam
凸轮廓线　cam profile
凸轮廓线绘制　layout of cam profile
凸轮理论廓线　pitch curve
凸缘联轴器　flange coupling
推程　rise
推力球轴承　thrust ball bearing
推力轴承　thrust bearing
退刀槽　tool withdrawal groove
退火　anneal
陀螺仪　gyroscope
V带　V belt
外圈　outer ring
外形尺寸　boundary dimension
万向联轴器　Hooks coupling; universal coupling
外齿轮　external gear
腕部　wrist
往复移动　reciprocating motion
往复式密封　reciprocating seal
位移　displacement
位移曲线　displacement diagram
位姿　pose, position and orientation
稳定运转阶段　steady motion period
稳健设计　robust design
蜗杆　worm
蜗杆头数　number of threads
蜗杆直径系数　diametral quotient

蜗杆旋向　hands of worm
蜗轮　worm gear
涡圈形盘簧　power spring
无级变速装置　stepless speed changes devices
系杆　crank arm, planet carrier
向心轴承　radial bearing
向心力　centrifugal force
相对速度　relative velocity
相对运动　relative motion
相对间隙　relative gap
细牙螺纹　fine threads
销　pin
小齿轮　pinion
小径　minor diameter
橡胶弹簧　balata spring
修正梯形加速度运动规律　modified trapezoidal acceleration motion
修正正弦加速度运动规律　modified sine acceleration motion
斜齿圆柱齿轮　helical gear
斜键、钩头楔键　taper key
泄漏　leakage
谐波齿轮　harmonic gear
谐波传动　harmonic driving
谐波发生器　harmonic generator
斜齿轮的当量直齿轮　equivalent spur gear of the helical gear
心轴　spindle
行程速度变化系数　coefficient of travel speed variation
行程速比系数　advance-to return-time ratio
行星齿轮装置　planetary transmission
行星轮　planet gear
行星轮变速装置　planetary speed changing devices
行星轮系　planetary gear train
虚约束　redundant (or passive) constraint
许用不平衡量　allowable amount of unbalance

许用压力角　allowable pressure angle
许用应力　allowable stress; permissible stress
悬臂结构　cantilever structure
悬臂梁　cantilever beam
循环功率流　circulating power load
旋转力矩　running torque
旋转式密封　rotating seal
旋转运动　rotary motion
选型　type selection
牙嵌式联轴器　jaw(teeth) positive-contact coupling
摇杆　rocker
一般化运动链　generalized kinematic chain
移动从动件　reciprocating follower
移动副　prismatic pair, sliding pair
移动关节　prismatic joint
移动凸轮　wedge cam
优化设计　optimal design
有害阻力　useless resistance
有益阻力　useful resistance
有效拉力　effective tension
有效圆周力　effective circle force
余弦加速度运动　cosine acceleration (or simple harmonic) motion
预紧力　preload
原动机　primer mover
圆带　round belt
圆带传动　round belt drive
圆弧齿厚　circular thickness
圆弧圆柱蜗杆　hollow flank worm
圆角半径　fillet radius
圆盘摩擦离合器　disc friction clutch
圆盘制动器　disc brake
原动机　prime mover
圆形齿轮　circular gear
圆柱滚子　cylindrical roller
圆柱滚子轴承　cylindrical roller bearing
圆柱副　cylindric pair
圆柱螺旋拉伸弹簧　cylindroid helical-coil extension spring
圆柱螺旋扭转弹簧　cylindroid helical-coil torsion spring
圆柱螺旋压缩弹簧　cylindroid helical-coil compression spring
圆柱凸轮　cylindrical cam
圆柱蜗杆　cylindrical worm
圆柱坐标操作器　cylindrical coordinate manipulator
圆锥螺旋扭转弹簧　conoid helical-coil compression spring
圆锥滚子　tapered roller
圆锥滚子轴承　tapered roller bearing
圆锥角　cone angle
运动失真　undercutting
运动设计　kinematic design
运动周期　cycle of motion
运动综合　kinematic synthesis
运转不均匀系数　coefficient of velocity fluctuation
运动粘度　kenematic viscosity
窄 V 带　narrow V belt
毡圈密封　felt ring seal
展成法　generating
张紧力　tension
张紧轮　tension pulley
振动力矩　shaking couple
振动频率　frequency of vibration
振幅　amplitude of vibration
正向运动学　direct(forward) kinematics
制动器　brake
直齿圆柱齿轮　spur gear
直齿锥齿轮　straight bevel gear
直径系数　diametral quotient
直径系列　diameter series
直廓环面蜗杆　hindley worm
直轴　straight shaft
执行构件　executive link; working link
质径积　mass-radius product
中间平面　mid-plane
中心距　center distance

中心距变动　center distance change
中心轮　central gear
中径　mean diameter
终止啮合点　final contact, end of contact
周节　pitch
周期性速度波动　periodic speed fluctuation
周转轮系　epicyclic gear train
轴承盖　bearing cup
轴承合金　bearing alloy
轴承座　bearing block
轴承高度/宽度/内径/外径　bearing height/width/bore diameter/outside diameter
轴承寿命　bearing life
轴承套圈　bearing ring
轴颈　journal
轴瓦、轴承衬　bearing bush
轴　shaft
轴端挡圈　shaft end ring
轴环/肩/角　shaft collar/shoulder/angle
轴向　axial direction
轴向齿廓　axial tooth profile
轴向当量动载荷　dynamic equivalent axial load
轴向当量静载荷　static equivalent axial load
轴向基本额定动载荷　basic dynamic axial load rating
轴向基本额定静载荷　basic static axial load rating
轴向接触轴承　axial contact bearing
轴向平面　axial plane
轴向游隙　axial internal clearance
轴向载荷　axial load
轴向载荷系数　axial load factor
轴向分力　axial thrust load
主动件　driving link
主动齿轮　driving gear
主动带轮　driving pulley
转速　swiveling speed; rotating speed
转动关节　revolute joint
转轴　revolving shaft
锥齿轮　bevel gear

Ⅲ.5　Metal Cutting

Cutting Tools

刀具　cutter; cutting tool
非标刀具　Special cutting tool; Special tool
标准刀具　Standard Tool
硬质合金钻头　Carbide Drills
硬质合金枪钻　Carbide Gun Drills
整体硬质合金锪钻　Solid Carbide Countersinks
整体硬质合金中心钻　Solid Carbide Center Drills
焊接式硬质合金扩孔钻　Carbide brazed core drills
整体硬质合金内冷麻花钻　Solid Carbide Drills with Internal coolant
整体硬质合金内冷麻花阶梯钻　Solid Carbide Step Drills with Internal coolant
硬质合金铣刀　Carbide Mills
滚刀　hob
硬质合金铰刀　Carbide Reamers
刀具修磨　Tool Regrinding
高速高钻头　HSS Drills
整体硬质合金铣刀　Solid Carbide End Mills
高速立铣刀　HSC End Mills
超硬材料刀具　Super Hard Tools
齿条插刀　rack cutter; rack-shaped shaper cutter
齿轮插刀　pinion cutter; pinion-shaped shaper cutter
齿轮滚刀　hob, hobbing cutter
铰刀　Reamer

机夹刀片　Cutting blade
前刀面　rake face
切削部分　cutting part
刀具角度　tool angle
退刀　tool backlash movement(tool retracting)
楔角　wedge angle
后角　clearance
切削平面　tool cutting edge plane
主偏角　tool cutting edge angle
几何前角　tool geometrical rake
法后角(法前角)　tool nomal clearance(rake)
刀尖　nose of tool
前角　rake angle
丝锥　Taps
刀夹系统/刀柄　Chucks
刀具平衡系统　Tool balancing systems
对刀仪　Tool Presetters
寻边器　Edge-Finders
刀柜　Tool Storages
刀架车　Tool Trollies
刀具使用寿命　tool life
刀库　tool magzine

Machine Tools
冲床　punch
车床　lathe
龙门刨床　double Haas planer
工具磨床　tool grinding machine
加工中心　machining center(MC)
镗床　boring machine
镗铣床　boring, drilling and milling machine
无心外圆磨床　centerless cylindrical grinder
齿轮加工机床,切齿机　gear cutting machine
磨床　grinding machine
滚齿机　hobbing machine
坐标镗床　jig boring machine
丝杠加工机床　laedscrew machine
铣床　milling machine
铣床主轴　milling spindle
数字控制　numerical control

数控车床　numerically controlled lathe
平面磨削　plain grinding
平面车床　plain turning
平面铣床　plane-mill
仿形铣削　profile mill
摇臂钻床　radial drilling machine
转塔式六角车床　turret lathe
万能车床　universal lathe
立式铣床　vertical-spindle milling machine
插齿机　gear shaper

Fixtures & Inspection tool
夹具　jig and fixture
镗孔夹具　boring fixture
定位　position;location
定位误差　position error
定位装置　locating device
定位元件　locating element
定位面　locating face
定位销　locating pin
定位板　locating plate
定位圈　locating ring
齿轮加工机床夹具　fixture of gear cutting machine
铣床夹具　fixture of milling machine
磨床夹具　fixture of grinding machine
刨床夹具　fixture of planing machine
插床夹具　fixture of slotting machine
真空夹具　vacuum fixture
通用夹具　universal fixture(jig)
固定夹具　stationary fixture
标准夹具　standard fixture(jig)
气动夹具　pneumatic fixture(jig)
卡盘　Chucks
夹紧系统　Clamping systems
气动夹紧　Pneumatic Clamping
液压夹紧　Hydraulic Clampin
检具　Inspection tool
百分表带表座　Dial Indicator with Mag. Base
游标卡尺　Vernier Calipers
千分尺　Micrometer

数字高度尺　Digital height gage
杠杆百分表　Lever type Dial indicator
丝规　Thread gage
塞规　Plug gage
深度尺　Depth gage
门线直径规　Diameter gage for valve line
球室角度量规　Angle gage for shpere sapce
坐标综合检具　Coordination comprehensive gage
合金标棒　Alloy master gage
三坐标测量机　Coordinate Measuring Machine, CMM

cutting process and control

切削加工　machining
切削深度　depth of cut
切削速度　cutting speed
退刀　return pass
进刀　pass
多次进刀　multiple passes
紧急停止　emergency stop
滚花　knurl
倒角　chamfer
车螺纹　threading
打中心孔　centering
车锥面　taper turning
车外圆　cylindrical turning
车端面　face turning
割槽　groove cutting
自动进给　automatic feed

待切削工件　work to be machined
机械加工余量　machining allowance
加工循环　machining cycle
连续切屑　continuous chip
卷状切屑　coil chip n
连续螺旋切屑　continuous spiral chip
切削力　cutting force
深孔钻削　deep-hole drilling
深孔铣削　deep-hole milling
间断切屑　discontinuous chip
进给力　feed force
进给运动　feed motion
精加工　finish
粗加工　roughing
机械加工余量　machining allowance
磨损　wear(out)
工件　workpiece
工件运动　workpiece motion
核准/审核/承办　approved by/checked by/prepared by
初审　checked by
核准　approved by
部门　department
生产确认　production control confirmation
原料　raw materials
物料　materials
成品　finished product
半成品　semi-finished product

Ⅲ.6　Metal material & heat treatment

合金工具钢　alloy tool steel
合金铸铁　alloyed cast iron
碳素钢　carbon steel
碳素工具钢　carbon tool steel
铸铁　cast iron
铸钢　cast steel
模具材料　die material

高合金钢　high alloy steel
高碳钢　high carbon steel
低合金钢　low alloy steel
低碳钢　low carbon steel
抗冲击工具钢　shock resistant tool steel
球墨铸铁　nodular graphite iron
可锻铸铁　malleable cast iron

麻口铸铁	mottled cast iron
淬透性曲线	hardenability curve
淬硬性(硬化能力)	hardening capacity
"U"形曲线	hardness penetration diagram
硬度分布(硬度梯度)	hardness profile
热处理规范	heat treatment procedure
热处理设备	heat treatment installation
热处理炉	heat treatment furnace
热处理工艺周期	heat treatment cycle
加热时间	heat time
加热系统	heat system
升温时间	heating up time
加热曲线	heating curve
高温渗碳	high temperature carburizing
高温回火	high temperature tempering
等温退火	isothermal annealing
分级时效处理	interrupted ageing treatment
局部热处理	local heat treatment
过热组织	overheated structure
固体渗碳	pack carburizing
氧氮碳共渗	Oxynitrocarburizing
不完全退火	partial annealing
再结晶温度	recrystallization temperature
热处理	heat treatment
退火	anneal
正火	normalizing
脱碳	decarburization
渗碳	carburization
淬火	quenching
硬化	hardening
热浴淬火	hot bath quenching
离子渗碳氮化	ion carbonitriding
离子渗碳处理	ion carburizing
离子电镀	ion plating
低温退火	low temperature annealing
回火	tempering
马氏体/硬化铁炭	martensite
真空涂膜	metallizing
软氮化	nitrocarburizing
喷砂处理	sand blast
时效处理	seasoning
喷丸处理	shot blast
调质处理	thermal refining

Ⅲ.7 Modern manufacturing

全面质量管理	Total Quality Management-TQM
柔性制造	Flexible Manufacturing
计算机集成制造	Computer Integrated Manufacturing(CIM)
敏捷制造	Agile Manufacturing
柔性制造系统	flexible manufacturing system;FMS
柔性自动化	flexible automation
产品数据管理	product data management (PDM)
并行工程	Concurrent Engineering(CE)
精益生产	Lean Production(LP)
敏捷制造	Agile Manufacturing(AM)
虚拟制造	Virtual Manufacturing,(VM)
网络制造	Networked Manufacturing(NM)
快速原型制造	Rapid Prototyping and Manufacturing
纳米技术	Nanotechnology and Micro-machine
高速加工	High speed machining
干切削加工	dry machining
准干式切削	(Near Dry Machining)
微量润滑系统	(Minimal Quantity of Lubrication)
产品数据交换	Standard for the Exchange of Product Model Data;STEP
计算机辅助设计	computer aided design,CAD
计算机辅助制造	computer aided manu-

facturing, CAM
计算机集成制造系统　computer integrated manufacturing system, CIMS
虚拟现实　virtual reality
虚拟现实技术　virtual reality technology, VRT
虚拟现实设计　virtual reality design, VRD
主生产计划　master production scheduling (MPS)
粗能力计划　Rough-cut capacity planning
物料需求计划　material requirement planning(MRP)
材料表　Bill of Materials(BOM)
产能需求计划　capacity requirement planning(CRP)
制造资源计划　Manufacturing Resource Planning(MRP Ⅱ)
企业资源计划　Enterprise Resource Planning（ERP）
制造执行系统　manufacturing execution system(MES)
供应链管理　Supply Chain Management (SCM)
物流　Physical Distribution; Logistics
物流系统　Logistics System
自动导引车　AGV-Automated guided vehicle
供应链管理　（Supply chain management, SCM）
自动立体仓库　Automatic Storage
自动托盘交换装置　Automatic Pallet Exchanger APC
自动换刀装置　Automatic Pallet changer APC
带式输送机　Belt Conveyor
桥式起重机　bridge crane
辊式输送机　roller Conveyor
叉车　forklift
牛鞭效应　Bullwhip Effect
客户关系管理　Customer Relationship Management(CRM)

Ⅲ.8　Non-traditional machining

激光束加工　Laser Beam Processing
电子束加工　Electron Beam Machining
电子束光刻系统　E-Beam Lithiograpgh
离子束加工　ion beam machining
电火花加工　Electrical Discharge Machining(EDM)
快走丝　Wire Cut Electrical Discharge Machining(WEDM-HS)
慢速走丝　Wire Cut Electrical Discharge Machining(WEDM-LS)
电化学加工　Electrochemical Machining, ECM
电解加工　Electrolytic Machining
电铸加工　Electrotyping
磨料流加工　abrasive flow machining

Appendix IV
Terms of Automatic Control

IV.1 Fundamental

变频器　frequency converters
变频调速　frequency control of motor speed
自动化　automation
交-直-交变频器　AC-DC-AC frequency converter
控制精度　control accuracy
控制柜　control cabinet
控制仪表　controlling instrument
控制屏，控制盘　control panel
差压液位计　differential pressure level meter
差压变送器　differential pressure transmitter
差动变压器式位移传感器　differential transformer displacement transducer
微分环节　differentiation element
数字滤波器　digital filer
数字信号处理　digital signal processing
数字化　digitization
数字化仪　digitizer
定值控制　fixed set point control
变频器　frequency converter
频域响应　frequency response

主成分分析法　PCA(principal component analysis)
脉冲调频控制系统　pulse frequency modulation control system
脉冲调宽控制系统　pulse width modulation control system
电容式位移传感器　capacitive displacement transducer
电-液转换器　electric hydraulic converter
电-气转换器　electric pneumatic converter
电液伺服阀　electrohydraulic servo vale
电磁流量传感器　electromagnetic flow transducer
反馈补偿　feedback compensation
前馈通路　feedforward path
现场总线　field bus
递阶规划　hierarchical planning
递阶控制　hierarchical control
人机协调　man-machine coordination
光电式转速传感器　photoelectric tachometric transducer

Appendix IV Terms of Automatic Control

压电式力传感器　piezoelectric force transducer
示教再现式机器人　playback robot
可编程序逻辑控制器　PLC(programmable logic controller)
整流器　rectifier
鲁棒控制　robust control
鲁棒性　robustness

步进控制　step-by-step control
阶跃函数　step function
零输入响应　zero-input response
零状态响应　zero-state response
z变换　z-transform
惠特克-香农采样定理　Whittaker-Shannon sampling theorem
维纳滤波　Wiener filtering

IV.2 Computer numerical control

计算机数值控制　Computerized Numerical Control, CNC
轴　Axis
五轴联动数控系统　five-axis simultaneously NC system
自动换刀装置　automatic tool changer (ATC)
数控车床　numerically controlled lathe
光栅尺　grating scale
机床坐标系　machine coordinate systerm
机床坐标原点　Machine Coordinate Origin
工件坐标系　Workpiece Coordinate System
工件坐标原点　Work piece Coordinate Origin
机床零点　machine zero
回零点　return zero
参考位置　Reference Position
绝对尺寸　Absolute Dimension
绝对坐标值　Absolute Coordinates
增量尺寸　Incremental Dimension
增量坐标值　Incremental Coordinates
最小输入增量　Least Input Increment
命令增量　Least command Increment
插补　Interpolation
直线插补　Line Interpolation
圆弧插补　Circula Interpolation
顺时针圆弧　Clockwise Arc
逆时针圆弧　Counterclockwise Arc
手工零件编程　Manual Part Programming

计算机零件编程　Computer Part programming
绝对编程　Absolute Programming
增量编程　Increment programming
字符　Character
控制字符　Control Character
地址　Address
程序段格式　Block Format
指令码　Instruction Code
程序号　Program Number
程序名　Program Name
指令方式　Command Mode
程序段　Block
零件程序　Part Program
加工程序　Machine Program
程序结束　End of Program
程序暂停　Program Stop
准备功能　Preparatory Function
辅助功能　MiscellaneouS Function
刀具功能　Tool Function
进给功能　Feed Function
主轴速度功能　Spindle Speed Function
进给保持　Feed Hold
刀具轨迹　Tool Path
零点偏置　Zero Offset
刀具偏置　Tool Offset
刀具长度偏置　Tool Length Offset
刀具半径偏置　Tool Radius Offset

刀具半径补偿　Cutter Compensation
刀具轨迹进给速度　Tool Path Feedrate
固定循环　Fixed Cycle,Canned Cycle
子程序　Subprogram
工序单　Planning sheet
执行程序　Executive Program
倍率　Override
分辨率　Resolution

Ⅳ.3 机 器 人

机器人　robot
机器人操作器　manipulator
机器人学　robotics
关节型机器人　jointed robot; articulated robot
机械手　manipulator
关节型操作器　jointed manipulator
位姿　position and orientation
变换矩阵　transformation matrix
移动机器人　mobile robot
运动规划　motion planning
运动学　kinematics
动力学　dynamics
多传感器融合　multi-sensor
视觉测量　visual measurement
双目视觉　stereo vision
定位　localization
导航　navigation
固定顺序机械手　fixed sequence manipulator
平面关节型机器人　SCARA (selective compliance assembly robot arm)
敏感元件　sensing element
伺服控制，随动控制　servo control
伺服马达　servomotor
定常系统，非时变系统　time-invariant system
时序控制器　time schedule controller
直角坐标型机器人　Cartesian robot
圆柱坐标型机器人　cylindrical robot
示教再现式机器人　playback robot
点位控制　point-to-point control
极坐标型机器人　polar robot
反向运动学　inverse (or backward) kinematics
直角坐标操作器　Cartesian coordinate manipulator

Appendix V
Hydraulic Transmission

流体传动	hydraulic power
液压技术	hydraulics
液力技术	hydrodynamics
气液技术	hydropneumatics
运行工况	operating conditions
额定工况	rated conditions
极限工况	limited conditions
瞬态工况	instantaneous conditions
稳态工况	steady-state conditions
许用工况	acceptable conditions
连续工况	continuous working conditions
实际工况	actual conditions
效率	efficiency
旋转方向	direction of rotation
公称压力	nominal pressure
工作压力	working pressure
进口压力	inlet pressure
出口压力	outlet pressure
压降	pressure drop; differential pressure
背压	back pressure
启动压力	breakout pressure
充油压力	charge pressure
开启压力	cracking pressure
峰值压力	peak pressure
运行压力	operating pressure
耐压试验压力	proof pressure
冲击压力	surge pressure
静压力	static pressure
系统压力	system pressure
控制压力	pilot pressure
充气压力	pre-charge pressure
吸入压力	suction pressure
调压偏差	override pressure
额定压力	rated pressure
耗气量	air consumption
泄漏	leakage
内泄漏	internal leakage
外泄漏	external leakage
层流	laminar flow
紊流	turbulent flow
气穴	cavitation
流量	flow rate
排量	displacement
额定流量	rated flow
供给流量	supply flow
流量系数	flower factor
滞环	hysteresis
图形符号	graphical symbol
液压气动元件图形符号	symbols for hydraulic and pneumatic components
流体逻辑元件图形符号	symbols for fluid logic devices
逻辑功能图形符号	symbols for logic functions

回路图	circuit diagram	工作行程	working stroke
压力—时间图	pressure time diagram	负载压力	induced pressure
功能图	function diagram	输出力	force
循环	circle	实际输出力	actual force
自动循环	automatic cycle	单作用缸	single-acting cylinder
工作循环	working cycle	双作用缸	double-acting cylinder
循环速度	cycling speed	差动缸	differential cylinder
工步	phase	伸缩缸	telescopic cylinder
停止工步	dwell phase	阀	valve
工作工步	working phase	底板	sub-plate
快进工步	rapid advance phase	油路块	manifold block
快退工步	rapid return phase	板式阀	sub-plate valve
频率响应	frequency response	叠加阀	sandwich valve
重复性	repeat ability	插装阀	cartridge valve
复现性	reproducibility	滑阀	slide valve
漂移	drift	锥阀	poppet valve
波动	ripple	阀芯	valve element
线性度	linearity	阀芯位置	valve element position
线性区	linear region	单向阀	check valve
液压锁紧	hydraulic lock	液控单向阀	pilot-controlled check valve
液压卡紧	sticking	梭阀	shuttle valve
变量泵	variable displacement pump	压力控制阀	pressure relief valve
泵的控制	control of pump	溢流阀	pressure relief valve
齿轮泵	gear pump	顺序阀	sequence valve
叶片泵	vane pump	减压阀	pressure reducing valve
柱塞泵	piston pump	平衡阀	counterbalance valve
轴向柱塞泵	axial piston pump	卸荷阀	unloading valve
法兰安装	flange mounting	直动式	directly operated type
底座安装	foot mounting	先导式	pilot-operated type
液压马达	hydraulic motor	机械控制式	mechanically controlled type
刚度	stiffness	手动式	manually operated type
中位	neutral position	液控式	hydraulic controlled type
零位	zero position	流量控制阀	flow control valve
自由位	free position	固定节流阀	fixed restrictive valve
缸	cylinder	可调节流阀	adjustable restrictive valve
有杆端	rod end	单向节流阀	one-way restrictive valve
无杆端	rear end	调速阀	speed regulator valve
外伸行程	extend stroke	分流阀	flow divider valve
内缩行程	retract stroke	集流阀	flow-combining valve
缓冲	cushioning	截止阀	shut-off valve

Appendix V Hydraulic Transmission

球阀	global(ball)valve	控制管路	pilot line
针阀	needle valve	泄油管路	drain line
闸阀	gate valve	放气管路	bleed line
膜片阀	diaphragm valve	接头	fitting; connection
蝶阀	butterfly valve	焊接式接头	welded fitting
噪声等级	noise level	扩口式接头	flared fitting
放大器	amplifier	快换接头	quick release coupling
模拟放大器	analogue amplifier	法兰接头	flange connection
数字放大器	digital amplifier	弯头	elbow
传感器	sensor	异径接头	reducer fitting
阈值	threshold	流道	flow pass
伺服阀	servo-valve	油口	port
四通阀	four-way valve	闭式油箱	sealed reservoir
喷嘴挡板	nozzle flapper	油箱容量	reservoir fluid capacity
液压放大器	hydraulic amplifier	气囊式蓄能器	bladder accumulator
颤振	dither	空气污染	air contamination
阀极性	valve polarity	固体颗粒污染	solid contamination
流量增益	flow gain	液体污染	liquid contamination
对称度	symmetry	空气过滤器	air filter
流量极限	flow limit	油雾气	lubricator
零位内泄漏	null(quiescent)leakage	热交换器	heat exchanger
遮盖	lap	冷却器	cooler
零遮盖	zero lap	加热器	heater
正遮盖	over lap	温度控制器	thermostat
负遮盖	under lap	消声器	silencer
开口	opening	双筒过滤器	duplex filter
零偏	null bias	过滤器压降	filter pressure drop
零漂	null drift	有效过滤面积	effective filtration area
阀压降	valve pressure drop	公称过滤精度	nominal filtration rating
分辨率	resolution	压溃压力	collapse pressure
频率响应	frequency response	填料密封	packing seal
幅值比	amplitude ratio	机械密封	mechanical seal
相位移	phase lag	径向密封	radial seal
传递函数	transfer function	旋转密封	rotary seal
管路	flow line	活塞密封	piston seal
硬管	rigid tube	活塞杆密封	rod seal
软管	flexible hose	防尘圈密封	wiper seal; scraper
工作管路	working line	组合垫圈	bonded washer
回油管路	return line	复合密封件	composite seal
补液管路	replenishing line	弹性密封件	elastomer seal

丁腈橡胶	nitrile butadiene rubber; NBR
聚四氟乙烯	polytetrafluoroethene; PTFE
优先控制	override control
压力表	pressure gauge
压力传感器	electrical pressure transducer
压差计	differential pressure instrument
液位计	liquid level measuring instrument
流量计	flow meter
压力开关	pressure switch
脉冲发生器	pulse generator
液压泵站	power station
空气处理单元	air conditioner unit
压力控制回路	pressure control circuit
安全回路	safety circuit
差动回路	differential circuit
调速回路	flow control circuit
进口节流回路	meter-in circuit
出口节流回路	meter-out circuit
同步回路	synchronizing circuit
开式回路	open circuit
闭式回路	closed circuit
管路布置	pipe-work
管卡	clamper
联轴器	drive shaft coupling
操作台	control console
控制屏	control panel
避震喉	compensator
粘度	viscosity
运动粘度	kinematic viscosity
密度	density
含水量	water content
闪点	flash point
防锈性	rust protection
抗腐蚀性	anti-corrosive quality
便携式颗粒检测仪	portable particle counter
电磁阀	Solenoid valve
单向阀	Check valve
插装阀	Cartridge valve
叠加阀	Sandwich plate valve
先导阀	Pilot valve
液控单向阀	Pilot operated check valve
板式安装	Sub-plate mount
集成块	Manifold block
压力溢流阀	Pressure relief valve
流量阀	Flow valve
节流阀	Throttle valve
双单向节流阀	Double throttle check valve
旋钮	Rotary knob
节流板	Rectifier plate
伺服阀	Servo valve
比例阀	Proportional valve
位置反馈	Position feedback
渐增流量	Progressive flow
电磁铁释放	De-energizing of solenoid
卡套式管接头	Bite type fittings
接管接头	Tube to tube fittings
直通接管接头	union
直角管接头	union elbow
三通管接头	union tee
四通管接头	union cross
端直通管接头	Mal stud fittings
长直通管接头	Bulkhead fittings
焊接式管接头	Weld fittings
接头螺母	Female connector fittings
变径管接头	Reducers extenders
铰接式管接头	Banjo fittings
旋转接头	Adjustable fittings/swivel nut
动态频响	Dynamic response
直动式伺服阀	DDV-direct drive valve
美国流体控制学会	NFPA-National Fluid Power Association
相位滞后	Phase lag
喷嘴挡板阀	Nozzle flapper valve
射流管阀	Servo-jet pilot valve
颤振电流	Dither
线圈阻抗	Coil impedance
流量饱和	Flow saturation
线形度	Linearity
对称性	Symmetry
滞环	Hysterics

Appendix Ⅴ Hydraulic Transmission

灵敏度　Threshold
滞后　Lap
压力增益　Pressure gain
零位　Null
零偏　Null bias
零飘　Null shift
频率响应　Frequency response
曲线斜坡　Slope
液压系统　hydraulic system
执行元件　actuator
液压缸　cylinder
液压马达　motor
液压回路　circuit
压力控制回路　pressure control
流量(速度)控制回路　speed control
方向控制回路　directional valve control
安全回路　security control
定位回路　position control
同步回路　synchronise circuit
顺序动作回路　sequent circuit
液压泵　pump
阀　valve
压力控制阀　pressure valve
流量控制阀　flow valve
方向控制阀　directional valve
液压辅件　accessory
普通阀　common valve
插装阀　cartridge valve
叠加阀　superimposed valve

Appendix VI
Enterprise Promotion

企业宣传　Corporation/Enterprise Promotion
有限公司　Co., Ltd
项目简介　project profile
工业园　Industry Park
致力于　main effort focus on
最先进的技术　State-of-the-Art Technology
最先进的设备　the most advanced machines
经过严格训练的高素质员工　the well trained workers
可以信赖的合作伙伴　trustable partner
德国技术　German Know How
专业制造　Professional Manufacturing
技术咨询　Technical consulting
提供优质服务　provide services of high quality
中国名牌　China Top Brand
最具有成长力的自主品牌　the most powerful self-growth brands
中国驰名商标　the well-known trademarks in China
福布斯"中国顶尖企业"　Forbes top Chinese enterprise
中国企业500强　the top 500 companies in China
企业文化　Corporate Culture
企业架构　Corporate Structure,
企业荣誉　Corporate Honour,
企业展望　Corporate Expectation
可持续发展　sustainable development
责任感　responsible
关爱环境　environmental care
前瞻　forward thinking
领导者/领头羊　leader/leading
创立于1984年　Founded in 1984
坚持创业和创新精神　be dedicated to innovation and creating
创世界名牌　create a world famous brand
营业额1500亿元　realize a turnover of 150 billion yuan
全球化集团公司　international group
第一品牌　the world's No. 1 brand
申报专利1000项　file for 1000 patent applications
发明专利　invention patent
标准化良好行为企业　an enterprise of good behavior in Standardization
博士后工作站　post-doctoral workstation
国家863计划　the National 863 Programs
国家科技进步奖　national science and technology progress award
国家科技支撑计划项目　project of the National Science and Technology Support Program
国家自然科学基金　the National Natural

Science Foundation
自主产权　self-proprietary, owned-proprietary
创新型企业　innovative enterprise
目标和使命　Goal and Mission
资源整合　resource integration
核心竞争力　core competences
为客户创造价值　create value for customers
节能降耗　saving energy and reducing cost
合作共赢　cooperation win-win
回馈社会　contributing to the society
前沿技术　Cutting-edge technology
拳头产品　key product; product champion
竞争优势　competitive advantage
产品设计与开发　Product design and development
市场拉动　market-pull
开发过程与组织　Development Processes and Organizations
产品规划　Product Planning
确认客户需求　Identifying Customer Needs
产品规格　Product Specifications
概念生成　Concept Generation
概念选择　Concept Selection
概念测试　Concept Testing
产品体系　Product Architecture
面向制造的设计　Design for Manufacturing
面向环境的设计　Design for Environment
原型制作　Prototyping
稳健设计　Robust Design
专利和知识产权　Patents and Intellectual Property
项目管理　Managing Projects
人因与人机工程学　Human Factors and Ergonomics
定制产品　customized product
技术推动型产品　technology-push product
平台型产品　platform product
工艺密集型产品　process-intensive product
高风险产品　high-risk product
速建产品　quick-bulit product
复杂系统　complex systems
项目组织　project organization
项目团队　project team
阶段门开发流程　stage-gate product development process
产品集成开发　integrated product development
TRIZ 意译为发明问题的解决理论　(Teorijz Rezhenija Izobretatel'Skitch Zadach)
产品及周期优化法　Product And Cycle-time Excellence—PACE
产品创新与设计方法　Product Innovation and Design Method-PIDM
任务书　mission statement
投放市场　launch
董事长　president
总经理　general manager
特助　special assistant manager
厂长　factory director
部长　department director
副理　deputy manager(vice manager)
作业员　operator
品管　QC(quality control)
课长　supervisor
制造工程师　ME(mechanical engineer)
制造技术员　MT(mechanical technician)
课长　section supervisor(department head)
注明：日韩的部门叫做课长，相当中国大陆的科长
副课长　deputy/vice section supervisor
组长　group leader/supervisor
线长　line supervisor
助理　assistant manager

Appendix VII
Mathematic Symbols and Expressions

$+$: plus(positive 正的)
$-$: minus(negative 负的)
$*$: multiplied by
$\div$: divided by
$=$: be equal to
$\approx$: be approximately equal to
( ) : round brackets(parenthess)
[ ] : square brackets
{ } : braces
$\because$: because
$\therefore$: therefore
$\leqslant$: less than or equal to
$\geqslant$: greater than or equal to
∞ : infinity
LOGnX : logx to the base n
x^n : the nth power of x
$f(x)$: the function of x
dx : differential of x
$x+y$: x plus y
$(a+b)$: bracket a plus b bracket closed
$a=b$: a equals b
$a \neq b$: a isn't equal to b

$a > b$: a is greater than b
$a \gg b$: a is much greater than b
$a \geqslant b$: a is greater than or equal to b
$x \to \infty$: x approaches infinity
x^2 : x square
x^3 : x cube
$\sqrt{x}$: the square root of x
$\sqrt[3]{x}$: the cube root of x
3‰ : three peimill
$\sum_{1}^{n} x_i$: the summation of x where i goes from 1 to n
$\prod_{1}^{n} x_i$: the product of x sub i where i goes from 1 to n
$\int_{a}^{b}$: integral betweens a and b

分母　denominator
分子　numerator
单位矢量　unit vector
导数　derivative
矩阵　matrix

Appendix VIII
Final Examination Sample

1. E-C Translation(30points)

(1) The objective of this study is to develop an automated flank wear measurement scheme using vision system for a microdrill. (10points)

(2) The ability of the heat pipe to affect the temperature of the carbide cutting insert and the elongation of the toolholder is inferred from the response of thermocouples and strain gauges mounted on the toolholder to the heat generated during various cutting conditions. (10points)

(3) We understand exactly the important role the cutting tools have to play at modern metal cutting. The most advanced machines, the well trained workers, the special

2. C-E Translation(50points)

(1) 未注明拔模斜度5°(3 points)

(2) 熟悉CAD产品设计和CAM产品加工(3 points)

(3) 车床是车间里最有用最通用的机床之一。(4 points)

(4) 轴可以有非圆形截面,而且不一定需要旋转。(5 points)

(5) 攻美国固定特种螺纹M1″,每英寸牙数14,精度等级为二级(5 points)

(6) X轴和Y轴均由交流伺服电机控制,可实现两轴联动控制;Z轴由步进电机控制,可实现开环控制。(10points)

(7) 该公司从事各类高品质精密金属切削刀具的制造和修磨服务。产品有硬质合金刀具和超硬刀具,如硬质合金钻头、铰刀、铣刀、刀片和PCD/CBN超硬刀具。(10points)

(8) 我打算做的报告分三个部分:第一部分关于激光加工的现状,第二部分关于激光加工的关键技术,第三部分是本人的最新的研究结果。(10points)

3. Write a paragraph on "What have I learned in this class(describe three topics covered in the class),how will this class help me in my future study and career,and any suggestions for future improvement of the course?"(300 words,20points)

All good things come to an end
——天下没有不散的筵席

参 考 文 献

[1] Karl T. Ulrich, Steven D. Eppinger. Product Design and Development(影印版)[M]. 北京：高等教育出版社, 2006.
[2] http://meche.mit.edu/about/.
[3] http://wumrc.engin.umich.edu/history.html.
[4] http://www.imts.com/.
[5] http://www.haier.net/en/careers/.
[6] http://en.smtcl.com/Aboutsmtcl/JoinUs/index.html.
[7] http://www.careers.siemens.com.cn/Career/Professionals_en.html.
[8] Serope Kalpakjan, Steven R. Schmid. Manufacturing Engineering and Technology—Hot Processe. Prientice-Hall, Inc. 2011.
[9] http://en.wikipedia.org/wiki/Job_interview.
[10] http://en.smtcl.com/Aboutsmtcl/JoinUs/index.html.
[11] http://www.careers.siemens.com.cn/Career/Professionals_en.html.
[12] http://www.nanotechsys.com.
[13] http://en.wikipedia.org/wiki/Manufacturing.
[14] http://meche.mit.edu/about/.
[15] http://wumrc.engin.umich.edu/history.html.
[16] http://en.wikipedia.org/wiki/Patent.
[17] http://en.wikipedia.org/wiki/Academic_conference.
[18] http://blizzard.cs.uwaterloo.ca/keshav/home/Papers/data/07/paper-reading.pdf.
[19] 唐一平. 机械工程专业英语[M]. 北京：电子工业出版社, 2009.
[20] 冯锦春. 试论大学生机械工程专业英语的学习[J]. 职业时空, 2011(9).
[21] 刘峰, 尹飞鸿. 机械工程专业英语教学研究[J]. 考试周刊, 2008(12).
[22] 章跃. 机械制造专业英语[M]. 北京：机械工业出版社, 2004.
[23] 夏明涛, 刘亚楼. 科技英语的长句分析与翻译[J]. 华北煤炭学院学报, 2005(5).
[24] 杨晓红, 尹明德. 机械工程专业英语词汇教学方法研究[J]. 科技信息(科学教研), 2007(22).
[25] 冯英, 蔡进. 科技英语文体特征及其翻译[J]. 中山大学学报论丛, 2006(07).
[26] 孙超平, 刘心报, 巩惠玲. 对提高学术期刊论文标题英译质量的思考[J]. 合肥工业大学学报：社会科学版, 2003(04).
[27] 张国君. 培养工程技术人员担任现场翻译[J]. 上海科技翻译, 1993(1).
[28] 冯治安. 谈谈施工现场英语口译[J]. 甘肃科技, 2010(4).
[29] 武力. 科技汉译英中词的选择和表达[J]. 上海科技翻译, 1996(02).
[30] 白俊文. 科技汉译英中常见接通/断开 15 例[J]. 中国科技翻译, 1990(4).
[31] 常国鸿. 科技汉译英中的概念不准确问题[J]. 中国科技信息, 2005(11).
[32] 蔡颢. 科技汉译英管见[J]. 中国科技翻译, 1994(3)：26-29.
[33] 吴云兴. 科技汉译英技能的提高[J]. 江苏技术师范学院学报, 2006, 12(5).

[34] 于建平. 科技论文汉译英中若干问题分析［J］. 中国翻译，2001，22(1).

[35] 曾剑平. 机械设备使用说明书的文体特点及其翻译［J］. 中国翻译，2004(6).

[36] 陈杰. 仪器设备英文说明书的文体特征及其翻译［D］. 长春：长春理工大学，2009.

[37] 蔡育红. 浅谈工业设备使用说明书的文体特点及其翻译［J］. 岱宗学刊，2005，9(3).

[38] 孙超平, 褚伟. 基于设备类使用说明书文体特征的汉译英要点刍议［J］. 合肥工业大学学报：社会科学版，2008，22(5).

[39] 莫群俐, 刘坚. 英文产品说明书中的非谓语动词结构及其翻译［J］. 湖南工程学院学报：社会科学版，2003(4).

[40] 何光明. 透析外企面试(15)：如何成功打造英文简历［J］. 新东方英语(大学版)，2011(4).

[41] 关开澄. 科技论文标题拟定：偏颇"五现象"与求美"七原则"［J］. 大庆石油学院学报，2008(2).

[42] 任秋生. 谈谈施工现场英语口译［J］. 中国翻译，1988(6).

[43] 化学工业部施工技术信息总站. 英日汉对照工程现场英语500句［M］. 北京：化学工业出版社，1998.

[44] 黄映秋. 工程图纸英语缩略表达与翻译［J］. 中国科技翻译，2009(1).

[45] 张越东, 刘百才. 看英文机械工程图纸的几点经验［J］. 机械工程师，1999(1).

[46] 薄丽媛. 英文工程图纸的常用尺寸标注及技术要求表示方法［J］. 机械制造，1986(11).

[47] 王永泉, 任柏林, 罗宁, 张桂英. 浅谈英文图纸读图的一些关键点［J］. 装备维修技术，2008(03).

[48] 曹晓艳. 国外机械图纸的识读方法. 无锡商业职业技术学院学报［J］. 2007(06).

[49] 杨玉华. 科技论文标题_关键词及摘要的撰写与英文翻译［J］. 焦作大学学报，2009，(23)2.

[50] 崔鲸涛. 科技论文英文标题中尽量不用赘词冗语［J］. 矿山机械，2008(05).

[51] 郭雪珍. 科技论文英文摘要语言应用常见问题［J］. 编辑之友，2011(S2).

[52] 李继民. 科技论文英文摘要的时态、语态问题探析［J］. 山东建筑大学学报，2010(02).

[53] 董琇. 国际会议交流英语［M］. 上海：同济大学出版社，2001.

[54] 刘汉龙. 国际会议英语［M］. 北京：中国水利水电出版社，2002.

[55] 全燕鸣. 制造工程与技术(热加工)学习辅导［M］. 北京：机械工业出版社，2010.

[56] 陈慧媛. 专业英语中长复合句译法初探［J］. 青海大学学报：自然科学版，2001(06).

[57] 阚子振, 吴传山. 浅谈机械工程专业英语翻译方法及技巧郑勇［J］. 科技信息(学术研究)，2008(11).

[58] 汤彩霞. 机械专业交际英语［M］. 北京：电子工业出版社，2011.

[59] http://bbs.jiyifa.cn/read.php?tid=1132.

[60] http://recruitment.naukrihub.com/recruitment-process.html.

[61] http://search.51job.com/hot/12882866,49148745.html.

[62] http://en.wikipedia.org/wiki/R%C3%A9sum%C3%A9.

[63] http://career-advice.monster.com/resumes-cover-letters/resume-writing-tips/engineering-resume-tips/article.aspx.

[64] http://www.airfel.com.

[65] http://www.bosch-trading.com.cn/web/product/product_braking_.jsp?lan=en.

[66] http://en.wikipedia.org/wiki/Technical_drawing.

[67] Kishawy, H. A. Wilcox, J. Tool Wear and Chip Formation During Hard Turning with Self-propelled rotary tool[J]. International Journal of Machine Tool and Manufacture,2003.43:433-439.

[68] Chiou,Richard,Lu. Investigation of dry machining with embedded heat pipe cooling by finite element analysis and experiments[J]. The International Journal of Advanced Manufacturing Technology,2007(9-10):905-914.

[69] http://www.sipo.gov.cn.

北京大学出版社教材书目

✧ 欢迎访问教学服务网站 www.pup6.com，免费查阅已出版教材的电子书（PDF 版）、电子课件和相关教学资源。
✧ 欢迎征订投稿。联系方式：010-62750667，童编辑，13426433315@163.com，pup_6@163.com，欢迎联系。

序号	书 名	标准书号	主 编	定价	出版日期
1	机械设计	978-7-5038-4448-5	郑 江，许 瑛	33	2007.8
2	机械设计	978-7-301-15699-5	吕 宏	32	2013.1
3	机械设计	978-7-301-17599-6	门艳忠	40	2010.8
4	机械设计	978-7-301-21139-7	王贤民，霍仕武	49	2014.1
5	机械设计	978-7-301-21742-8	师素娟，张秀花	48	2012.12
6	机械原理	978-7-301-11488-9	常治斌，张京辉	29	2008.6
7	机械原理	978-7-301-15425-0	王跃进	26	2013.9
8	机械原理	978-7-301-19088-3	郭宏亮，孙志宏	36	2011.6
9	机械原理	978-7-301-19429-4	杨松华	34	2011.8
10	机械设计基础	978-7-5038-4444-2	曲玉峰，关晓平	27	2008.1
11	机械设计基础	978-7-301-22011-5	苗淑杰，刘喜平	49	2013.6
12	机械设计基础	978-7-301-22957-6	朱 玉	38	2013.8
13	机械设计课程设计	978-7-301-12357-7	许 瑛	35	2012.7
14	机械设计课程设计	978-7-301-18894-1	王 慧，吕 宏	30	2014.1
15	机械设计辅导与习题解答	978-7-301-23291-0	王 慧，吕 宏	26	2013.12
16	机械原理、机械设计学习指导与综合强化	978-7-301-23195-1	张占国	63	2014.1
17	机电一体化课程设计指导书	978-7-301-19736-3	王金娥 罗生梅	35	2013.5
18	机械工程专业毕业设计指导书	978-7-301-18805-7	张黎骅，吕小荣	22	2012.5
19	机械创新设计	978-7-301-12403-1	丛晓霞	32	2012.8
20	机械系统设计	978-7-301-20847-2	孙月华	32	2012.7
21	机械设计基础实验及机构创新设计	978-7-301-20653-9	邹旻	28	2014.1
22	TRIZ 理论机械创新设计工程训练教程	978-7-301-18945-0	蒯苏苏，马履中	45	2011.6
23	TRIZ 理论及应用	978-7-301-19390-7	刘训涛，曹 贺等	35	2013.7
24	创新的方法——TRIZ 理论概述	978-7-301-19453-9	沈萌红	28	2011.9
25	机械工程基础	978-7-301-21853-2	潘玉良，周建军	34	2013.2
26	机械 CAD 基础	978-7-301-20023-0	徐云杰	34	2012.2
27	AutoCAD 工程制图	978-7-5038-4446-9	杨巧绒，张克义	20	2011.4
28	AutoCAD 工程制图	978-7-301-21419-0	刘善淑，胡爱萍	38	2013.4
29	工程制图	978-7-5038-4442-6	戴立玲，杨世平	27	2012.2
30	工程制图	978-7-301-19428-7	孙晓娟，徐丽娟	30	2012.5
31	工程制图习题集	978-7-5038-4443-4	杨世平，戴立玲	20	2008.1
32	机械制图(机类)	978-7-301-12171-9	张绍群，孙晓娟	32	2009.1
33	机械制图习题集(机类)	978-7-301-12172-6	张绍群，王慧敏	29	2007.8
34	机械制图(第 2 版)	978-7-301-19332-7	孙晓娟，王慧敏	38	2014.1
35	机械制图	978-7-301-21480-0	李凤云，张 凯等	36	2013.1
36	机械制图习题集(第 2 版)	978-7-301-19370-7	孙晓娟，王慧敏	22	2011.8
37	机械制图	978-7-301-21138-0	张 艳，杨晨升	37	2012.8
38	机械制图习题集	978-7-301-21339-1	张 艳，杨晨升	24	2012.10
39	机械制图	978-7-301-22896-8	臧福伦，杨晓冬等	60	2013.8
40	机械制图与 AutoCAD 基础教程	978-7-301-13122-0	张爱梅	35	2013.1
41	机械制图与 AutoCAD 基础教程习题集	978-7-301-13120-6	鲁 杰，张爱梅	22	2013.1
42	AutoCAD 2008 工程绘图	978-7-301-14478-7	赵润平，宗荣珍	35	2009.1
43	AutoCAD 实例绘图教程	978-7-301-20764-2	李庆华，刘晓杰	32	2012.6
44	工程制图案例教程	978-7-301-15369-7	宗荣珍	28	2009.6
45	工程制图案例教程习题集	978-7-301-15285-0	宗荣珍	24	2009.6
46	理论力学（第 2 版）	978-7-301-23125-8	盛冬发，刘 军	38	2013.9
47	材料力学	978-7-301-14462-6	陈忠安，王 静	30	2013.4

序号	书 名	标准书号	主 编	定价	出版日期
48	工程力学(上册)	978-7-301-11487-2	毕勤胜,李纪刚	29	2008.6
49	工程力学(下册)	978-7-301-11565-7	毕勤胜,李纪刚	28	2008.6
50	液压传动（第2版）	978-7-301-19507-9	王守城,容一鸣	38	2013.7
51	液压与气压传动	978-7-301-13179-4	王守城,容一鸣	32	2013.7
52	液压与液力传动	978-7-301-17579-8	周长城等	34	2011.11
53	液压传动与控制实用技术	978-7-301-15647-6	刘 忠	36	2009.8
54	金工实习指导教程	978-7-301-21885-3	周哲波	30	2014.1
55	工程训练（第3版）	978-7-301-24115-8	郭永环,姜银方	38	2014.5
56	机械制造基础实习教程	978-7-301-15848-7	邱 兵,杨明金	34	2010.2
57	公差与测量技术	978-7-301-15455-7	孔晓玲	25	2012.9
58	互换性与测量技术基础(第2版)	978-7-301-17567-5	王长春	28	2014.1
59	互换性与技术测量	978-7-301-20848-9	周哲波	35	2012.6
60	机械制造技术基础	978-7-301-14474-9	张 鹏,孙有亮	28	2011.6
61	机械制造技术基础	978-7-301-16284-2	侯书林,张建国	32	2012.8
62	机械制造技术基础	978-7-301-22010-8	李菊丽,何绍华	42	2014.1
63	先进制造技术基础	978-7-301-15499-1	冯宪章	30	2011.11
64	先进制造技术	978-7-301-22283-6	朱 林,杨春杰	30	2013.4
65	先进制造技术	978-7-301-20914-1	刘 璇,冯 凭	28	2012.8
66	先进制造与工程仿真技术	978-7-301-22541-7	李 彬	35	2013.5
67	机械精度设计与测量技术	978-7-301-13580-8	于 峰	25	2013.7
68	机械制造工艺学	978-7-301-13758-1	郭艳玲,李彦蓉	30	2008.8
69	机械制造工艺学(第2版)	978-7-301-23726-7	陈红霞	45	2014.1
70	机械制造工艺学	978-7-301-19903-9	周哲波,姜志明	49	2012.1
71	机械制造基础(上)——工程材料及热加工工艺基础(第2版)	978-7-301-18474-5	侯书林,朱 海	40	2013.2
72	制造之用	978-7-301-23527-0	王中任	30	2013.12
73	机械制造基础(下)——机械加工工艺基础(第2版)	978-7-301-18638-1	侯书林,朱 海	32	2012.5
74	金属材料及工艺	978-7-301-19522-2	于文强	44	2013.2
75	金属工艺学	978-7-301-21082-6	侯书林,于文强	32	2012.8
76	工程材料及其成形技术基础（第2版）	978-7-301-22367-3	申荣华	58	2013.5
77	工程材料及其成形技术基础学习指导与习题详解	978-7-301-14972-0	申荣华	20	2013.1
78	机械工程材料及成形基础	978-7-301-15433-5	侯俊英,王兴源	30	2012.5
79	机械工程材料（第2版）	978-7-301-22552-3	戈晓岚,招玉春	36	2013.6
80	机械工程材料	978-7-301-18522-3	张铁军	36	2012.5
81	工程材料与机械制造基础	978-7-301-15899-9	苏子林	32	2011.5
82	控制工程基础	978-7-301-12169-6	杨振中,韩致信	29	2007.8
83	机械制造装备设计	978-7-301-23869-1	宋士刚,黄 华	40	2014.12
84	机械工程控制基础	978-7-301-12354-6	韩致信	25	2008.1
85	机电工程专业英语(第2版)	978-7-301-16518-8	朱 林	24	2013.7
86	机械制造专业英语	978-7-301-21319-3	王中任	28	2014.12
87	机械工程专业英语	978-7-301-23173-9	余兴波,姜 波等	30	2013.9
88	机床电气控制技术	978-7-5038-4433-7	张万奎	26	2007.9
89	机床数控技术(第2版)	978-7-301-16519-5	杜国臣,王士军	35	2014.1
90	自动化制造系统	978-7-301-21026-0	辛宗生,魏国丰	37	2014.1
91	数控机床与编程	978-7-301-15900-2	张洪江,侯书林	25	2012.10
92	数控铣床编程与操作	978-7-301-21347-6	王志斌	35	2012.10
93	数控技术	978-7-301-21144-1	吴瑞明	28	2012.9
94	数控技术	978-7-301-22073-3	唐友亮,余 勃	45	2014.1
95	数控技术及应用	978-7-301-23262-0	刘 军	49	2013.10
96	数控加工技术	978-7-5038-4450-7	王 彪,张 兰	29	2011.7
97	数控加工与编程技术	978-7-301-18475-2	李体仁	34	2012.5
98	数控编程与加工实习教程	978-7-301-17387-9	张春雨,于 雷	37	2011.9
99	数控加工技术及实训	978-7-301-19508-6	姜永成,夏广岚	33	2011.9
100	数控编程与操作	978-7-301-20903-5	李英平	26	2012.8
101	现代数控机床调试及维护	978-7-301-18033-4	邓三鹏等	32	2010.11
102	金属切削原理与刀具	978-7-5038-4447-7	陈锡渠,彭晓南	29	2012.5
103	金属切削机床(第2版)	978-7-301-25202-4	夏广岚,姜永成	42	2015.1

序号	书名	标准书号	主编	定价	出版日期
104	典型零件工艺设计	978-7-301-21013-0	白海清	34	2012.8
105	模具设计与制造(第2版)	978-7-301-24801-0	田光辉，林红旗	56	2015.1
106	工程机械检测与维修	978-7-301-21185-4	卢彦群	45	2012.9
107	特种加工	978-7-301-21447-3	刘志东	50	2014.1
108	精密与特种加工技术	978-7-301-12167-2	袁根福，祝锡晶	29	2011.12
109	逆向建模技术与产品创新设计	978-7-301-15670-4	张学昌	28	2013.1
110	CAD/CAM 技术基础	978-7-301-17742-6	刘 军	28	2012.5
111	CAD/CAM 技术案例教程	978-7-301-17732-7	汤修映	42	2010.9
112	Pro/ENGINEER Wildfire 2.0 实用教程	978-7-5038-4437-X	黄卫东，任国栋	32	2007.7
113	Pro/ENGINEER Wildfire 3.0 实例教程	978-7-301-12359-1	张选民	45	2008.2
114	Pro/ENGINEER Wildfire 3.0 曲面设计实例教程	978-7-301-13182-4	张选民	45	2008.2
115	Pro/ENGINEER Wildfire 5.0 实用教程	978-7-301-16841-7	黄卫东，郝用兴	43	2014.1
116	Pro/ENGINEER Wildfire 5.0 实例教程	978-7-301-20133-6	张选民，徐超辉	52	2012.2
117	SolidWorks 三维建模及实例教程	978-7-301-15149-5	上官林建	30	2012.8
118	UG NX6.0 计算机辅助设计与制造实用教程	978-7-301-14449-7	张黎骅，吕小荣	26	2011.11
119	CATIA 实例应用教程	978-7-301-23037-4	于志新	45	2013.8
120	Cimatron E9.0 产品设计与数控自动编程技术	978-7-301-17802-7	孙树峰	36	2010.9
121	Mastercam 数控加工案例教程	978-7-301-19315-0	刘 文，姜永梅	45	2011.8
122	应用创造学	978-7-301-17533-0	王成军，沈豫浙	26	2012.5
123	机电产品学	978-7-301-15579-0	张亮峰等	24	2013.5
124	品质工程学基础	978-7-301-16745-8	丁 燕	30	2011.5
125	设计心理学	978-7-301-11567-1	张成忠	48	2011.6
126	计算机辅助设计与制造	978-7-5038-4439-6	仲梁维，张国全	29	2007.9
127	产品造型计算机辅助设计	978-7-5038-4474-4	张慧姝，刘永翔	27	2006.8
128	产品设计原理	978-7-301-12355-3	刘美华	30	2008.2
129	产品设计表现技法	978-7-301-15434-2	张慧姝	42	2012.5
130	CorelDRAW X5 经典案例教程解析	978-7-301-21950-8	杜秋磊	40	2013.1
131	产品创意设计	978-7-301-17977-2	虞世鸣	38	2012.5
132	工业产品造型设计	978-7-301-18313-7	袁涛	39	2011.1
133	化工工艺学	978-7-301-15283-6	邓建强	42	2013.7
134	构成设计	978-7-301-21466-4	袁涛	58	2013.1
135	设计色彩	978-7-301-24246-9	姜晓微	52	2014.6
136	过程装备机械基础(第2版)	978-301-22627-8	于新奇	38	2013.7
137	过程装备测试技术	978-7-301-17290-2	王毅	45	2010.6
138	过程控制装置及系统设计	978-7-301-17635-1	张早校	30	2010.8
139	质量管理与工程	978-7-301-15643-8	陈宝江	34	2009.8
140	质量管理统计技术	978-7-301-16465-5	周友苏，杨 飒	30	2010.1
141	人因工程	978-7-301-19291-7	马如宏	39	2011.8
142	工程系统概论——系统论在工程技术中的应用	978-7-301-17142-4	黄志坚	32	2010.6
143	测试技术基础(第2版)	978-7-301-16530-0	江征风	30	2014.1
144	测试技术实验教程	978-7-301-13489-4	封士彩	22	2008.8
145	测控系统原理设计	978-7-301-24399-2	齐永奇	39	2014.7
146	测试技术学习指导与习题详解	978-7-301-14457-2	封士彩	34	2009.3
147	可编程控制器原理与应用(第2版)	978-7-301-16922-3	赵 燕，周新建	33	2011.11
148	工程光学	978-7-301-15629-2	王红敏	28	2012.5
149	精密机械设计	978-7-301-16947-6	田 明，冯进良等	38	2011.9
150	传感器原理及应用	978-7-301-16503-4	赵 燕	35	2014.1
151	测控技术与仪器专业导论(第2版)	978-7-301-24223-0	陈毅静	36	2014.6
152	现代测试技术	978-7-301-19316-7	陈科山，王燕	43	2011.8
153	风力发电原理	978-7-301-19631-1	吴双群，赵丹平	33	2011.10
154	风力机空气动力学	978-7-301-19555-0	吴双群	32	2011.10
155	风力机设计理论及方法	978-7-301-20006-3	赵丹平	32	2012.1
156	计算机辅助工程	978-7-301-22977-4	许承东	38	2013.8
157	现代船舶建造技术	978-7-301-23703-8	初冠南，孙清洁	33	2014.1

如您需要免费纸质样书用于教学，欢迎登陆第六事业部门户网(www.pup6.com)填表申请，并欢迎在线登记选题以到北京大学出版社来出版您的大作，也可下载相关表格填写后发到我们的邮箱，我们将及时与您取得联系并做好全方位的服务。